SITTING BULL

AND HIS WORLD

Tatan'ka Iyota'ke

SITTING BULL

AND HIS WORLD

ALBERT MARRIN

DUTTON CHILDREN'S BOOKS

NEW YORK

Library of Congress Cataloging-in-Publication Data
Marrin, Albert.
Sitting Bull and his world/Albert Marrin.—1st ed.
p.   cm.
At head of title: Tatan'ka Iyota'ke.
Includes bibliographical references.
Summary: Discusses the life of the Hunkpapa chief
who is remembered for his defeat of Custer at Little Big Horn.
ISBN 0-525-45944-8 (hc)
1. Sitting Bull, 1831–1890—Juvenile literature. 2. Dakota Indians—Juvenile literature.
3. Hunkpapa Indians—Biography—Juvenile literature. (1. Sitting Bull, 1831–1890. 2. Hunkpapa
Indians—Biography. 3. Indians of North America—Great Plains—Biography.) I. Title.
E99.D1 S6124   2000   978'.004975'0092—dc21   [B]   99-042367

Published in the United States by Dutton Children's Books,
a division of Penguin Putnam Books for Young Readers
345 Hudson Street, New York, New York 10014
http://www.penguinputnam.com/yreaders/index.htm

Designed by Amy Berniker
Maps by Richard Amari
Printed in China
First Edition
10 9 8 7 6 5 4 3 2 1

For our dear friends, the Weinbergs—
Fran, Larry, Paul, and Joel

Contents

"A people without history is like wind on the buffalo grass."
—Lakota saying

SITTING BULL

AND HIS WORLD

Prologue

THEY SAY THEY ARE INDIANS

"A powerful and warlike people, proud, haughty and defiant [with] strong muscular frames and very good horsemen, well dressed, principally in skins and robes; rich in horses and lodges; [they] have great abundance of meat, since buffalo, elk, antelope and deer abound in their country. They say they are Indians and do not wish to change their mode of living."
—WILLIAM BLACKMORE, North American Indians, 1869

OLD MEN SAID it happened in present-day South Dakota around the year 1828. The sun had just set behind the western mountains. It was early fall, and already a cold wind whistled across the Great Plains, kicking up little clouds of dust. The stars of the Milky Way sparkled like diamonds scattered on black velvet, and a full moon hung like a golden lantern in the cloudless sky. The air was so pure that if you looked at any point in the heavens for a few minutes, you would have seen scores of meteorites speeding earthward, each trailing a silvery banner of light.

Four warriors sat around a smoky fire of buffalo chips—lumps of dried dung—the only "firewood" on the treeless Plains. The smoke had a strong, pungent odor, but they did not mind; for them, it added to the flavor of the meat. All were hungry and tired, wanting nothing more than to enjoy the roasting buffalo ribs, smoke their pipes, and curl up in their sleeping robes.

Yet interrupting this serene, crisp nightfall, they heard a strange shuffling noise in the distance. As minutes passed, the noise grew louder. Grabbing their weapons, the warriors turned to face the intruder.

Suddenly a *tatanka,* a bull buffalo, emerged from the darkness and came into the circle of light cast by the fire. *Tatanka* shook his massive head, snorting and grunting, his beard sweeping the ground. Since fire often attracted animals at night, and the warriors had already made a kill, three of them returned to their places; they knew that the *tatanka* would leave when he had satisfied his curiosity. But their companion, Returns Again, could not tear himself away. Cautiously, he walked toward the animal, drawn to it by something he felt but could not express in words.

Returns Again and the other warriors were members of the Teton Lakota, or Dakota. Teton means "western" and Lakota "alliance of friends," "us folks," or "Plains people." Thus, the Teton Lakota were the People of the Western Plains. Returns Again had a name feared by his enemies. Whenever Returns Again went on a successful raid, he always *returned again* to strike the enemy a final blow before heading home. Yet he was more than an able warrior. Returns Again had special powers, or "medicine." His people believed his gifts enabled him to understand animal speech, and to speak to them in return.

Returns Again stared at the intruder, listening intently. Gradually, his ears became attuned to the bull buffalo's grunts—and he realized what they meant. These were not random sounds, but the Lakota language spoken slowly and in a deep "voice." This is what he heard: *"Tatan'ka Iyota'ke, Tatan'ka Psi'ca, Tatan'ka Winyu'ha Najin', Tatan'ka Wanji'la."* When the bull buffalo had finished, he turned away, shook his head furiously for a few seconds, then ambled off into the darkness.

Returns Again stood there, trembling with emotion. *Tatanka's* words had struck him like a lightning bolt. This visitor was not merely one of the four-leggeds. Oh, no! He was none other than the buffalo god! He had come to give him, Returns Again, a precious gift. Those four phrases he had spoken were really names. Returns Again realized that each name signified a "divide," or stage, in a man's life: Sitting Bull, Jumping Bull, Bull Standing with Cow, and Lone Bull. Infancy, youth, maturity, and old age.

An Indian took several names during a lifetime. Mastering a new skill, doing a notable deed, or having an unusual experience might cause a person to change his or her name, or have the members of the tribe change it.

After that nighttime visit, Returns Again took the name Tatan'ka Iyota'ke: Sitting Bull. Later, he took the second name, Jumping Bull, and gave the name Sitting Bull to his teenage son.

The life of that Sitting Bull, the son of Returns Again, is the subject of this book.

The Teton Lakota depended upon the buffalo to satisfy nearly every spiritual and material need. They considered the buffalo brave and generous, strong and wise, so it was also an ideal model for human beings. By following the buffalo's example, Sitting Bull the son gave that name its fullest meaning. Tatan'ka Iyota'ke stood for more than life's first divide. It also meant "The Buffalo Bull Who Resides Among Us." In other words, a strong and wise being had come to "sit"—live— among the Lakota.

Sitting Bull, around 1885.

There had been other renowned Indian leaders. In the 1760s, during the French and Indian War, the Ottawa chief Pontiac nearly drove the British out of Michigan. During the War of 1812 between Britain and the United States, Tecumseh of the Shawnee tried to unite all Indian people against the Americans in the Ohio Valley. Among the great chiefs of Sitting Bull's day, Geronimo led the Chiricahua Apache in a dogged defense of his homeland in Arizona and New Mexico against invading whites. Chief Quanah Parker, who had a white mother and a Comanche father, fought to save the buffalo from extermination on the Texas plains. Crazy Horse of the Oglala Lakota was a master tactician who devised a new strategy for fighting the U.S. Cavalry.

None of these leaders was as respected as Tatan'ka Iyota'ke. He, too, was a warrior—one of the best. But he was much more. His people knew him as a *wichasha wakan;* that is, a seer, a holy man, one with an inborn ability to understand the past and see into the future through dreams and visions. Sitting Bull's songs, sayings, and speeches not only revealed a keen intelligence, but also help to explain the powerful hold he had on his people. A few whites—very few—recognized his unique qualities. Nelson A. Miles, his opponent and a future commander general of the U.S. Army, insisted, "Sitting Bull was the greatest Indian that has ever lived in this country." William F. Cody, better known as "Buffalo Bill," went further. He called Sitting Bull "the world's most famous Indian."[1]

Sitting Bull's life spans a stormy period in our country's history. When he was born, in 1831, the United States had not changed very much from colonial times. It was still a frontier society with a vast wilderness waiting, white people thought, to be tamed by the plow and the fence. Yet a few months before Sitting Bull's death in 1890, the government declared that the frontier no longer existed, because whites lived in every part of the United States.

During Sitting Bull's lifetime, the Wasichu, as the Lakota called white people, devoted enormous effort to the "winning of the West." The Lakota and other native peoples might have used other terms, however—such as the "losing," "stealing," "conquering," and "destroying" of the West. Make no mistake about it: The lands stretching westward from the Mississippi River to the Rocky Mountains were not bought for a few colorful trinkets. Americans gained these lands by a combination of force and fraud, hard work and courage, broken treaties and bad faith—and good intentions gone terribly wrong.

Force above all. Between 1862 and 1890 the United States fought eleven separate Indian wars, involving some two hundred military actions. These were not battles between massed armies, but hit-and-run raids, ambushes, and pursuits of fleeing tribes. Measured by the lives lost, these wars were "cheap." A typical action claimed the lives of fewer than ten men, often less, on either side. Historians believe American soldiers and civilians killed about four thousand Indians in *all* Indian wars since 1776. Indians may have killed seven thousand white soldiers and civilians during that same time. Yet numbers do not begin to tell the whole story. Expressed in terms of human values—kindness, mercy, justice—the Indian wars were the most brutal in our history.[2]

A historian, writing nearly a century ago, claimed that the Native Americans had to lose. He wondered only whether the whites could have won in a more humane way:

> That the . . . tribes were doomed to complete displacement on the soil of their nativity after once the European races had discovered this continent is a proposition that few will care to deny. A change so fundamental, involving loss of land, institutions, customs, and the innermost functions of social life, was not one that could be accomplished without pain and apparent wrong. The only ground for criticism of those concerned . . . is whether or not they have unnecessarily added to its burden of sorrow and suffering.[3]

Why didn't the white people just set a boundary and not push farther west? They tried to do just that, but failed every time. For example, in the early 1800s, President Thomas Jefferson did not believe whites could ever live on the Great Plains, a wild country with little water and no timber; he wanted to set aside the eastern border of the Plains as a "Permanent Indian Frontier," fit only for the wandering tribes. President Andrew Jackson agreed. Unfortunately, the Cherokee, Choctaw, Chickasaw, and Creek tribes held millions of acres of land in Georgia, Alabama, and Mississippi. Since whites wanted that land for growing cotton, in the 1830s Jackson sent them to a reservation in Indian Territory, now the state of Oklahoma. Thousands of Indians died along the horrible "Trail of Tears," the long walk westward. Oklahoma was supposed to belong to the Indians forever. Yet, when whites wanted that land, too, the Indians lost nearly all their holdings.

General Philip H. Sheridan, who masterminded the conquest of the Great Plains after the Civil War, knew the true reason behind the Indian wars. Sheridan admitted that brutality and the destruction of the Indian way of life were the inevitable results of white, not Indian, actions. "The government made treaties, gave presents, made promises, none of which were honestly fulfilled," he wrote in 1878. "We took away their country and their means of support, broke up their mode of living, their habits of life, introduced disease and decay among them, and it was for this and against this they made war." Yet Sheridan, as a professional soldier, felt that he could not choose his wars. Just as he obeyed his government's orders to crush the Confederacy during the Civil War, he fought the Indians with equal ruthlessness.[4]

None fought harder against that threatening doom than Tatan'ka Iyota'ke. An impressive figure, he stood five feet ten inches tall, weighed 175 pounds, and had reddish-brown skin. Sitting Bull's deep brown eyes, large and wide, set in a face painted red for good luck, had the mischievous twinkle of one who enjoyed a hearty laugh. Even so, when he stared at someone, his eyes seemed to stab into that person's soul, reading his or her deepest thoughts. Radiating self-confidence, Sitting Bull wore two long braids wrapped in badger skin, a challenge to anyone bold enough to go for them with a knife. A buckskin shirt fringed with clumps of human hair testified to his skill with that same weapon. On special occasions, he wore a warbonnet with nearly a hundred eagle feathers, each earned by a brave deed. Otherwise, he went about with a single feather in his hair.[5]

Sitting Bull was a man at peace with himself. He always had a sense of his destiny, always knew who he was and his reason for being. He once told a newspaper reporter:

Sitting Bull posing for an undated studio photograph. Although he wears a long warbonnet, each feather representing a war honor, he usually wore only a single eagle's feather in his hair.

> I am a free man. I see. I know. I began to see when I was not yet born; when I was not in my mother's arms, but inside my mother's belly. It was there that I began to study about my people. . . . [The Great Spirit] . . . gave me the power to see out of the womb. I studied there, in the womb, about many things. . . . I was so interested that I turned over

on my side. The [Great Spirit] must have told me at that time . . . that I would be the man to be the judge of all the other Indians—a big man to decide for them in all their ways.[6]

Did he mean this literally? Apparently so. Native Americans believed that the Great Spirit—God—visited people in dreams. During such visits He might give them magical powers and show them the future. Others might say that Sitting Bull believed so strongly in his mission that he convinced himself that the Great Spirit had chosen him before his birth. Or, perhaps, he made the story up simply to show his devotion in a dramatic way. For whatever reason, he spent his entire life "studying" his people and serving them.

Sitting Bull had strict moral principles. Although a brave warrior, he fought honorably, by the Lakotas' time-honored rules. The violence of the warpath ended when he returned to his village. At home he lived as peaceably as anyone could wish. A loyal friend, he never broke a promise or deceived anyone. A kind and gentle man, the sight of a sick child—any child—filled his eyes with tears. Above all, he was a patriot who insisted that Native Americans must be free to choose their way of life. Had he been a white man, fellow citizens would have praised him, as they once praised Patrick Henry, for declaring: "Give me liberty or give me death!"

These qualities gave Sitting Bull enormous influence among the Lakota. Wooden Leg, a warrior who fought beside him, said it best: "He had . . . a kind heart and good judgement as to the best course of conduct. . . . He was strong in religion—the Indian religion. . . . He had a big brain and a good one, a strong heart and a generous one."[7]

Most white Americans hated Sitting Bull. To them, he was the wildest of "wild" Indians. They saw him as the "monster" who destroyed the "gallant" Colonel George Armstrong Custer and his regiment at the Battle of the Little Bighorn. An army officer described him as a wolf in human form. "He is a ferocious beast!" whose only aim "is to kill whites."[8] The officer forgot to mention (if he ever knew) that Sitting Bull never attacked a white settlement and that he freed white women and children captives. He fought only when whites invaded his homeland. He refused to come under the rule of the U.S. government.

There are serious problems in learning about Sitting Bull—indeed, in learning about all Indians, or Native Americans, the term commonly used today. Europeans coined the word "Indian" after their first contact with native peoples in 1492.[9] In using this word, they lumped native peoples into a single category, despite their thousands of tribal groupings. When they first met white people, natives identified themselves with their tribal names. Later, they borrowed the whites' term and called themselves Indians. "Native American" is an invention of the late twentieth century. We will use both terms interchangeably.

Scientists have collected thousands of native costumes, weapons, utensils, and sacred objects. Objects, however, cannot literally speak for themselves. They do not directly reveal what their creators thought or the view of the world, the customs and beliefs, behind that thinking. The written word is our chief means of learning about the past. Lacking written languages, Native Americans could not in that fashion record events as they happened or their impressions of them.

Tribes preserved accounts of past events in story form. Storytellers were usually elderly men who repeated stories they had been told years earlier. Still, human memory fades with time. Old incidents and details are forgotten; new "facts" manage to creep in, gradually changing the story. When the storytellers died, or other matters occupied listeners' attention, memory of the original events faded away.

"Winter counts" also helped in recalling the past. These consisted of tanned animal skins on which tribal elders painted pictures. Each picture served as a reminder of that year's most memorable event. Years had names like "Dish Face Died," "Plenty Buffalo," and "Enemies Come to the Hunting Ground." The term "winter count" comes from the custom of reckoning time by "winters" instead of by years. For example, Sitting Bull had fifty-nine winters at the time of his death.

Some Native Americans created pictorial "autobiographies." Before the white man came, they painted their exploits on their tipi cover in natural dyes. Later, they traded for writing tools. Sitting Bull used crayons to draw his autobiography in a notebook during the 1860s. It consists of forty-one pictures depicting his war honors. He "signed" his drawings with a line connecting a picture of a seated *tatanka* to the outline of a human head. Most winter counts and autobiographies have vanished on account of time and neglect; many others burned during the wars. Those that survive tell little of what historians most want to know. Who? What? When? Where? Why? How? Pictures cannot answer such questions.

The written word enabled whites to explain events in detail and, through printing, preserve their explanations unchanged into the future. As a result, the history of the West is, and will remain, largely one-sided. By *writing* the history, whites controlled how future generations would understand what happened. The history we have is the winners' story, seen through their eyes and colored by their needs. It, too, is filled with inaccurate and incomplete information.

Even the most unprejudiced whites had difficulty understanding Native Americans. The tribes of the Great Plains alone have more than thirty different languages and scores of local dialects. These are so difficult to learn that, to make themselves understood, tribes developed a common sign language. Based on hand signals and gestures, not words, sign language enabled people from different backgrounds to "talk" easily and became the basis for modern deaf speech.[10]

Statements by Indians were not recorded by the speakers themselves, but by whites listening through interpreters. Frontier interpreters were not linguists—far from it. Most were "half-breeds," men of mixed parentage. Although they could get by using certain words and phrases, they frequently missed the fine points. Thus, in translating for their employers, they often misinterpreted. For example, the famous warrior Tashunka Witko, or Untamed Horse, they called Crazy Horse, the name by which he is known in our history books. "Man of Whose Very Horses the Enemy Is Afraid" became Man Afraid of His Horses. Somehow Sitting Bull came out as "Slightly Recumbent Gentleman Cow." Some whites thought his name meant "enemy." And while an interpreter's misunderstandings could be innocent, he could also interpret in a self-interested, prejudiced, or deliberately manipulative way.

Because context is so important to meaning, even a "correct" translation can mislead. Depending on who uses a certain word and how, it can foster pride or destroy self-respect. In describing American slavery, historian Julius Lester reminds us that the word "nigger" has meant different things to different people at different times. Spoken by bigots, it was (and is) a gross insult, a verbal slap in the face. Under slavery, however, blacks adopted this hateful word for their own purposes. They found that, by calling themselves "nigger," they drew its sting, making it an act of free will and therefore a form of resistance.[11]

Until recently, the word "squaw" (woman) appeared in countless writings about Native Americans. It, too, cannot be taken at face value. The word comes from the Algonquian family of languages spoken by the Eastern Woodland tribes and means "woman." There is no such word in the language of Sitting Bull's people. The Lakota used *winyan* for "woman" and *wakanyuza* for "wife." Whites borrowed "squaw," a perfectly honorable word in its original context, and used it—or misused it—in various ways.

In the mouths of some whites, "squaw" meant "an overworked hag," a woman of low morals, or even a prostitute. Yet other whites used it without any negative meaning. For example, soldiers referred to "squaw camps"; that is, camps in which women and children lived while the men were away hunting buffalo or fighting. Army officers even applied it to their wives. Captain Francis M. Gibson, an officer and a gentleman if there ever was one, had once helped a Lakota warrior's family. The warrior never forgot his kindness. When the captain's wife gave birth to a daughter, the warrior gave him valuable furs to keep them warm. In parting, Gibson grasped the warrior's arm. "Let me thank you for your gift," he said. "Also my squaw thanks you, and may the Great Spirit prosper you and bring you good hunting."[12]

Despite language difficulties and differing ways of life, the story of Sitting Bull is worth pursuing and learning about for two important reasons. First, biography shapes history. History is really about *people,* not about official reports and statistics. Thus, the story of individual lives puts a human face on otherwise meaningless events and dates. Second, Sitting Bull's story allows us to take a closer look at white Americans and their values at a crucial time in our nation's history. Through his experiences we can gain a larger perspective on such continuing problems as racism, violence, and human rights.

In writing this book, I strove to avoid telling the story in terms of saints and sinners, "good guys" and "bad guys." A whole people cannot be all good or all bad, despite our inclination sometimes to judge groups or nations that way. If Sitting Bull's life teaches us anything, it is the danger of judging one society by the ideas of another. In the winning and losing of the West, each side acted according to its own beliefs and customs. Few people deliberately set out to do wrong. By the standards of their own societies, most individuals acted decently and responsibly. In this, both Indians and whites showed their common humanity. I hope to bring home that truth by telling a uniquely *American* story through the life of a fascinating human being. For the first Americans, no less than the later arrivals to these shores, share a common land and a common history and, now, a common destiny.

One

GROWING UP LAKOTA

"What I am, I am."
—SITTING BULL, 1877

THE TIME: A DAY DURING the Moon When the Grain Comes Up, in the Winter When Yellow Eyes Played in the Snow. The place: a campsite at Many Caches. By white folks' reckoning, that was March 1831, at some caches, or storage pits, located on the south bank of the Grand River in Dakota Territory, the future states of North and South Dakota.

Her Holy Door, big with child, knew that her time had come. Rather than trouble her husband—as giving birth was a woman's duty—she asked her six-year-old daughter, Good Feather Woman, to run to the birth-helper a few tipis, or lodges, away.

Moments later, an elderly woman pushed aside the door flap and stepped inside. Kneeling, she began to massage Her Holy Door's belly with gentle circular motions while softly chanting prayers. When the labor pains grew intense, she drove two three-foot stakes into the ground with a stone-headed mallet. Her Holy Door then squatted before the stakes, grasped the tops hard, and pushed with the muscles of her lower body. Her son arrived moments later.

The birth-helper wrapped the infant in a square of soft deerskin. Tenderly she washed him with sweet grass soaked in water, oiled him with bear grease, and lay him in his mother's arms. Then she left to tell the father, Sitting Bull, who once called himself Returns Again, that a healthy son had just been born. As it turned out, this would be his only son, although the couple had another daughter, Brown Shawl Woman, a year or two later.

Lakota children were fortunate. It was not a matter of material luxuries, as the Lakota had few of these, but of emotional security. Newborns came into a world of welcoming adults who loved them. An Indian tribe—and not just the Lakota—resembled a large family. Although not everyone was related by blood, members felt bound to one another in ways that modern city dwellers can scarcely imagine. Nobody had the right to do his or her "own thing." Instead, everyone belonged to a tightly knit community. Each person knew his or her place—what to expect from family and tribe, and what was expected in return.

Besides parents, the Lakota child was surrounded by doting grandparents, uncles, aunts, cousins, and family friends. Everyone felt responsible for children and treated them as their own. A toddler, wherever she or he wandered, never strayed beyond the watchful eyes of a caring adult. Nor did children have to seek affection: That was their birthright. They could walk into any lodge, sure of a warm welcome. White visitors described how toddlers would stop playing to nurse from the nearest woman, then rejoin their playmates.[1] Orphans did not exist among the Lakota. If children lost their parents, relatives took them in or another family adopted them. Families did not complain of having too many children. Each child was a blessing sent by the Great Spirit.

The son of Sitting Bull was no exception. We do not know the details of his upbringing, and he may vanish from our story for pages at a time. But no matter. We can easily fill in the gaps, since his upbringing could not have been very different from that of any other Plains Indian child.

Since the birth of a son was an important event, Sitting Bull naturally wanted to share his joy. He did this through the news-walker, a sort of human newspaper who carried word of the latest events—births, deaths, marriages, battles, gossip—from band to band and tribe to tribe. Whites dubbed the news-walker's activities the "moccasin telegraph."

A few days after the birth, people gathered for the naming ceremony. Sitting Bull named his infant son Jumping Badger for reasons we do not know. Before long, however, everyone was calling him Hunkeshnee, or "Slow." Not that Slow was slow in the sense of unintelligent. On the contrary, he seemed wise beyond his age; perhaps "Thoughtful One" would be a better translation of his Lakota name. When other infants had food placed in their hands, they ate it right away. Not Slow. He turned it over, studying it from every angle before putting it into his mouth.[2]

Slow spent his first six months strapped tightly in a cradleboard, a stiff leather basket fastened to a board. Wherever Her Holy Door went, he went, too. When she worked, she hung the cradleboard on a lodgepole or rested it against a rock. At night, he slept in it between his parents. Although it had a hole to allow urine to drain, Slow still got messy. So, once a day, Mother bathed him, greased him, and changed his "diaper" of dried moss. Uncomfortable as it may have been, the cradleboard allowed his bones to grow strong and straight.

Once freed from the cradleboard, Slow could do much as he pleased. Lakota parents did not boss their children around. Slow ate when hungry; no one made him eat "on time" or worried if he missed a meal. He slept when he felt tired, since Indian children were never "put to bed."

Plains Indian women carrying their babies in cradleboards, as portrayed by the artist George Catlin.

Best of all, Slow's parents gave him the freedom to crawl around, to explore and, yes, to get hurt. Nobody said "don't" when he reached toward the fire, much less ran over to pull him away. "One must learn from the bite of the fire to let it alone," Lakota parents said.[3] Every mishap, provided it did not threaten serious harm, became a learning experience. Parents thought it better to comfort a whimpering child than have the child remain ignorant of the world.

Whimper, but not cry! Like all Lakota children, Slow never had the freedom to cry. Enemies might be lurking about, particularly at night, and a crying child could easily reveal the camp's location. If Slow started to cry, Her Holy Door picked him up, cuddled him, or nursed him. If that failed, she pinched his nose with her thumb and forefinger, placing her palm over his mouth. After a few "lessons," he got the idea and did not cry. Mothers also dripped water into their infants' nostrils, so they would breathe through their mouths and stop crying.

When Slow acted up, his parents did not yell at him, much less hit him. The Lakota thought that hitting a child was an unforgivable act of brutality. "We never struck our children, for we loved them," a parent recalled. "Rather we talked to them, gently, but never harshly. If they were doing something wrong, we asked them to stop."[4] Adults whipped dogs, not children.

If persuasion failed, parents disciplined their children in other ways. Fear was one method. Parents told unruly youngsters, "Be quiet, or a witch might hear you."[5] Witches were bad enough, but almost kindly compared to Big Owl. Large as a cloud and silent as a falling snowflake, Big Owl tore mischievous children apart with his hooked beak. Parents also promised to feed mice to bed wetters who did not control themselves. Finally, if all else failed, they embarrassed the child before the entire community. Painful as that may have been, it usually worked.

Even as a toddler, Slow joined other children in the lodge of the camp storyteller. Most likely, that person was his uncle Four Horns. An important man in his own right, Four Horns had a marvelous way with words. At night he sat cross-legged near a fire, explaining moral principles through stories and proverbs. "A Lakota may lie once," he would say, "but after that no one will believe him." Other proverbs were: "The life of a greedy person is short," "The lazy person gets into mischief," and "There is a hole at the end of a thief's path."[6]

The storyteller also told about geography, natural history, and astronomy in story form. He described how Wakantanka, the Great Spirit, made the world and everything in it. Wakantanka created Wasiya, the Giant of the North, whose icy breath brings winter, and the Itkomi, the tiny spider people who leave flint arrowheads for their human friends to find. Some stories recalled tribal history, although memories of past events seldom went back more than two or three lifetimes. Modern scholars, like Royal B. Hassrick, have traced Lakota history back to the 1600s.[7]

French explorers from Canada were the first whites to meet Slow's ancestors. They found them living in the forests of Minnesota, the "land of sky-colored waters." There, by the headwaters of the Mississippi River (or "great water") and Lake Superior, they had thirty villages of timber-framed cabins covered with slabs of bark. The men hunted deer in the forests and fished in the streams. The women paddled canoes along the waterways to gather wild rice.

Other tribes lived nearby and often fought over territory. Although expert fighters, Slow's ancestors seem not to have gone looking for trouble. "They never attack till attacked," wrote Father Jacques Marquette, adding, "they keep their word strictly." Another explorer wrote that "they release the prisoners they take."[8]

Their chief enemies were the Cree and Chippewa tribes, who called them Nadowe-is-in, or "Little Snakes." Frenchmen heard the name as *Nadowes-sioux,* which they shortened to *Sioux.* Since the old-time Lakota never called themselves by this name, we will use it only in quotations.

Things started going wrong in the 1660s. French traders met the Cree and Chippewa, exchanging guns and ammunition for beaver skins. Slow's ancestors had only bows and arrows. Outmatched in battle, most abandoned their villages. They left the forests, trekking westward and southward across Minnesota toward the valley of the Missouri River.

That journey lasted not weeks or months, but years—in fact, decades. Along the way, the Lakota separated into the Santee, Yankton, and Teton; that is, eastern, central, and western groups. Each group, or division, consisted of several tribes. The Teton Lakota, the most westerly division, had seven tribes, also known as the Seven Council Fires. These were the Oglala ("Those Who Scatter Their Own"), Brulé ("People with Burnt Thighs"), Miniconjou ("Those Who Plant by the Stream"), Oohenunpa ("Two-Kettles People"), Sans Arc ("Without Bows"), Sihasapa ("Blackfeet"), and Hunkpapa ("Those Who Camp by the Entrance to the Camp Circle"). Each tribe in turn consisted of several family groups, or bands. Slow's ancestors, the Hunkpapa, had bands with names like Sleepy Kettle, Sore Backs, and Those That Carry Bad Bows. His family belonged to the band called Icira (pronounced *Itchy-krah*), or "Those Who Laugh at Each Other."[9]

Each band had its peace chief or headman. White people imagined chiefs as powerful rulers, like their own kings and presidents. Yet native peoples had no "government" or "law" as whites understood these terms. A chief did not inherit his office, win it by election, or seize it by force. He grew into it; that is, band members accepted him as their chief because of his forceful personality and accomplishments. A chief did not rule his people. He could not tax, jail, or punish anyone. At most, he gave advice, which anyone could ignore. With other leading men, he discussed important matters in council meetings. Discussions might last for days, since all decisions required a unanimous vote. Councils were models of decorum and fair play. No one thought of interrupting a speaker, shouting, or using abusive words. The Lakota language has no swear words.

Slow's ancestors moved ever westward, living by hunting small animals and gathering edible plants. About the year 1700, they reached the Missouri River. The name derives from *mini sose*, Lakota for "Big Muddy Water."[10] At 2,464 miles, flowing from its source in southern Montana to its junction with the Mississippi at St. Louis, Missouri, it is the longest river in North America. Over a mile wide in places, the Missouri is often so shallow that a person can stand midstream up to the knees. At certain times of the year, it flows lazily; at other times, it is a raging torrent. Its main tributary is a stream the Lakota called the "Yellow Rock River"; whites called it the Yellowstone. This river originates in the Lakotas' "Large Plain," or Wyoming. Other rivers—the Bighorn, Rosebud, Tongue, Powder—flow northward into the Yellowstone from the Bighorn Mountains in Wyoming.

After crossing the Missouri, Slow's ancestors entered a new world as strange as any the Europeans found when they first reached these shores. The line formed by the Missouri and Mississippi rivers is a natural boundary, clearly visible from a low-flying airplane. Gently rolling prairies of tall grasses fall away to the east. To the west lie the Great Plains, a flat, treeless region covered by short grasses. At nearly one million square miles, the Great Plains is one-third the area of the United States and includes all or part of ten states.[11]

Ancient rivers, carving out broad valleys, gave the Great Plains their few high places. Millions of years of rushing streams, rain, and wind eroded the valley walls to form ridges and bluffs. Washington Irving, author of "The Legend of Sleepy Hollow" and "Rip Van Winkle," visited the area four years after Slow's birth. Like most travelers from the East, he called it "the great American desert." No one believed whites would ever settle there in large numbers.

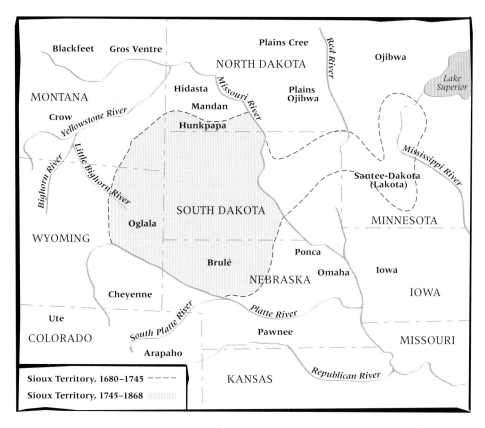

The westward expansion of the Lakota.

[The entire region] spreads forth into undulating and treeless plains, and desolate sandy wastes wearisome to the eye from their extent and monotony. . . . Occasionally the monotony of this vast wilderness is interrupted by mountainous belts of sand and limestone, broken into confused masses; with precipitous cliffs and yawning ravines, looking like the ruins of a world; or is traversed by lofty and barren ridges of rock, almost impassable. . . . Such is the nature of this immense wilderness of the far West. . . . Some portions of it along the rivers may partially be subdued by agriculture . . . but it is to be feared that a great part of it will form a lawless interval between the abodes of civilized man, like the wastes of the ocean or the deserts of Arabia.[12]

Although normally mild and dry, summers on the Great Plains can be wicked. With nothing to block them, strong winds blow northward from the deserts of Mexico and the American Southwest, shriveling plants, turning streams to dust, and killing animals with thirst. In winter, the North

Pole governs the weather. Arctic winds sweeping down across Canada bring subzero temperatures, blinding blizzards, and mountainous snowdrifts. From time to time, as if for variety, hailstorms, cloudbursts, and tornadoes batter the plains.

During Slow's childhood, the Great Plains teemed with wildlife. Deer and antelope numbered in the *millions,* fearing only the wolf. The grizzly bear, with its daggerlike teeth and razor-sharp claws, feared nothing. Prairie dogs, a type of ground squirrel, lived in vast underground "towns." Game birds—grouse, prairie chicken, geese, wild turkey—were everywhere. Flocks of passenger pigeons, extinct since 1914, blackened the sky for hundreds of miles on either side of the Missouri and Mississippi rivers. Washington Irving wrote:

> They appear absolutely in clouds, and move with astonishing velocity, their wings making a whistling sound as they fly. . . . When they alight, if on the ground, they cover whole acres at a time; if upon trees, the branches often break beneath their weight. If suddenly startled while feeding . . . the noise they make in getting on the wing is like the roar of a cataract or the sound of distant thunder.[13]

The buffalo, however, were the true lords of the Great Plains. A full-grown bull stands seven feet at the shoulder, measures twelve feet from his nose to his rump, and weighs over two thousand pounds. A mature cow is smaller; perhaps five feet tall, seven feet long, and weighing up to fifteen hundred pounds. Despite their bulk and weight, buffalo can run thirty-five miles an hour; a racehorse goes about forty miles an hour.[14]

When Slow was born, roughly forty million buffalo roamed the Great Plains. They moved in herds so large that today we can scarcely imagine them. The naturalist N. P. Langford described an "average" herd in 1862. Langford and some friends had just camped when

> We saw a cloud of dust rising in the east, and the rumbling grew louder and I think it was about half an hour when the front of the herd came into view. . . . From an observation with our field glasses, we judged the herd to be 5 or 6 (some said 8 or 10) miles wide, and the herd was more than an hour passing us at a gallop. . . . The

whole space, say 5 miles by 12 miles, as far as we could see, was a seemingly solid mass of buffaloes.[15]

An adult buffalo needs thirty pounds of grass each day. Since a herd could pick a place clean within hours, it had to keep moving or starve. The herds moved with the seasons. In the spring, they migrated northward, following the new grass. In the fall, they migrated southward toward the milder climate and more open grazing; that is, dry grass only partially covered by drifting snow.

Those Indians who hunted the buffalo did so only part-time. The largest group formed an alliance called the Three Tribes. For centuries, the Hidatsa, Mandan, and Arikara lived in solidly built villages of mud and thatch along the upper reaches of the Missouri. Able farmers, they grew squash, beans, and maize. Yet, despite their best efforts, they never had enough to eat. So, after planting their crops in the spring, they headed for buffalo country.

It took all their strength and ingenuity to follow the herds. On moving day, women placed their family's belongings on a travois or "dog-drag," a wooden frame slung between two poles. A strong dog could pull thirty-five pounds, which did not allow for many possessions. Lacking vehicles of any sort, everyone traveled on foot, barely covering six miles a day. Scouts walked several miles ahead to locate the buffalo. Behind them came the main body, surrounded by warriors ready for trouble. At the center were the women, each with a bundle on her back, hurrying the dogs along. Dogs also made for good eating, and no feast was complete without a serving of boiled or roasted puppy.

The "buffalo jump" was the Three Tribes' favorite method of killing buffalo. Coming to a high bluff or a steep-sided gully, they hid as best they could, waiting for a grazing herd. When it came within range, everyone—men, women, children—leaped up, shouting and waving blankets. The herd stampeded. Pressed from behind and unable to turn back, the animals went over the edge, bouncing, sliding, and tumbling downward. By the time they hit bottom, most were dead or dying. Women cut the meat into long, narrow strips, which they hung on racks to dry in the wind. Dried buffalo meat could keep for months without spoiling. Women also selected the best skins for tanning. Fastening them to the ground with wooden pegs, they scraped them smooth and over the next ten days applied a mixture of

Plains Indians air-drying strips of buffalo meat on racks. When prepared this way, the meat weighed little, could easily be transported, and held its nutritional value for years.

buffalo brains and water. Finally, they softened the skins by rubbing them with their hands.

So it went, century after century. At the end of the hunting season, the tribes returned to their villages to harvest their crops. And then, seemingly in the blink of an eye, everything changed. The Plains tribes discovered the horse.

Horses had once lived in North America, along with woolly mammoths, camels, and saber-toothed tigers. About fifteen thousand years ago, during the last Ice Age, they all died out. In the 1520s, the Spanish conquistadors reintroduced the horse when they invaded Mexico. Native warriors could not resist the charge of an armored knight on horseback. The horse was a war-winning weapon.

Moving northward from Mexico, the Spanish invaders crossed the Rio Grande River into Texas, Arizona, and New Mexico to start cattle ranches with animals brought from Spain. Since there were many cattle and few Spaniards, they taught local Indians to work as mounted herdsmen. Slaves in all but name, these Indian cowboys, called *vaqueros,* ran away whenever they got the chance. To hinder pursuit, they took the fastest horses and set many others free. These freed horses headed for the open grasslands. There, lacking natural enemies, they multiplied into vast herds. Spaniards called them *broncos mesteños,* "wild horses," the origin of the English word "mustang."

Vaqueros often fled to the Apache, a warlike tribe of farmers and hunters. To win acceptance, the fugitives brought gifts of stolen horses, which they taught their hosts to ride. That was not easy. At first the Apache feared the strange beasts. Gradually, however, they learned to sit on a horse's back without falling off. Some riders balanced themselves with two long sticks, pushing them against the ground on each side. Before long, the Apache were stealing Spanish horses on their own. As their herds grew, they traded their older mounts to neighboring tribes and taught them to ride. In this way, horses and riding skills spread from south to north and west to east.

The desire for horses acted as a magnet, drawing tribes to the Great Plains from the Rocky Mountains to the west and the lands bordering the Mississippi on the east. The story of these "horse Indians" is a familiar one of adventure, of people challenging the unknown in search of better lives. Just as whites moved westward seeking more farmland, Indians sought to escape farming. In little more than a century, from 1640 to 1770, thirty-seven tribes abandoned their gardens and began using horses to hunt the buffalo full-time. These tribes included the Teton Lakota, Cheyenne, Arapaho, Crow, Assiniboin, Comanche, Kiowa, Pawnee, Shoshone, and Blackfeet.

The buffalo became their staff of life. Its meat provided good food, having 50 percent less cholesterol, 70 percent less fat, and 30 percent more protein than beef. Since each person ate, on average, ten pounds of buffalo meat a day, a typical band consumed 3,600 tons of meat a year, or about 30,000 animals. Indians also had more than eighty nonfood uses for the buffalo. For example, they turned its skin into blankets, robes, clothing, shields, packs, bags, and lodge covers; horns became spoons and cups; sinew, a sturdy muscle fiber, supplied thread for sewing and bowstrings. Al-

Artist Frederic Remington specialized in Western themes. He painted this picture of a Plains Indian warrior in 1901. Such men learned to ride and fight at high speed on horseback from childhood.

together, the hunting tribes killed about two million buffalo each year. Yet the yearly birth of calves was so high that Indians believed they could hunt the shaggy beasts forever.[16]

Although the Missouri River tribes kept to their old ways, their villages became markets for Plains horses and European trade goods. Slow's ancestors got their first horses from the Arikara in 1750. They set out upon the sea of grass gladly, without any regrets. Horses allowed a few men to take more food in an hour than an entire village grew in a season of farming. Equally important, the horse and the buffalo changed their mental outlook. Command of these powerful animals gave them self-confidence and a sense of superiority. It was a good feeling, knowing they were masters of their own destiny.

Yet, before mastering their destiny, the young had to master themselves. Males and females had their own roles to play. These roles were totally different, but Slow's people did not consider one sex inferior or superior to the other. Children had no doubts about the path to follow in life, since there was only one path. They learned from their elders. A girl learned all she needed from her mother, female relatives, and older girls. A boy learned from his father, male relatives, and older boys.

Girls were destined to become wives, mothers, and homemakers. After Slow's sister, Good Feather, learned to walk, she followed her mother everywhere and imitated her in everything. Her Holy Door gave her a doll and a doll cradleboard, which she carried on her back like any other "wife." As she grew, Her Holy Door taught her to cook, tan buffalo skins, sew, and make household articles, including the house itself. On moving days, she helped strike the lodge and load it along with the family's other belongings on a horse travois—a load of about 125 pounds. At the next campsite, she helped unpack the lodge, raise it, and carry everything inside. Striking and raising a lodge took about ten minutes.

A man would not dream of helping a woman with her chores any more than she would dream of asking him to help. Yet she was no drudge. Husband and wife were equal partners with different duties. A wife was the "glue" that held the family together. Guided by the motto "An industrious woman lives in a good lodge," she owned the home and everything in it. If

MEAT
every part eaten, including:
hump
blood
liver and inner organs preserved for later use:
pemmican
jerky

BRAIN
hide-tanning

SKULL
ceremonies
Sun Dance

TAIL
fly brushes
whips

CHIPS
fuel
ceremonial smoking signals

HOOVES, FEET
glue
rattles

HORNS
cups
fire carrier
gunpowder flasks
spoons
ladles
headdresses
toys
rattles

MUSCLES (SINEW)
thread
bow backings
bindings
bowstrings

BLADDER, PAUNCH, STOMACH
cooking vessels
water vessels
basins
pouches
buckets
cups

PAUNCH LINING
buckets
cups
basins

BEARD
ornaments for clothing and weapons

HAIR
headdresses
saddle pad filler
pillows
ropes

HIDE
moccasins
cradles
winter robes
bedding
clothing
pouches

quivers
tepee covers
gun cases
shields
dolls
buckets
rattles
drums
cinches
ropes
thongs
saddles
stirrups
knife cases
bridles
masks
snowshoes
ornaments

BONES
knives
arrowheads (ribs)
shovels
splints
sleds
arrow straighteners
saddle trees
war clubs
scrapers
quirts
awls
paintbrushes

Diagram of a buffalo showing only some of its many uses.

Plains Indians used the horse travois, or drag, to haul their belongings from place to place.

the marriage failed, or if she fell in love with another man, she left without saying a word. Everyone expected the former husband to accept his loss gracefully. He must pass over it with a casual remark like "A dog has pissed on my lodge."[17]

Boys were destined to become providers, protectors, and warriors. Slow grew up knowing that one day he would have to kill, and go on killing until the day he died. A man who could not kill animals for food and enemies for protection or revenge could not survive on the Great Plains, much less support a family.

Killing was serious business. Slow's father taught him never to kill carelessly or for "pleasure." Hunters led exciting lives, but they were not sportsmen. Indians believed that all life was sacred, a gift from the Great Spirit. Slow learned always to beg an animal's forgiveness for taking its life and to explain that he needed it for food. If he did not, or if he failed to treat its remains with respect, its spirit would get angry. It would tell other animals of the insult, and they would not allow themselves to be killed, leaving the tribe to starve.

When Slow was big enough to bend a thin piece of wood with his hands, Sitting Bull gave him a miniature bow and arrows. The boy started by shooting at easy targets. Each time his arrow hit the mark, his father praised him warmly. If he missed, his father held his hands to show him the right way. About the age of three, Slow joined the gangs of little boys who ran around the camp, tormenting the dogs with blunt arrows and bringing home birds for cooking.

Slow and his friends trained long and hard. Their games were demanding, often dangerous contests disguised as "play." Each game had a set purpose. Boys developed their ability to endure pain by rolling in the snow or diving into icy water. In summer, they stood naked, allowing horseflies to bite them. Should they catch one of these tiny terrors, in revenge they stuck a straw in its backside and set it free. Oglala boys, said Black Elk, a famous religious leader, put dry sunflower seeds on their own wrists. "They were lit at the top, and we had to let them burn clear down to the skin. They hurt and made sores, but if we knocked them off or cried Owh!, we would be called women."[18]

Team games taught cooperation. For example, two teams faced each other in the Swing-Kicking game, a violent brawl. It began only after each side shouted this question: "Shall we grab them by the hair and knee them in the face until they bleed?"[19] In the Fire-Throwing game, each team attacked its opponent's base with hot coals thrown with willow sticks; the side that retreated, lost. Other games fostered courage, agility, endurance, and speed. Boys held footraces at noon, when the sun was hottest. Slow became the fastest runner in the tribe; only his friend Crawler beat him, but not often.

Slow's father told him that a Lakota man must study the animals and model himself upon them. He should be brave as the elk, watchful as the frog, patient as the spider, quiet as the snake, swift as the dragonfly, elusive as the coyote, and strong as the buffalo. Accordingly, Slow learned to sniff the air for buffalo or grizzly-bear scent. He picked up animal droppings, felt them, and crumbled them in his hand; their shape, hardness, and warmth told what animal had left them, what it had eaten, and whether it was nearby. He put his ear to the ground, listening for the echo of a distant buffalo herd on the move. A wolf's off-key howling or a flock of screeching magpies meant trouble.

Most of all, Slow became a keen observer. When one followed a trail, every bent blade of grass, every footprint and out-of-place stone, had meaning. Lots of shallow tracks close together told him that deer were calmly grazing, while sand thrown up in piles suggested playful fawns. Slow could even "read" a patch of dried urine. The position of urine in relation to a horse's hoofprints revealed its sex and its rider's mission. Mares urinated toward the rear of their hind legs, while stallions projected their urine forward. Now, women rode only mares, men only stallions. Many women meant that a band was moving camp. An all-male party was likely to be a war party.

Sitting Bull taught his son everything he knew about horses. Having obtained their first horses by trade, the Lakota soon found other ways of getting them. One way was to capture mustangs by lassoing pregnant mares or nursing mares with colts. Another was to lasso them at water holes, after they had drunk deeply and their sagging bellies kept them from galloping away at top speed.

All Plains Indian tribes commonly preferred to get their horses by stealing from other tribes. A successful thief proved his courage and earned the respect of his band. Few activities required more courage than sneaking into a camp at night and taking a prize horse tied in front of a lodge.

Since horses were a form of wealth, a man rich in horses attracted young women. If the man liked a woman, and she agreed, he offered to "buy" her from her father for a string of horses; social scientists call this a "bride price." The Lakota regarded generosity as a key virtue, saying: "A man must help others as much as possible, no matter who, by giving him horses, food, or clothing."[20] Those with many horses gained respect and influence by giving them away. Yet not all horse thieves lived to enjoy their

During one exciting afternoon, artist George Catlin watched Indians lasso wild horses.

riches. Getting caught meant certain death—but the danger made life more exciting.

Almost before Slow could walk, his father put him on a gentle stallion, which he led around for an hour every day. In this way, Slow got used to the animal's smell and movements. By the age of three, he could mount on his own, if necessary, by climbing a horse's foreleg much as a squirrel goes up a tree. When he turned five, his father gave him a horse to care for by himself. He also gave him some good advice: "Son, it is cowardly to be cruel. Be good to your pony."[21] When Slow was seven, his father asked him to look after the family's horse herd.

Slow spent days alone with dozens of horses. Except for a breechcloth, a piece of buckskin worn around the waist, he rode naked. "You are my gods," boys used to tell their horses. "I take good care of you." To amuse himself, Slow swam with his favorite horse in a stream. Or, perhaps like the youngster an American army officer once watched through his field glasses, Slow chased a wild horse at top speed. Catching it with his lasso, he mounted and went after another, and another, until sunset.[22]

When young riders got together, they passed the time with horse races and games like Throwing-Them-off-Their-Horses.[23] This game was not for weaklings. It had one object: to push an opponent off his galloping horse. Anyone who fell was "out," perhaps literally—knocked unconscious. That was too bad, but nobody showed him any pity or sympathy. The best he could do was get up, put on a brave face, and remount. If he lost some blood, that was to be expected. Bruises and scars were badges of honor with the Lakota. Boys liked to paint scars on their bodies.

Slow could not wait to try his skills for real. His chance came in 1841, at the age of ten. That spring, his father invited him to join the village hunters.

During the winter, with luck, hunters might trap a few buffalo in deep snow. But the main hunt took place in late summer or early fall, after the buffalo had grown their winter coats. At such times, the Lakota bands assembled as complete tribes to hunt and worship together. Every hunt followed a set pattern.

For the Lakota, hunting meant more than just killing for food. It was a religious activity blessed with offerings of smoke. Plains Indians smoked a blend of red willow bark and tobacco. Each band had a sacred pipe made of a stone bowl representing the earth and a wooden stem signifying all life. While waiting for the scouts to return, a holy man blew a puff of smoke in the four directions as an offering to Wakantanka. Then he prayed: "Grandfather, be merciful that my people may live."

When scouts located a herd, each hunter mounted his buffalo horse. He had trained this animal, used only for hunting, to stop short and make quick turns. Since he had to let go of the reins to free his hands during the chase, he had also trained it to respond to his voice or to pressure from his knees. A man's buffalo horse and his war horse were his prized possessions. If either of them were killed, it was the same as though a member of his family had been murdered, demanding vengeance in kind.

A seriously wounded buffalo could run over a mile before collapsing. Therefore, the hunter had to ride in close and aim for the heart or lungs to cause instant death. Some hunters carried a fourteen-foot lance tipped with a flint point. The object was to thrust the lance downward and forward into a vital organ. Since it took exceptional courage to kill a buffalo this way, carrying only a lance was a show of supreme confidence.

Hunter's buffalo magic. This hunter has painted a buffalo design on his face and chest to encourage buffalo and other animals to allow themselves to be killed for food. From a painting by George Catlin.

Most hunters preferred the bow and arrow. In the right hands, these weapons were as deadly as any gun. Until the invention of the repeating rifle in the 1870s, guns were difficult to aim and reload on a galloping horse. Shot from a bow at fifty feet, however, a flint-tipped arrow could penetrate a board one inch thick. Most hunters could send an arrow into a buffalo up to the feathers, even drive it completely through, downing a second buffalo running alongside. And they did it quickly. Hunters grasped eight arrows in one hand and had loosed them all before the first found its mark. Each arrow had a long tapering head, its rear sloping backward for easy recovery and reuse. A groove along the shaft allowed the animal's blood to flow freely, hastening its death.

The hunters left camp at sunrise. Nobody was allowed to ride out ahead of the group, since they might start a stampede, spoiling the others' chances. Special hunt guards rode on either side of the group to enforce the rules. If anyone went off on his own, the guards knocked him off his horse and beat him with their bows. If he resisted, they killed him on the spot.

Sighting their prey, the hunters separated into two groups, forming an arc to the right and left of the herd. The idea was to create a "horse surround"; that is, to charge and encircle the herd, then drive inward from all directions at once.

Excitement rose. The pipe bearer blew more smoke toward the heavens. Men whispered into their horses' ears, telling them to run fast and not

Buffalo Hunt, a painting by Charles M. Russell. Hunting buffalo was very dangerous. Notice how close the riders must get to be able to land a deadly blow with a lance or shoot an arrow.

be afraid. Many fixed their eyes on a single buffalo, praying silently: "Grandfather, my children are hungry. You were created for that. So I must kill you."[24]

"Hopo! Hopo!" the chief cried. "Let's go!"

The hunters charged. Hearing hoofbeats, the buffalo realized their danger and stampeded, running forward in a mass.

Each man rode into the herd, lancing or shooting as he went. *"Yuhoo!"* he yelled as each buffalo fell.

Galloping into a stampeding herd was dangerous. A bull could easily turn and charge its pursuer, or, if wounded, drop in the horse's path, causing the horse to fall and throw its rider under other buffalo's pounding hooves. At such times all that stood between life and death was your friends' ability to pick you up quickly. Artist George Catlin watched a hunt in 1832:

> A cloud of dust was soon raised, which in parts obscured the throng where the hunters were galloping their horses around and driving the whizzing arrows or their long lances to the hearts of these noble animals; which in many instances, becoming infuriated with deadly wounds in their sides, erected their shaggy manes over their blood-shot eyes and furiously plunged forwards at the sides of their assailants' horses, sometimes goring them to death at a lunge, and putting their dismounted riders to flight for their lives. . . . Many were the bulls that turned upon their assailants and met them with desperate resistance; and many were the warriors who were dismounted, and saved themselves by the superior muscles of their legs; some who were closely pursued by the bulls, wheeled suddenly around and snatching the part of a buffalo robe from around their waists, threw it over the horns and the eyes of the infuriated beast, and darting by its side drove the arrow or the lance to its heart.[25]

Each carcass, easily identified by markings on the arrows in its side, belonged to the man who downed it. As the hunters examined their kill, the rest of the village arrived for the butchering. People knelt beside the carcasses to lap up the oozing blood, which they regarded as highly nutritious

Strange things would sometimes happen during buffalo hunts. George Catlin saw an angry buffalo butt a horse while its owner stood on the horse's back and on that of another buffalo.

(so did white fur trappers). Using flint knives, they slit open bellies, thrust in their arms up to the elbows, and dragged out coils of intestines. These they held to their lips while squeezing the vitamin-rich mush, partially digested grass, into their mouths. The naturalist John James Audubon witnessed such a feast by white hunters: "Now one breaks in the skull of the bull, and with bloody fingers draws out the hot brains and swallows them with peculiar zest; another has now reached the liver, and is gobbling down enormous pieces of it."[26] Infants in their cradleboards solemnly chewed pieces of raw meat.

Slow killed a calf during his first hunt. His father thought that fitting, since his boy was small, like a calf. That success brought Slow to a milestone in this life. The time had come for his "vision quest."

The Lakota believed that everything in nature was really two things at once. There was a physical being that you saw and the invisible spirit that controlled its actions. When a boy approached manhood, he sought the spirits in a vision quest. If he succeeded, a spirit revealed itself to him, became his guardian, and lent him its "medicine," or magical power. Those men who received unusual powers became holy men. People relied upon holy men for everything from curing illness to foretelling the future. Women seldom went on vision quests.

Slow prepared for the experience by purifying his body and mind. Guided by a holy man, he entered a sweat lodge, the Plains Indian version of a steam bath. There he chanted prayers while sprinkling water on hot stones. The stones gave up their "breath" as steam, cleansing his body by causing him to sweat. After several days of this, Slow went by himself to a lonely spot, most likely a high bluff, wearing just moccasins and a breech-cloth. Seated on a buffalo robe, he neither slept nor ate, but smoked a pipe and prayed for a vision. If he was lucky, it came within a few days.

A spirit could take any shape. It might be something connected to the weather, the elements: wind rustling the grass, a shadow cast by a passing cloud, the rumble of distant thunder, the sun's rays reflecting on a stone, a shooting star. Most visions, however, took animal form. There were count-less possibilities, such as a wolf howling, a woodpecker hammering at a tree, a cricket chirping, or a gnat buzzing. Whatever form the spirit took, it spoke to the youngster, promising to be his guardian. It taught him magical songs that would protect him and bring success. It gave him a list of taboos, or things to avoid—places he must not visit, foods he should not eat, and words he dare not say.

Although invisible to others, visions were real to those who experi-enced them. We do not know where Slow went on his vision quest or how long he waited for the vision to appear. Only Slow and the holy man who guided him knew what he saw during his special time. All we can say is that it must have left a profound impression. Acting on the spirit's instruc-tion, Slow began to keep a "medicine bag," a collection of sacred objects— body paints, bear claws, eagle talons, odd-shaped stones—he believed had magical powers. These objects, together with future visions and dreams, en-abled him to see into the future, he believed.

Animals "spoke" to Slow, and he to them. Fellow Hunkpapas recalled that he spoke to buffalo and wolves. One day, when he was about fifteen, he met a wolf with two arrows sticking in its side. "Boy," said the animal, "if you will relieve me, your name shall be great." Slow pulled out the arrows, cleaned the wounds with water, and sent the wolf away with a song he composed on the spot, dedicated to the wolf tribe:

An Oglala medicine man offering smoke to Wakantanka, the Every-where Spirit. Photo by Edward S. Curtis.

Alone in the wilderness I roam
With much hardship in the wilderness I roam
A wolf said this to me.[27]

The youngster had a special relationship with the meadowlark, a song-bird with a yellow breast and a black crescent-shaped marking beneath the throat. One day, Slow left his friends to rescue a wounded meadowlark. "Let us," he said, "be kind to birds, especially to our meadowlark friends that speak to us in our language."

"Brother Meadowlark," as he called it, returned the favor. While Slow lay asleep under a tree, he dreamed that a meadowlark landed on an over-hanging branch. The bird said, "Lie still! Lie still!" Sure enough, when he awoke, he saw a grizzly bear standing beside him. Following the bird's "advice," he lay motionless until it lumbered away.[28] Slow looked up at the bird and sang a song he made up in its honor:

Pretty bird you have seen me and took pity on me
Amongst the tribes to live, you wish for me
Ye bird tribes from henceforth, always my relation shall be.[29]

Grizzlies, however, were not as dangerous as people. Although grizzlies fought for food and in self-defense, they never joined together to make war.

TWO

WAR AND MORE

"I will give my flesh and blood that I may conquer my enemies!"
—LAKOTA SUN DANCE VOW

"The western Dahcotah have no fixed habitations. Hunting and fighting, they wander incessantly, through summer and winter. . . . War is the breath in their nostrils. Against most of the neighboring tribes they cherish rancorous hatred, transmitted from father to son, and inflamed by constant aggression and retaliation."
—FRANCIS PARKMAN, <u>The Oregon Trail</u>, 1846

WHITE PEOPLE DID NOT bring war to the Great Plains. Long before they arrived, the Plains tribes themselves participated in what seemed an eternal cycle of violence. Children inherited their parents' wars, like family heirlooms passed down through generations. Tribes fought to protect their hunting grounds and seize new ones, to defend themselves, and to avenge past losses. For example, the Crow constantly fought the Blackfeet. In turn, the Blackfeet battled the Crow, Shoshone, and Assiniboin, who also fought other tribes. Yet, despite their conflicts, all agreed that they hated the Lakota more than any other tribe.

Lakota history is a story of loss and then conquest. After losing their own lands and learning to hunt buffalo on horseback, Slow's ancestors became aggressors. First to feel their power were the Mandan, Hidatsa, and Arikara, the very tribes that had introduced them to the horse. By the 1740s, Lakota warriors were stealing villagers' horses and attacking their hunting parties. Eventually, the Lakota forced them to abandon their homes and move in with other tribes for safety. The Lakota then claimed their hunting grounds for themselves.

After crossing the Missouri, Slow's ancestors fanned out, always pushing in a westerly direction. Some bands headed northwest, toward the Yellowstone country in present-day Montana. Other bands headed southward and westward into the Dakota Territory, future states of North and South Dakota.

This advance was no peaceful excursion. It was a march of conquest. Wherever they went, the Lakota found other groups already using the land. Ignoring their claims, they fought no fewer than twenty-six tribes. Of these, they "buried the hatchet," made peace, with only the Cheyenne and Arapaho. The others became their sworn enemies, who hated and feared Slow's ancestors while the Lakota boasted of their victories. Like a powerful vision, success in war was a gift of the Great Spirit, proof of their supremacy.

A century later, by the time of Slow's birth in 1831, the Lakota territory stretched west from the Missouri River to the Rocky Mountains and south from the Yellowstone River to the Platte River in Wyoming. Since the seasonal migrations of the buffalo herds crossed Lakota land, they ruled the heart of the northern buffalo range. This was not an area the Lakota wished to share, much less surrender. Later, even as they fought white invaders, they continued to expand their holdings by conquest.

War was a daily reality for the Lakota. When Slow was small, his mother dressed his feet in tiny moccasins before going to bed, since they might have to run from the lodge if an enemy attacked. A model youngster, he later killed buffalo and had a vision. Yet he was still not a complete person. Although each successful hunt brought him a step closer to manhood, hunting could not make him a man. War alone could do that.

If Plains Indians hunted to live, they lived to fight. War was part of Slow's mind-set, his expectations of life, ingrained in him from infancy. The idea that people should prefer peace to war would have struck him as strange. Peace, to him, was merely a time between wars. Fighting was natural. Success in battle was the true measure of a man's worth; courage the supreme virtue. Victory in battle brought the greatest rewards. These were not material things, but the admiration of his people. Only the successful warrior, Slow knew, could advise others, speak in tribal councils, and become a chief. No woman would marry a man who had not proven himself in battle.[1]

The Lakota excused only the *winkte,* or the "halfmen-halfwomen," from battle. These were male homosexuals who dressed as women, spoke in "women's" voices, and did women's work. *Winkte* were not uncommon among the Plains tribes. In the 1500s, Spanish explorers reported "men who marry other men and serve as their wives."[2] Plains Indians accepted— no, valued—*winkte* as members of the community. Skilled at tanning and clothing decoration, they were also persuasive "love-talkers"; that is, they delivered the proposals of young men too shy to speak for themselves. Although they did not fight, they joined war parties to care for the wounded.

From what we know about Slow's early life, he had no intention of becoming a *winkte.* His destiny, he knew, lay on the warpath. Successful warriors were the village darlings. He remembered how, when he was a little boy, his mother pointed them out, describing their deeds with admiration in her voice. Slow's father could match his war honors with anyone's, and Slow listened intently to stories of his adventures. Father enjoyed the company of warriors. Often he asked his wife to prepare a meal worthy of his friends. They'd eat heartily, boasting of their deeds between mouthfuls of buffalo meat. Warriors were supposed to boast, for it reminded everyone that they were special—"braves." Humility, the Lakota believed, was a sign of weak character.[3]

Of course, warriors died. That was natural, and the younger they died, the better. Each time members of the Kit Fox—Young Fox—warrior society paraded, they sang as onlookers cheered:

> *I am a Fox.*
> *I am supposed to die.*
> *If there is anything difficult,*
> *If there is anything dangerous,*
> *That is mine to do.*[4]

Fathers repeated proverbs such as "The brave die young." "Son," they would say earnestly, "I never want to see you live to be an old man. Die young on the battlefield. That is the way a Lakota dies."[5]

How strange all this sounds to us! The twentieth century has been the bloodiest in human history, and many of us do not see war as such a necessary or marvelous activity. Nevertheless, Lakota fathers spoke out of pride and love for their sons. Nomadic hunters lived hard lives, with old age nothing to look forward to. Failing health—bad teeth, arthritis, blurred vision, stomach troubles—meant pain without any hope of relief. Worse, aging brought loss of self-esteem. Hunters unable to hunt became burdens to their families. Warriors unable to fight became objects of ridicule. Better to die bravely in the prime of life than to wither away slowly, they believed.

War required skills above and beyond those of the hunter's. For example, boys practiced sneaking up on the "enemy" by stealing meat off the drying racks. If they were caught, the young women laughed at them. Games taught them to avoid arrows. Friends chose a boy to be "it." Armed only with a play shield, he had to stand before a hailstorm of blunt-tipped arrows. The trick was always to keep the shield in motion. A shield had on its rim a circle of feathers that fluttered with each movement of the arm, confusing an enemy's aim. Even so, you could not dodge every arrow. These did not break the skin, but caused painful bruises. Even a blunt arrow could take out an eye. Boys also played the Spear-and-Hoop game. Its object was to train the hand and eye; a boy would throw a spear through a wooden hoop thrown into the air.

Young warriors practicing with lances. Notice how the two warriors on the right are using their horses as moving shields. Painting by George Catlin.

The warrior had to master certain riding skills. By the age of twelve, Slow would have been the envy of any American circus rider. He could mount a horse as it galloped past him and then leap from its back onto the back of another. He could ride at top speed, lean over, and snatch a white pebble off the ground. Riding side by side, he and a friend could pick up a fallen comrade at full gallop. Slow became expert at using his charging horse as a shield. He would drop down to one side, holding on by a heel hooked over its back and an elbow hooked into a loop of braided buffalo hair woven into its mane. This maneuver allowed him to shoot arrows over the animal's back or from under its neck without showing himself to the enemy.

Youngsters had to overcome their natural fear of dead people. To help them, warriors paraded between the lodges with enemy heads, ears, hands, and feet skewered on sharp sticks. Sometimes they dragged dead bodies through camp by ropes tied to their feet. Parents encouraged their sons to shoot the bodies with arrows and crush their skulls with rocks. Black Elk recalled how, when he was a child, warriors killed a Crow horse thief. "The women," he said, "cut him up with axes and scattered him around. It was horrible. Then the people built a fire right there beside the Crow and had a kill dance. Men, women and children danced right in the middle of the night, and they sang [victory] songs." Although such sights sickened him at first, Black Elk got used to such spectacles. So did Slow and other young-sters. Later, Black Elk became a respected warrior and an able medicine man. We do not know how Slow reacted to his very first sight of a dead en-emy. We do know, however, that when he was ten, warriors dared the boys to touch the bloody remains of a Crow warrior. Slow went first, winning praise as the bravest boy in camp that day.[6]

Warriors scalped or mutilated the dead, but never did both. Scalping had a long history. Some white people still believe that the New England Puritans introduced the practice in the 1600s. To encourage the killing of Native Americans, the story goes, they offered bounty hunters money for scalps; Indians simply copied the practice. That is only partially true. Whites, as we shall see, often took Indian scalps. But scalping existed in North America long before the arrival of Europeans. Scientists have found skulls, some over a thousand years old, bearing the marks of scalping. A warrior grasped an enemy's hair with one hand, cut around the hairline with a knife, and pulled the scalp off the skull.[7] Explorers described how the Eastern Woodland tribes dried scalps by stretching them over hoops made of twigs.

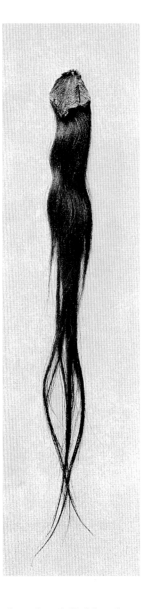

This scalp probably belonged to a Plains Indian and was taken by an-other Indian. White men also took scalps during the Indian wars.

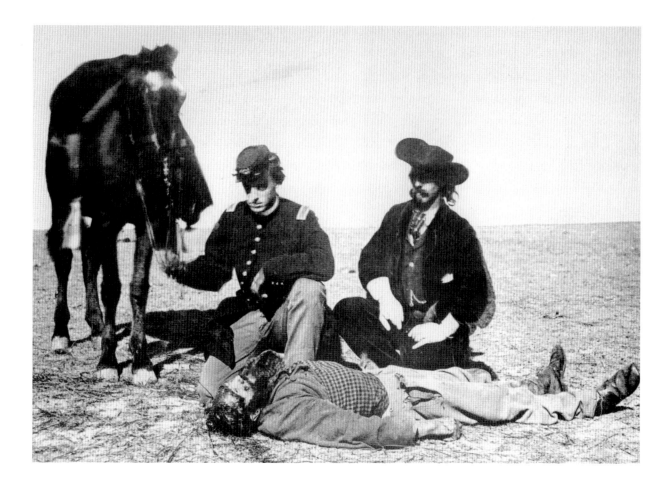

The scalped body of a hunter named Ralph Morrison was found by army scouts near Fort Dodge, Kansas, in 1868.

The custom of scalping probably originated in certain religious beliefs. Some Native Americans noticed that hair is the only part of the body that grows continuously over a person's lifetime. Thus, they reasoned, it must be an extension of the human life force, or soul. Out of respect for their souls, they spent hours each day combing their hair and greasing it with bear fat or buffalo dung. Wives parted their hair down the center of their heads and painted the line red for good luck in childbirth. Scalping, therefore, destroyed the victim's soul, preventing it from entering the next world. Other tribes, like those in California, Oregon, and Washington, never practiced scalping.

Mutilation without scalping was worse than scalping. Plains Indians believed that the soul kept its human shape after death. Thus, you entered the next world as you were at the time of death. For example, a woman who died while pregnant carried her unborn baby throughout eternity, while dying with a toothache meant everlasting pain. Similarly, warriors cut victims to pieces to ensure their eternal agony. Comrades risked their lives to save the bodies of friends from scalping or mutilation. It was the ultimate favor one man could do for another.[8]

Plains Indians also killed, scalped, and mutilated women and children for the sake of honor. That made sense to them. Since men fought desperately to defend their families, warriors believed that killing loved ones in front of their defender showed courage.[9]

By their early teens, boys would sneak away in groups of three or four to experience killing people for themselves. A Lakota warrior named Wooden Leg claimed his first victim, a Shoshone, at the age of thirteen. He and some friends once found a lodge with an elderly Shoshone man inside. Taken by surprise, the poor fellow never had a chance. "We cut up the body of the old Shoshone man," Wooden Leg recalled. "We cut off his hands, his feet, his head. We ripped open his breast and his belly. I stood there and looked at his heart and his liver. We tore down the lodge, built a bonfire of it and its contents and piled the remnants of the dead body on this bonfire. We stayed there until nothing was left but ashes and coals." Then they rushed home to brag about their deed.[10]

Slow (as far as we know) never joined such a group. Instead, in 1845 he invited himself along on a genuine war party. He had just turned fourteen.

His band was camping along the Powder River in northern Wyoming—Crow territory. One day, his father's friend, Good Voiced Elk, decided to lead a raid. Anyone could be a "war chief" if he could get others to follow him. Since Good Voiced Elk had a fine war record and strong medicine, he began to drum up interest. He sat in front of his lodge, beating a drum and singing war songs. One by one, those who wished to join "signed up" by puffing his black war pipe, black being the color of death. When perhaps thirty men had joined up, they left camp early the next morning.

Each rode a saddle horse and led his warhorse by a buffalo-hair rope. Like the buffalo horse, this animal was specially trained and used only for battle. To make it long-winded, its owner had widened its nostrils by slitting them on either side. Fast and agile, a warhorse could leap over a fallen enemy and allow a wounded Lakota to hold on to its tail for support while it dragged him out of harm's way.

Each warrior carried versions of hunting weapons adapted to fighting on horseback. Unlike the heavy hunting lance, the war lance was lightweight, measuring only eight feet. While a hunting arrow might be pulled out for reuse, war arrows had barbed points resembling fish hooks. Attached loosely to the shaft, the head easily broke off inside the victim. The only way to remove it was to push it entirely through the body and out the other side, causing further harm. In addition, each man carried a knife, a tomahawk or hatchet, and a war club. The war club had a fourteen-inch handle with an egg-shaped stone fastened to the end by rawhide. This vicious weapon could crack a man's skull as easily as a hen's egg. Some war clubs had tapered wooden handles with three flint blades set in the handle. Finally, every warrior carried a shield. Fashioned from thick layers of buffalo hide, a shield could stop any arrow. Shields could even stop bullets if they hit at an angle rather than straight on.

Warriors believed that shields had supernatural power. A shield's design, revealed by one's guardian spirit in a dream, offered magical protection. Eagle feathers, for example, gave their owner the courage of that bird. The painted figure of a grizzly, or its claws attached to the shield's rim, gave the owner the bear's fierceness. Knights during the Middle Ages decorated their shields with the sign of the cross for the same reason: to gain God's favor in battle. Like the Christian knight, when a Lakota warrior held his shield, he dared not tell a lie or think bad thoughts. If he did, it would fail him when he needed it most. Throughout his life, Slow carried a blue shield with eagle feathers fluttering from the rim and a black bird painted in the center.

Although Sitting Bull used a picture of a buffalo as his "signature," he always had a sacred-bird design painted on his shield.

The youngster watched his father leave camp with his friends. Burning with envy, he mounted his horse and set out after them alone. He did not tell his mother or sisters, knowing they would object.

Following the trail of horse tracks, Slow kept out of sight, fearing his father would send him back if he appeared too soon. Toward evening, after the war party had gone a long way, he rode into its night camp. "We are going, too," Slow declared, patting his horse's head.[11]

His father had a stern look on his face, but inwardly his heart swelled with pride. "You have a good running horse," he said. "Try to do something brave."[12]

However, Good Voiced Elk had the last word. In joining a war party, its members agreed to follow the leader only in certain matters. A war chief appointed the war party's scouts, selected its route, and set its objective. Yet he could not give orders, let alone punish disobedience. At best, he was a role model who had good medicine. During battle, he shouted advice and led by personal example, which a warrior was free to ignore. Now, since every boy had to prove himself sometime, Good Voiced Elk decided to let his friend's son come along.

Lakota war parties took no special precautions while in their own country. They traveled by day, eating freshly killed buffalo meat. All that changed when they neared enemy territory. Moving cautiously, at night they lit no fires and ate only dried meat. If the leader wanted to cover ground quickly, they rode all night, taking turns sleeping in the saddle; while one slept, a comrade led his horse. Scouts usually rode a day ahead of the main force. Covered with wolf skins, they lay on tops of buttes and examined the countryside for hours before going farther. If all seemed well, they signaled by waving blankets, riding their horses in various patterns, and imitating animal calls. War parties seldom used smoke signals, because these were visible to friend and enemy alike.[13]

Some warriors probably quit and went home after entering enemy territory. They left honorably, without anyone accusing them of cowardice. A warrior might take anything—the hooting of an owl, the barking of a coyote, an odd-shaped stone, a dream—as a sign from his guardian spirit to leave at once. If enough men saw bad signs, it meant their medicine was not working right. Then everybody turned back.

Their caution made sense. Hunting bands could not afford severe losses from battles. A warrior's death might impoverish his family, burdening the entire band. Worse, no band was big enough to survive heavy and constant losses. For that reason, warriors thought it foolish to attack if even one man was sure to die. "They will not venture an engagement," wrote an American officer, "unless they hold all the winning cards. To risk as little as possible—such is their fundamental maxim."[14] When not protecting their families, warriors never fought if outnumbered. Nor did they ignore losses to make repeated charges, or stand to receive an enemy charge, or die to the last man to hold a position, as sometimes happened when American and European armies fought. The best attack was a surprise attack, preferably an ambush, since that reduced the chance of loss.

Warriors did not try to annihilate an entire tribe. True, a small band, caught by surprise, might suffer dreadfully. Yet that was unusual. Generally, when half the enemy was killed, the victors allowed the others to escape. More than one fight ended with the chief shouting: "That is enough!"[15]

Plains Indians saw the warpath as, above all, the path of honor. No warrior ever gained honor merely through shedding blood. Any halfway decent archer could shoot from a safe distance; a coward could kill with a stab in the back. Tribes valued each deed in proportion to the danger involved. A warrior gained honor by risking his own life. Scouting ahead of a war party took courage, as did stealing horses from an enemy camp. Both brought respect.

Good Voiced Elk's scouts located a small band of Crow hunters near the Red Water River. Immediately, the war party hid behind a low hill and prepared for action. Each warrior began by making medicine; that is, checking that his spiritual "armor" was in good shape. (Stonewall Jackson, the great Civil War general, did this by getting down on his knees and praying before each battle.) The Lakota warrior prepared himself by painting his face and body with bold, exciting designs. "War paint" was not supposed to scare the enemy, but to give the wearer magical protection. Each warrior had his own pattern—stripes, dots, circles, zigzags, sunbursts—given him by his guardian spirit in a dream.

After painting himself, the warrior did the same for his horse. Here, too, decoration was a form of magic. The warrior might paint his mount in a solid color, or add designs such as lightning bolts, snowflakes, and hailstones. He tied eagle feathers, symbols of freedom and power, to its tail to give it speed. For sharp vision, he painted circles around its eyes. Still other decorations advertised the rider's war record. Painted hoofprints represented successful horse-stealing raids. Red handprints on the horse's hips showed the number of scalps its owner had taken. Straight lines, one above the other, were coup marks. The rider himself wore an eagle feather for each coup; some had enough coup feathers to make an elaborate warbonnet with two streamers of feathers running down their backs.

Slow wore no feathers. Nevertheless, he painted his horse, a gray stallion, red and his own body yellow from head to foot. Besides his weapons, he carried a coup stick, a gift from his father. He intended to use that stick or die trying.

As the Crows neared the hill, Slow's enthusiasm overcame his good sense. Without waiting for Good Voiced Elk's signal, the boy shouted a war cry and broke cover at a gallop. Having lost the element of surprise, the others could only follow in his dust. "Yip, yip, yip!" they yelled, slapping their open mouths to make their war cry.

Outnumbered, the startled Crows turned and fled. One Crow, with a lame horse, however, could not keep up the pace. As Slow's cries grew louder, the Crow thought it better to stand and fight rather than die with his back to the hated Lakotas. Suddenly, he drew rein, dismounted, and notched an arrow on his bowstring.

An experienced warrior would have flung himself to one side of his horse to avoid the arrow. Not Slow. He came like a whirlwind, leaning forward with the outstretched coup stick. Before the Crow could shoot, he whacked him across the arm, spoiling his aim. The arrow flew off harmlessly. *"On-hey!"* the boy shouted at the top of his voice. "I, Slow, have conquered him!" The others arrived seconds later. They killed the Crow and went on to kill a few more of his companions. Next morning they started back.[16]

A few days later, the war party reached its home village. At dawn, it galloped in yelling and waving scalps at the end of sticks. The whole village turned out to celebrate. Mothers patted their sons' faces, tears of joy streaming down their cheeks. Old people shouted the warriors' names. Young women hoped to marry such brave men. Boys cheered, hoping their chance would come soon.

That night the village held a Dance-Until-Morning dance, or "Hair-Kill dance," around a roaring campfire. Later a woman or a *winkte* would dry each scalp on a hoop. The warrior could then display it on a pole outside his lodge or use it to decorate his shield or clothing.

Sitting Bull's first coup. Although he drew the event for his pictorial autobiography with colored crayons, we have reproduced it and several other of his drawings in black and white.

Slow did not take the Crow warrior's scalp. He got something better. He had scored a first coup—the highest honor—his first time in battle. No Lakota could have wished for more.

That night, his father gave away horses as a tribute to his son. The best gift, however, he saved for last. He led Slow around camp on his best warhorse. Slow smiled. Like the mighty buffalo bull, he was strong and fearless.

"My son has struck the enemy! He is brave!" his father shouted. Then he gave him the most precious thing he owned: his own name. "I dub him *Tatan'ka Iyota'ke!*"[17]

Thus, at the age of fourteen, the boy Slow vanished and the man Sitting Bull took his place.

Sitting Bull loved fighting. After counting coup for the first time, he seldom missed a chance to take the warpath. His pictorial autobiography records many battles with Crows, Assiniboins, and other enemies during the 1840s and 1850s, all ending in victory. Each time, before setting out, he composed a song. Years later, his companions sang those songs for white visitors to the tribal reservation. Among these visitors was Walter S. Campbell, who wrote under the name Stanley Vestal. As a professor at the University of Oklahoma, Vestal often visited Indian reservations, where he collected their drawings and translated their stories and songs. These translations are historical "documents," windows into their author's mind and soul. Sitting Bull believed entirely in the Lakota ideal of war. Although he had good medicine, he expected to die fighting, as a brave man should. In one song, a favorite, he prepared his mother for bad news:

> No chance for me to live;
> Mother, you might as well mourn.[18]

The young man's exploits became famous not only among his own people, but across the entire northern Great Plains. Always the first to charge the enemy, he drew their attention by shouting *"Tatan'ka Iyota'ke he miye"*—"Sitting Bull, I am he!"[19]

Once he and some friends cornered a lone Crow warrior. After an exchange of shots, the Crow ran out of arrows. Sitting Bull had three arrows left. Rather than take unfair advantage, he shot two of them into the ground within reach of the Crow. As the Crow put an arrow to his bowstring, Sitting Bull shot him dead with his remaining arrow. Ultimately, he wore thirty coup feathers in his warbonnet. Even older men thought it a privilege to fight at his side. *"Tatanka-Iyotanka tahoksila!"* they shouted as they charged. "We are Sitting Bull's boys!"[20]

The band's elders decided to honor Sitting Bull. In 1852, after he turned twenty-one, they elected him to the Kit Fox and Strong Heart warrior societies. These societies, composed of the tribe's bravest fighters, had various duties: policing the buffalo hunts, protecting the camp, giving advice on key matters.

During Sitting Bull's initiation into the Strong Hearts, members chanted in unison: "If you get killed, that will be good. For this is the rule."[21] In the ultimate show of confidence, they also made him one of their two sash-wearers.

A sash-wearer was a warrior's warrior—the bravest of the brave. He wore a long strip of red cloth draped over his shoulder as a badge of office, with the remainder rolled up under his arm. In battle, he dismounted from his horse, unrolled the sash, pinned the free end to the ground with an arrow, and sang his war songs. With the battle raging all around, he never moved from that spot, preferring to die rather than save his life by retreating. Only a fellow society member could release him by pulling out the arrow.

Sitting Bull's hunting skills and war honors made him a "good catch" for any woman. He married at least five times and fathered perhaps fifteen children, including three sets of twins. We know little about his family life. Light Hair, his first wife, apparently died in childbirth in 1852, their first year of marriage. After a while, he married Snow On Her and Scarlet Woman, and then two others.[22]

Like all Plains Indians, the Hunkpapa practiced polygamy; that is, a man was allowed to have more than one wife at a time. What with hunting accidents and war, there were never enough men to go around; women in some bands outnumbered men three to one.[23] Polygamy gave most women a protector and a chance at motherhood. It also made economic sense. A man's wives shared the hard work of tanning hides and homemaking. Wives, therefore, often asked their husband to marry as many women as he could support. If he did not, they called him selfish, an insult among the Lakota. Some men had six wives.

Sitting Bull's first set of wives did not get along. Old-timers told Stanley Vestal that Snow On Her refused to share. Rather than let Scarlet Woman have Sitting Bull to herself on certain nights, she insisted that the three of them sleep together. This gave Sitting Bull little rest, forcing him to lie flat on his back. If he tried to turn his face to one wife, the other pulled at him. Finally, Snow On Her became so quarrelsome that he "threw her away"— divorced her. Yet Scarlet Woman did not have him to herself for long. She died, leaving him with a young son. Eventually, he married Four Robes and her sister, Seen by Her Nation. This arrangement worked, and these two women lived with him until his death.[24]

Everyone liked Sitting Bull. The man had personal magnetism, an inborn ability to connect with others on an emotional level. Mary Collins, a Christian missionary who knew Sitting Bull in the last years of his life, spoke from experience. "He had," she recalled, "some indefinable power which could not be resisted by his people, or even others who came in contact with him."[25] That power was due to the self-assurance he learned from his spirit-helpers.

Sitting Bull illustrates how he stole a drove of horses from the Crow. Captured horses not only brought wealth to the tribe, but honor to the thief who showed exceptional courage by getting close to an enemy village at night.

Sitting Bull laughed easily and enjoyed hearing others laugh. Yet, at heart, he was a serious person. A natural leader, he knew that leadership brought responsibility for those who trusted him. In daily life, he lived up to his obligations in countless ways. A generous man, he always gave meat to the needy; nor, for that matter, would he allow a dog to go hungry. A peacemaker, he spoke calmly and sensibly, helping people to settle their quarrels. When they did, he gave them gifts and had a dance in celebration.

Youngsters knew they had a friend in Sitting Bull. They sought his advice about everything from hunting to courting. Once he taught a bashful fellow named Otter Robe how to get along with the opposite sex. Otter Robe was dancing between two young women, his arms dangling awkwardly at his sides, a solemn expression on his face. Sitting Bull draped the youth's arms across their shoulders, saying, "You'll have more fun if you dance that way."[26]

Sitting Bull seemed to have a charmed life. Although always in the thick of the fight, he never received more than a scratch from an enemy arrow. That changed in 1856.

He and some friends had stolen horses from a Crow camp. The raiders moved as fast as they could, but keeping the horses together slowed their getaway. That allowed a dozen mounted Crows to gain on them. Rather than set the horses free, a few warriors drove them onward while the others turned to meet the enemy. When the Crows saw that the Hunkpapas meant to fight, they halted. The enemies eyed one another from a few yards away, each waiting for the other to make the first move.

Suddenly, three Crows charged. The first darted among the Hunkpapas, counted coup on a warrior, and galloped away. The second killed a Hunkpapa and escaped without a scratch. The third wore the red buckskin shirt of a Crow war chief. He took his time. Reining in his horse, he dismounted and advanced on foot. That fellow yonder, with the warbonnet and red sash: the chief wanted to meet him in single combat.

Sitting Bull accepted the challenge. He did not pin his sash to the ground this time; he wanted to get at the enemy right away, not wait until he came to him. Following his opponent's example, he also dismounted. Both men had flintlock muskets, old guns that fired a lead ball. As they ran toward each other, Sitting Bull sang a Strong Heart song:

Sitting Bull, dismounted and crouching behind his shield, shoots a Crow warrior at the same time as the enemy shoots him in the foot.

> *Comrades, whoever runs away,*
> *He is a woman, they say;*
> *Therefore, through many trials,*
> *My life is short!*[27]

The Crow aimed carefully. Seeing that, Sitting Bull dropped to one knee, held up his shield, and raised his musket. *BANGBANG!* Both men fired at once. Sitting Bull's bullet hit the Crow in the stomach, its force hurling him backward. The Crow's bullet tore through Sitting Bull's left foot. Ignoring the pain, he

ran up to his victim, plunged his knife into his heart, and took his scalp. The death of their chief broke the Crows' war medicine. They ran away. Sitting Bull remounted and rejoined his friends. He would never forget that brave warrior. The wound the Crow had given him did not heal properly. Although he could still hunt and fight with the best of them, he walked with a limp for the rest of his life.

Sitting Bull's victory over the Crow chief brought him to another one of life's divides. In times of trouble or danger, warriors vowed to do the Sun Dance in tribute to Wakantanka. The Sun Dance was the Plains Indians' holiest ceremony, the most sacred ritual they could conceive. In it, men (but never women) offered their flesh and blood to show gratitude for past blessings and to gain wisdom for the future. This ceremony grew out of their belief that all things came forth in pain. So it was with the buffalo cow giving birth to her calf, and the stone "groaning" as the hunter shapes it into an arrowhead. Since Wakantanka had created the universe, the sacrifice of a horse, for example, was nothing special; it merely gave Wakantanka something he already owned. A man's body, however, belongs to himself alone. When he literally gave part of himself, he gave the only thing that was truly his. "I must give something that I really value to show that my whole being goes with the lesser gifts," explained a Lakota named Chase by Bears. "Therefore I promise to give my body."[28]

The Lakota held their Sun Dance in the summer, when all the hunting tribes gathered for the main buffalo hunt. In July 1856, they camped by the Little Missouri River in Montana. Sitting Bull watched as young men felled a cottonwood tree and cut off the branches, leaving only a fork at the top. While chanting prayers, they planted the tree in the center of a circular enclosure of brushwood. Near the base of the tree they cleared a space and set out buffalo skulls decorated with sacred markings.

On the day of sacrifice, Sitting Bull and his companions solemnly walked to the enclosure wearing only breechcloths. One by one they sat under the tree, facing the buffalo skulls. Holy men painted their hands and feet red and blue, colors of the sun and sky, and painted stripes across their shoulders to represent the sun's rays. Then the holy men cut two sets of parallel slits on each side of the dancers' breasts. Slowly, carefully, they passed a wooden skewer under the skin between each pair of slits. After that, they tied a rope to the end of each skewer and attached it to the fork

The sacred Sun Dance as drawn by a Plains Indian named No Heart.

of the Sun Dance tree. Some dancers had skewers placed not in their chests, but in their backs. These the holy men tied to four or five heavy buffalo skulls.

The dancers stood up.

The drums throbbed.

Circling the tree, the dancers kept time with the drumbeats while staring into the sun and blowing on eagle-bone whistles. Each moved quickly, twisting his body and leaning backward so that the skewers tore into his flesh.

An hour passed. Two hours. Streams of blood and perspiration rolled down the painted bodies. Each dancer gritted his teeth, not daring to cry out; any cry of pain would have marked him as unworthy of the Great Spirit's blessing. Witnesses later told interviewers that the dancers chanted this prayer: "Wakantanka, have mercy on me, let the tribe live long and let us have lots of buffalo. Let no one get sick so the tribe will increase."[29] Gradually, the skewers tore through the flesh, or the holy men cut the

flesh, freeing the dancers. Dropping to the ground, still staring into the sun, many had visions more vivid than any experienced during a vision quest.

Sitting Bull danced often in the years ahead. He gave his flesh so generously that his nephew, White Bull, remembered the scars on his arms, back, and chest. His visions amazed everyone. They helped him become more than a mighty hunter, more even than a brave warrior. Those visions marked him as a *wichasha wakan,* or a holy man. Fellow tribesmen described him as "a man medicine seemed to surround."[30] His spirit-helpers gave him certain magical objects, including a charm to control the weather. In times of crisis, they visited him in his dreams to foretell the future. Lakota people, who saw these visions come true, later reported that they always told the truth. In the end, Sitting Bull's visions correctly predicted his death.

During the winter of 1857, Sitting Bull and three others set out to raid the Assiniboins. They found a lone lodge occupied by a father, mother, and three children. This helpless family hardly seemed worthy of a Strong Heart sash-wearer. Yet, to Plains warriors, an enemy was an enemy. So, after making medicine—praying to his spirit-helpers and following their advice—Sitting Bull led the attack.

The mother fled, holding an infant in her arms and dragging a toddler by the hand. The father and his eleven-year-old son, a tall, thin boy armed with a small bow, tried to cover their escape. Moments later, all except the boy lay in pools of blood. But the boy stood his ground, shooting arrows at his family's killers. The warriors counted coup on him and were about to strike the death blow when he did the unexpected. Grabbing hold of Sitting Bull's leg, he called him "older brother" and begged for mercy.

Artist Frederic Remington's portrayal of the Sun Dance in Harper's Weekly for December 13, 1890. Notice how far the skewers pull the flesh away from the dancer's chest.

Sitting Bull's friends later recalled that those words went to his heart.

"Don't shoot him!" he cried. "Don't shoot! This boy is too brave to die. I have no brother. I take this one for my brother. Let him live."[31] He called his adopted brother Little Assiniboin. The following year, he dubbed him Jumping Bull in honor of his father, who did not need that name anymore.

Sitting Bull depicts himself killing the Crow warrior who killed his father.

The death of Jumping Bull happened this way: Old Jumping Bull had an awful toothache. His jaw swelled to twice its normal size, and the gentlest touch felt like a bolt of lightning blasting through his skull. The pain grew so bad that, after a sleepless night, he wished himself dead. Next day, his wish came true.

The band was moving camp when fifty Crows swarmed over a ridge. They quickly cut off two boys riding ahead of the main group, killing them in front of the horrified onlookers. Sitting Bull organized the counterattack and drove them away in a running fight.

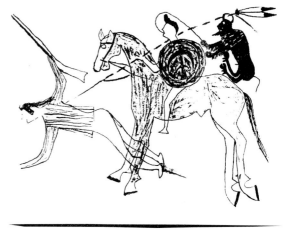

During the pursuit, his father overtook a Crow warrior whose horse had gone lame. Jumping Bull, a man of over sixty winters, was not up to fighting a vigorous warrior eager to count coup. Yet this was probably his last chance to die with honor. Dismounting, he raised his bow and arrow, only to have the Crow shoot first. As he fell, mortally wounded, the Crow plunged a knife into the top of his head.

Sitting Bull's version of the capture of three Crow women at the time of his father's death. Notice how a Crow warrior is trying to halt Sitting Bull's charge.

Sitting Bull arrived moments later. Too late to help his father, he struck the killer with his lance. Although Sitting Bull's friends drove their arrows into the Crow's body, Sitting Bull wanted more. He leaped off his horse and cut the body apart, tossing the bloody pieces over his shoulder. Meanwhile, his friends had captured three Crow women; and everyone expected him to have them killed as well. Yet his anger quickly cooled. It was one thing to kill women and children during a fight, another to murder prisoners in cold blood. "It is not right," he said. "Treat them well, and let them live. My father was a man, and death is his."[32]

A medicine man painted the old man's face in his medicine colors and dressed his body in his best clothes. To prevent wolves from digging up the body, the family did not bury it in the ground, but wrapped it in a buffalo robe. Then they placed it on a platform, or scaffold, resting on forked poles driven into the ground. Beneath the platform, they put his weapons and the body of his favorite horse, killed for the ceremony. The spirit of the slain man, they believed, then mounted the spirit of the slain horse for the journey to the next world. There, amid the stars, Jumping Bull's ancestors welcomed him, and together they hunted the buffalo forever.

Despite his father's death, Sitting Bull was content. He had become all that his father had wanted—all that the Lakota expected of a brave young hunter and warrior. By his late twenties, he was a respected leader of a proud warrior people. Yet the world was changing. Strangers began to appear on the Great Plains. The Lakota called them Wasichus—white people. Lakota society had shaped Sitting Bull. Now the Wasichus were about to shape Lakota society in ways he could scarcely imagine.

Three

HAIRY MEN FROM THE EAST

"We did not think of the great open plains, the beautiful rolling hills, and tangled growth, as 'wild.' Only to the white man was nature a 'wilderness' and only to him was the land 'infested' with 'wild' animals and 'savage' people. To us it was tame. . . . Not until hairy men from the east came and with brutal frenzy heaped injustices upon us and the families we loved . . . was it for us that the 'Wild West' began."

—LUTHER STANDING BEAR, LAKOTA,
WRITING ABOUT HIS YOUTH IN THE 1860s

WHEN SITTING BULL'S FATHER was a boy, the French claimed a vast territory they called Louisiana. It so happened that this territory included nearly the entire Great Plains, from what is now the east bank of the Mississippi River to the Rocky Mountains in the west, reaching south all the way to the Gulf of Mexico. A French city, St. Louis, lay at the junction of the Mississippi and Missouri rivers. Every spring, French traders from St. Louis traveled up the Missouri in keelboats, fifty-foot vessels powered by oars. Despite their country's claims, these men knew they were only guests in a country belonging to others. The Lakota told these traders where they could go, when, and what to charge for their goods; often they simply robbed the traders. The Frenchmen put up with this treatment because they still made high profits. Besides, France did not have enough soldiers to fight "horse Indians" on anything like equal terms.

In 1803, France sold the Louisiana Territory to the United States. President Thomas Jefferson appointed his private secretary, Meriwether Lewis, and William Clark, a former army officer, to explore the new lands. Their expedition left St. Louis in April 1804. Traveling by keelboat up the Missouri River to today's North Dakota, they crossed the Rocky Mountains on foot, a journey filled with hardship and danger. Finally, after two years, they reached the Pacific coast of Oregon and returned to St. Louis in September 1806.

Lewis and Clark met the Lakota along the upper reaches of the Missouri during the first year of their trip. Things did not go well. The chiefs explained that Wasichus traveled through this country only with Lakota permission. When the explorers objected, claiming the land belonged to the United States, tempers flared. Fortunately (for the explorers), a fight was avoided at the last moment. Yet, from the explorers' point of view, they had learned a valuable lesson. Although they resented the Lakota, they recognized their strength. As Lewis wrote in their journal, these "pirates of the Missouri" threatened American expansion. He predicted that the nation could never rule this vast domain unless it defeated these "vilest miscreants of the savage race."[1]

Upon returning, Lewis and Clark reported their findings to President Jefferson. The Louisiana Territory, they said, teemed with fur-bearing animals. That news signaled money to be made. John Jacob Astor, already the "king" of the fur trade, sent teams of white men to trap beaver in the streams of the northern Rockies. Along plains rivers, Astor built outposts, called "forts," where his agents traded with the hunting tribes for beaver pelts and buffalo robes.

Astor's agents provided the tribes with things they could not make for themselves. Iron arrowheads, sold six to a package, made hunting easier, as did guns and ammunition. Iron pots, knives, and axes lightened women's work. "Let me tell you," said a trader, "once a squaw used a steel needle she'd never go back to a bone awl. She'd harry her man 'til she had steel."[2] He was right. Trade created new desires—desires Indians very much wanted to satisfy.

Traders also brought "bad medicine," powerful forces for evil. Whites found that the biggest profits came from whiskey. The idea was to get Indians so drunk that they would give up their furs at a fraction of their true value.

Trader's whiskey, or "firewater," was raw alcohol and river water boiled with red pepper and black chewing tobacco, "for taste." Indians often became addicted to this poisonous brew. Some modern researchers think this may have been due to genetic factors. Men got crazy-drunk, even killing their families in uncontrollable rages. In exchange for a glass of whiskey, some even made their daughters sleep with the traders for a night.

Alcoholism weakened the tribes' respect for nature. Hunters slaughtered entire buffalo herds, not to eat, but to be able to trade for whiskey. In 1832, when Sitting Bull was scarcely a year old, the artist George Catlin witnessed a horrible scene near a trading post. He saw Lakota hunters "come into the Fort with *fourteen hundred fresh buffalo tongues,* which were thrown down in a mass, and for which they required but a few gallons of whiskey, which they soon demolished." They left the rest of the animals to rot.[3]

Nevertheless, during the 1820s and 1830s, the Plains Indians got along with the few Wasichus they met. Unlike Lewis and Clark, these men tended to think highly of the Lakota. Prince Maximilian, a German adventurer, claimed they were dangerous only as enemies. "As such they are cruel and bloodthirsty. As friends they are just as loyal and very grateful." The fur trader Joshua Pilcher agreed. "No Indians," he said in 1838, "ever manifested a greater degree of friendship for the whites in general, or more respect for our Government, than the Sioux." If whites respected their rights, Pilcher added, the Lakota would never cause trouble.[4]

Yet that was not to be. In the eighteenth and nineteenth centuries, European visitors often described Americans as a people who "never stay still." One reason was that there were more of them every year. The first census, in 1790, counted 3.9 million inhabitants of the United States. By 1840, there were 17 million, an increase of over 400 percent, thanks to a high birth rate at home and immigration from abroad. The majority lived not in cities but on farms and in small towns. Each year, rising population and the desire for an improved standard of living drew thousands to the frontier to find good land to farm.

About the time Sitting Bull killed his first buffalo, fertile farmlands became available in Oregon and gold was discovered in California. In 1843, the first wagon trains came rolling down the Oregon Trail, the most famous route in American history.

The Oregon Tail began at "jumping-off" towns along the Missouri River.

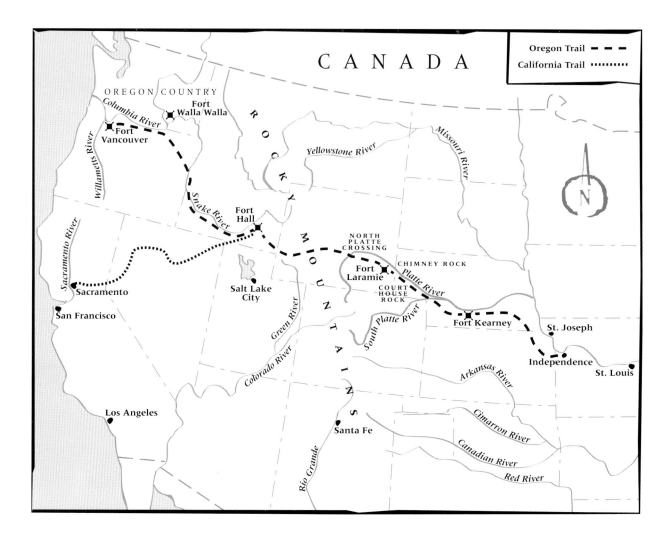

The Oregon Trail and the California Trail.

Pioneers, or emigrants, called their covered wagons "prairie schooners," because they resembled white-sailed ships crossing a sea of green grass. Groups of emigrants would set out in mid-May, when the prairie grass was high enough to feed their livestock. Their route ran for twelve hundred miles along the valley of the Platte River to a trading post in Wyoming called Fort Laramie. From there, the trail snaked through South Pass in the Rockies toward Oregon and California.

Around nine hundred emigrants used the Oregon Trail in 1843. Indians paid little attention to them. They seemed too few to worry about, their wagon trains merely thin lines amid the vastness of the Great Plains. After 1843, however, a human tidal wave surged westward, bound for the rich farmlands of Oregon and the California gold fields: 1,200 emigrants came in

1844, 3,000 in 1845, 1,600 in 1846, 9,500 in 1847, 42,000 in 1849, 55,000 in 1850.[5] On busy days, 500 wagons would pass Fort Laramie in the hours between sunrise and sunset. For white Americans, the Oregon Trail marked the birth of a continental nation that claimed the land from the east coast to the west. For Native Americans, it marked the beginning of the end of their way of life.

Emigrants changed the land itself. Their wagon wheels carved deep ruts in the ground (some still visible today). When the ruts got too deep, the wagons moved a few feet to the side, widening the trail to form an indelible scar across the continent. One stretch of trail was so trampled down that the Lakota called it *Nablaska*, the land "flattened out by the foot." Once a chief watched in disbelief as wagons rolled past Fort Laramie for a solid week. Finally, pointing to the east, he asked an emigrant, "Are there still any whites remaining there?" The number of Lakota people, the largest Plains Indian group, was tiny compared to the number of whites. In 1833, for example, all the Lakota tribes may have totaled 20,000 people, among them 5,000 warriors.[6]

Emigrants saw the Plains Indians in various ways. Some liked those they met, particularly the Lakota. They described them in letters and diaries as "a fine intelligent looking race" and "the best Indians on the prairies." An emigrant observed, "There can be no doubt of the friendliness of these people." Although painted warriors looked ferocious, they behaved well. Warriors often acted as guides, led emigrants to water holes, and returned lost children. "They appear to be perfectly harmless," Mrs. Harriet Ward wrote her son, adding, "You would be surprised to see me writing so quietly in the wagon alone . . . with a great wild-looking Indian leaning his elbow on the wagon beside me, but I have not a single fear except that they may frighten the horses."[7]

Most of Mrs. Ward's compatriots were seldom so trusting. They experienced culture shock, the anxiety and fear that comes from encountering people who are very different from themselves. Make no mistake about it: Indians and whites lived in separate worlds. Their experiences, beliefs, and customs were vastly different. Having almost nothing in common, each used the standards of their own society to judge the other. This opened the way to misunderstandings and, finally, to countless tragedies.

Native Americans believed in the unity and sanctity of nature. Human beings were part of Wakantanka's creation, they said, not its masters or owners. To Indians, the idea of owning land was just plain silly. People could not own the land any more than they could own the air they breathed, the rain that fell, or the sun's warming rays.

White people disagreed. The white culture believed that each person had a God-given right—an "inalienable" right, said the Declaration of Independence—to "life, liberty, and the pursuit of happiness." These words expressed the most revolutionary idea of modern times. White Americans understood that idea to mean more than freedom of religion or of the press, more even than democracy. Abraham Lincoln called it "the right to rise." It meant that in America a person's origins or family name was supposed to count for nothing. What mattered was equality, the ability of everyone to climb as high as talent and effort allowed. However, before the Civil War (1861–65) and for many years afterward, most whites did not apply these ideas to black people, whether slave or free.

Whites measured success in terms of ownership, or the individual possession of property. Property took many forms: land, buildings, animals, even other people—slaves. An individual could buy property, sell it, or exchange it. There was no end to the amount of property you could amass. The more property you had, the richer you were and the more power you had in the community.

Americans measured the value of property in dollars and cents. Money was a marvelous thing. You could accumulate it and invest it; that is, use it to create more wealth. Wealth was good. Wealth meant "progress," the steady improvement of you and your family, and perhaps of humanity.

For countless Americans, progress required the conquest of nature. Their God, speaking in the Bible, commanded them: "Be fruitful and multiply, and fill the earth and subdue it: and have dominion over . . . every living thing that moveth upon the earth."[8]

The popular idea of beauty followed this divine commandment. Beauty meant fields of golden grain and herds of domestic cattle. Thick forests and open prairies teeming with game were, to white people, "empty," "ugly," "wild," "desolate," and "useless." Such things had no right to exist. For that reason, the assault upon nature had been part of the "American way of life" from the moment the first European settlers landed on these shores. Perhaps you could say that subduing nature was as American as apple pie. So was hatred of Indians.

Most emigrants had made up their minds about Indians long before the Oregon Trail opened. Racism, the belief that one race is superior to all others, was widespread in the 1800s. Racial "superiority" justified the enslavement of black people and hatred of Native Americans. Emigrants often described Indians as "creatures," beasts in human form, little better than monkeys. Few could imagine that Indians, any more than blacks, had rights a white person must respect.[9]

Everything about Indians seemed inferior. To emigrants, an Indian camp was a rowdy, wicked place. Instead of worshiping the one true God,

A peaceful village scene on the Northern Plains, with horses drinking from a shallow river. The white man standing on the riverbank and the wagon in the background to the left indicate that the picture was probably taken on a reservation.

"red heathens" worshiped countless gods. Naked toddlers and grown men clad in breechcloths were proof of "indecency," "degeneracy," and "animal morality." Unlike whites, Indians supposedly did not believe cleanliness was next to godliness. Indians never washed with soap, but took sweat baths and painted their bodies in "devilish" patterns. Emigrants filled diary pages with comments about "painted, dirty and nauseous-smelling savages," "dirty, obnoxious-looking creatures," and "creatures [that] looked too filthy to live."[10]

A *dance, with enemy scalps, painted by George Catlin.*

Whites found Indian methods of raising children equally offensive. Emigrants condemned Indian parents for allowing their children to "run wild." And were they ever stupid! Why, said Miss Ellen Adams, "Some Indians do not understand a single word of English."[11]

Most emigrants never learned more than a few words in any native language, let alone how Indians related to one another. Whites assumed that Indian men had no respect for women. If they had, they would not "buy" wives with horses or practice polygamy, a "sinful" custom in the eyes of God. Indian women worked hard; anybody knew that at a glance. Thus, to emigrants, "a woman was but a kind of slave, or beast of burden."[12] Whites portrayed Indian cooking methods as "disgusting." The sight of puppies "roasted entire, intestines and all," made them nauseous.[13]

White disgust reinforced white fears. Fear of Indians was nothing new in American history. Since colonial times, newspapers and novels had bombarded readers with tales of Indian cruelty. Some of these tales were true. Yet most were exaggerations or lies intended to boost sales, the same way stories of space aliens do today.

Emigrants came west expecting the worst. The idea of scalping made their flesh crawl. Women sheared off their own and their children's hair before crossing the Missouri River. Even so, they lived in constant fear. "I just knew," a girl recalled, "that if one of those Indians had touched my hair, that my scalp would have come off without any pulling."[14]

Emigrants told of spending sleepless nights "filled with unspeakable terror." Children dreamed of being chased by Indians and running so fast their feet rose from the ground, making them airborne. "I'm Scairt," a teenager wrote in her diary. Another described herself as "a veritable little 'fraid cat—afraid of everything—of snakes, of wolves, of storms, but most of all, of Indians." Still another imagined a painted warrior hiding behind "every weed and bunch of grass." Some expressed their fear of scalping and suggested a solution to the "Indian problem":

> *The Injuns will catch you while crossing the Plains*
> *They'll kill you, and scalp you, and beat out your brains.*
> *Uncle Sam ought to throw them over the fence*
> *So there'll be no Red Injuns a hundred years hence.*[15]

Indians also experienced culture shock. Regarding the Wasichus' physical appearance, they found them both ugly and funny. White people had a pale, deathly color, like a skinned antelope drained of its blood. Constant perspiring gave them a musty, sour odor that turned Indians' stomachs. Unlike Indians, who by nature had little body and facial hair, white men had chests matted with dark hair and wore bushy beards, prompting the nickname Dog Faces. Wearing boots made whites turn out their toes while walking, earning the nickname Crooked Feet. And were whites ever stupid! Why, white women lacked the sense to demand that their husbands marry more wives to help with the chores.

White behavior, particularly as parents, offended Indians. Rather than "spoil" infants by soothing them, as Indians did, whites let them cry for hours. At other times, parents treated children like pets rather than little people who must learn to survive in a dangerous world. Wasichus coddled children, making them eat and sleep at set times.

What really horrified Indians was the whites' brutality. Parents slapped, spanked, and pulled youngsters' ears, making them cringe and whine like whipped dogs. Therefore, when Indians called whites Flop Ears, they were not simply poking fun. That nickname represented a type of cruelty Indians despised. Only crazy people, they said, struck their own flesh and blood. No decent person could tolerate such a beast. A child-beater had neither friends nor respect among Native Americans.

Finally, Indians regarded whites as irreligious. On Sundays, Wasichus sang and prayed to their God. To Indians, however, all that singing and praying seemed like gibberish. By their actions, whites showed contempt for Wakantanka's creation. Like huge, slithering maggots, their wagon trains gnawed their way across the Great Plains. Emigrants cut timber along the rivers, while their cattle ate the grass for miles on either side of the Oregon Trail. Wherever they camped, they left mounds of garbage and polluted water holes.

Most emigrants loaded their wagons with so much needless baggage that oxen could scarcely pull the heavy loads. Before long, discarded farm tools and household goods began to litter the trail. Weakened by overwork and lack of grass, oxen died in droves. One emigrant counted an average of one dead ox every half-mile. Another described the way west as an "open-air slaughterhouse." The stench of decaying flesh, he wrote, "is quite annoying, and with it the atmosphere seems everywhere to be charged."[16] Wagons became useless. Owners abandoned them and loaded whatever they could on the remaining animals.

The first wagon trains often found the trail blocked for days by migrating buffalo herds. That quickly changed. Wagon train noises frightened the buffalo and bullets killed them. Observers noted that emigrants had an irresistible urge to pull the trigger whenever a buffalo crossed their gun sights. Josiah Gregg, a veteran Plainsman, wrote: "Such is the excitement that generally prevails at the sight of these fat denizens of the prairies that very few hunters appear able to refrain from shooting as long as the game remains within reach of their rifles; nor can they ever permit a fair shot to escape them."[17]

Buffalo herds learned to avoid the Oregon Trail by grazing farther to the north and south. Every hunting tribe felt the change. As herds left their old ranges, Indians had to travel farther and search harder for food. For the first time in generations, signs of hunger appeared in the winter counts. So did the symptoms of disease.

America's crowded, dirty towns were breeding grounds for diseases. Although thousands of citizens died each year, over time the majority developed an immunity to old-world diseases like measles, whooping cough, and scarlet fever. Not the Native Americans. Lacking any exposure to these diseases, and therefore any immunity, they were helpless against what scientists call "virgin soil epidemics."[18] When white settlers moved inland from the coast, they brought their diseases with them. In this way, the Missouri River and the Oregon Trail became highways of death.

Nothing was deadlier than smallpox. This disease killed more Indians than all the white man's diseases and bullets combined. Caused by a virus, its symptoms are high fever and muscle aches, followed by pimples that become blisters, break open, ooze pus, and finally form scabs. The pimples cover the body, particularly the face, often leaving survivors blind and disfigured by deep pockmarks. Smallpox is highly contagious. Not only can the virus spread from person to person through the air and by touch, even the dried scabs are infectious.

Smallpox killed more Native Americans than all the white man's bullets. Here we see its horror depicted in an Oglala winter count.

Whites had learned to prevent smallpox through vaccination. Yet the law did not require vaccination, so there were outbreaks even in white communities. Plains Indians, however, knew nothing of vaccination. They had never experienced anything so devastating as smallpox. Because it spread with the speed of a prairie fire, no "medicine" could prevent it or halt it once it got under way. Smallpox destroyed entire bands, sending families fleeing in all directions. Overcome by panic, husbands abandoned wives, mothers infants, and children their aged parents. Men killed their loved ones to spare them the agonies of the disease, then killed themselves.

In 1833, when Sitting Bull was two years old, a "fire canoe," as the Lakota called the steamboat, came from St. Louis. A familiar sight along the Missouri River, the *Yellowstone* had always brought a wide selection of trade goods. This time she also brought smallpox to the Three Tribes. Within a few weeks, it cut their population to less than half. The Blackfeet, Pawnee, Crow, Arikara, and Lakota did not suffer as severely, because they did not all live together in permanent villages. Sitting Bull got the disease, although whether it was during this epidemic or at some other time we cannot say. The pockmarks on his face are visible in some photographs taken years afterward.

Plains tribes blamed the emigrants for their troubles. Gradually, their grievances turned to hostility. Emigrants' fears began to come true as warriors stampeded cattle, stole horses, and scalped stragglers from the wagon trains. Yet these incidents were nowhere near an "Indian war." Between 1840 and 1850, warriors killed 115 emigrants; emigrants killed 161 Indians. The way west, therefore, was safer than many city streets.[19]

All the same, government officials devised a plan to protect the emigrants. In 1849, soldiers built Fort Kearny, Nebraska, and took over Fort Laramie from the fur traders. From then on, the fort was a genuine "war house," a place manned by soldiers. Two years later, officials invited the northern Great Plains tribes to a treaty council.

In August 1851, 10,000 Lakotas, Cheyennes, Arapahos, Crows, Shoshones, Arikaras, Assiniboins, and Hidastas gathered at Horse Creek near Fort Laramie. After days of speeches by both sides, the chiefs "touched the pen," or accepted the Treaty of Horse Creek. This was the first agreement between the Plains Indians and the U.S. government. By accepting it, the tribes promised not to attack one another and to stay within certain boundaries. The whites gained the right to use the Oregon Trail in safety and build military posts on Indian lands. In return, the government agreed to give the tribes $50,000 in trade goods each year for ten years.

Neither side fully expected to live up to its promises. The problem was not dishonesty, but the fact that each side had its own ways and beliefs. In America, the people gave their representatives the power to make treaties. Representatives, however, could not enforce unpopular treaties against the people's will. If, for example, a majority later decided they needed Indian lands, any elected official who opposed them faced defeat at the polls. This is why the government had ended up breaking every treaty it had made with the Eastern Woodland tribes. Before long, that sad history would repeat itself in the West.

Tribal chiefs signed the treaty in good faith. Warring tribes had made peace among themselves countless times. They did so with speeches, gifts, and pledges of eternal friendship. Even so, they likened treaties to ripe fruit: both spoiled quickly. Treaties were good while they lasted. Peace gave tribes a breathing spell, a quiet time to rest and prepare for the next clash. Beyond that, treaties had no value to people who lived by hunting and fighting.

A sick cow triggered the first clash between warriors and soldiers on the Great Plains. In August 1854, the animal wandered into Camp Brulé of the Lakota near Fort Laramie, where a visiting Miniconjou Lakota shot it. Although the cow's owner had left it to die, he saw a chance to collect a few dollars from the government for his loss. An officer at the fort, however, decided to make a big deal of the matter. Lieutenant John J. Grattan, a recent graduate of West Point, thought himself God's gift to the U.S. Army. He needed a chance to prove it by carrying out a daring mission.

Grattan begged his commander to allow him to arrest the culprit. The commander agreed, so Grattan set out with twenty-nine Long Knives—cavalrymen—an interpreter, and two light cannons. By the time they reached the Brulé camp, the interpreter had emptied a bottle of whiskey and was roaring drunk. He approached the lodge of the chief, Conquering Bear, shouting that the soldiers meant to slaughter the Indians, cut them into little pieces, and eat their hearts raw.

Expecting trouble, women and children quietly slipped away from the camp, while warriors fixed arrows to their bowstrings. Chief Conquering Bear did not want to fight. He offered five valuable horses for the cow.

Grattan wanted the horses *and* the Miniconjou cow killer. Conquering Bear refused. The Lakota considered hospitality a sacred obligation, and no host dared turn away a guest. But the lieutenant did not care about Lakota customs. Without warning, he ordered his men to open fire, killing the chief.

Instantly the warriors released a shower of arrows in return, killing every white man. A rescue party found Grattan's body with twenty-four arrows in it, one of which had passed completely through his head. The only way to identify him was by the watch in his pocket.

Now, for the first time Plains Indians had fought American soldiers. The outcome was a blow to national pride. AVENGE THE GRATTAN MASSACRE! newspapers shouted in bold headlines. If "massacre" means the deliberate killing of defenseless people, the Brulé had done nothing of the sort. Grattan had ordered his men to fire on peaceful warriors in their own village. They defended themselves by destroying their attackers.

A year passed before the army made its move. Revenge came in the person of Colonel William S. Harney, a tough campaigner leading seven hundred troops. On September 3, 1855, Harney's scouts located an Indian band camped along Ash Hollow Creek in western Nebraska. The colonel did not know it was the camp of the Brulé chief Little Thunder, or that its inhabitants had nothing to do with the "Grattan Massacre." Nor did he care. Harney wanted to show that a provocation by *any* band automatically turned *all* bands into targets. Little Thunder tried to surrender, but the colonel attacked anyhow.

A true massacre occurred that day. Of the village's 250 inhabitants, 87 lay dead when the smoke cleared. Most of the dead were women and children. News-walkers carried the story of Ash Hollow across the northern Great Plains. It stunned Sitting Bull, as it did all Lakota people. Ash Hollow was the worst defeat the Lakota had suffered since leaving the forests of Minnesota. Sitting Bull had grown up believing the loss of even one or two warriors on a raid was terrible, and losing three or four a disaster. The tribe would miss them greatly as hunters and warriors. Now white soldiers had overrun an entire camp, leaving the survivors without food or shelter. Sitting Bull never forgot Ash Hollow. It disturbed him deeply, turning him against white people. From then on, he despised them.

"The Big Chief of the soldiers is an awful man," a warrior declared, "when he speaks he makes us tremble." The Lakota called Harney "Mad

Bear" because he seemed like a crazed grizzly who attacked women and children.[20]

The tragedy at Ash Hollow sent shock waves of hatred and fear across the Great Plains. We get a hint of this in the way mothers put their children to bed at night. "If you are not good the Wasichus will get you," said Lakota mothers. White mothers said much the same thing: "You behave or the Sioux will get you."[21] Yet the Lakota had learned their "lesson." Although they continued to kill a few emigrants each year, they allowed most wagon trains to pass safely. Meanwhile, in April 1861, whites began to fight among themselves. For the next four years, until April 1865, whites would spill more blood in a single battle than all the Great Plains tribes spilled in a decade of fighting.

Slavery had existed in America since colonial times. In 1619, a Dutch ship unloaded its cargo of Africans at Jamestown, Virginia. Although slavery was unprofitable in the North and had died out after the Revolution, it flourished in the South, mainly on cotton plantations. In November 1860, Abraham Lincoln won the presidential election. Fearing he would abolish slavery, eleven Southern states left the Union to form a new nation, the Confederate States of America. On April 12, 1861, Confederate gunners fired the first shots of the Civil War, against Fort Sumter, in South Carolina.

Those shots resounded all the way to the Great Plains. In the weeks after Fort Sumter, the frontier army all but collapsed as soldiers sympathetic to the Confederacy deserted. Of the units loyal to the Union, the best ones left for battlefields in the East. Troop shortages forced both sides to abandon frontier posts, igniting a war within the Civil War.

An uneasy truce had settled over the Great Plains after Ash Hollow. Yet it proved only the lull before the storm. The early emigrants had hurried across the sea of grass on their way to Oregon and California. Even had they wished to stop and farm on the Great Plains, it would have been impossible because their plows could not break through the hard-packed sod. That changed during the 1850s, thanks to inventions like John Deere's steel plow and Cyrus McCormick's mechanical reaper. As a result, large white settlements sprang up along the fringes of the Great Plains in what are now the states of Minnesota, Kansas, and Iowa. Such changes always brought hardship to the native peoples. The Civil War gave them a chance to even the score.

Whites everywhere felt the Indians' rage. The Utes struck in Idaho, the Navajos in New Mexico, the Apaches in Arizona, and the Shoshones in Utah. Fast-moving war parties shot up wagon trains, killed farmers, and looted trading posts. In Texas, the Comanches and Kiowas forced the line of settlement to retreat eastward by as much as two hundred miles. A fearless traveler, or a careless fool, might ride for a week without finding a living white person or an unburned farmhouse.

Indians attack a wagon train. From Fanny Kelly's <u>My Captivity Among the Sioux Indians</u>. Thanks to Sitting Bull, Mrs. Kelly was set free and safely returned to her own people.

In Colorado, the Cheyennes and Arapahos attacked wagon trains and mining camps. Colonel John M. Chivington struck back with the Third Colorado Volunteers, a unit of unruly frontiersmen. Chivington, a former Methodist preacher, was not interested in punishing the guilty; he wanted only to kill Indians—*any* Indians. "Kill and scalp all, big and little," he told his men. "Nits [insect eggs] make lice." In other words, the colonel did not see Indians as human beings, but as vile insects to be killed on sight.

On November 29, 1864, he attacked a sleeping Cheyenne camp at Sand Creek, a branch of the Arkansas River. As a sign that he wanted peace, Black Kettle, the band's chief, flew both a white surrender flag and the

Stars and Stripes over his lodge. No matter. When Chivington's guns fell silent, about 350 people, half the village's inhabitants, lay dead. The troopers topped their "victory" by shooting captives and mutilating the dead. Sergeant Lucian Palmer, an eyewitness, later told congressional investigators: "I think among the dead bodies one-third were women and children. The bodies were horribly cut up, skulls broken in a good many; I judge they were broken after they were killed, as they were shot besides. I do not think I saw any but what were scalped; saw fingers cut off, saw several bodies with privates cut off, women as well as men. . . . [A major] stood by and saw his men cutting fingers from dead bodies."[22]

The worst Indian uprising during the Civil War years took place in Minnesota. Over the years, the U.S. government had persuaded the Santee, the Lakota's eastern cousins, to sign treaties surrendering millions of acres of land. Unfortunately, the Santee saw little of the promised benefits. Supplies guaranteed by the government failed to arrive on time, or never arrived. Dishonest traders preyed on the Santee like vultures. When they complained, traders bribed officials to look the other way. When starving Santee asked for credit, shopkeepers refused. "Go and eat grass," declared Andrew Myrick.[23]

In 1862, Santee anger boiled over. The timing was no accident. That spring, Confederate generals Robert E. Lee and Stonewall Jackson had crushed a massive Union offensive in northern Virginia. With President Lincoln's armies in retreat, the Santee vowed to retake their lands by force.

On August 17, a quiet Sunday for whites, warriors struck dozens of places in Minnesota at once. In the days that followed, at least 700 whites died in this, the worst Indian uprising in American history. Dazed survivors stumbled into the nearest village or army post. An eyewitness reported: "Mothers came in rags, barefooted, whose husbands and children were slaughtered before their eyes. . . . The roads in all directions from [the town of] New Ulm are lined with the murdered men, women and children." The body of Mr. Andrew Myrick, shopkeeper, had its mouth stuffed with grass. Warriors taunted it, shouting: "Myrick is eating grass himself."[24]

Governor Henry H. Sibley led the counterattack with 1,600 army soldiers and civilian volunteers. Within a month, he routed the Santee, taking hundreds of prisoners. Whites were in no mood for generosity. Crowds stoned Santee prisoners. "O God let me at them," a grieving rock thrower

Refugees from the Santee uprising in Minnesota, 1862. These cousins of the Plains Lakota rebelled when the U.S. government refused to keep its treaty promises.

screamed. "They have killed my husband and all my children. They smashed out the brains of my little babe only four weeks old." Another shouted as she waved a butcher knife: "O let me! Let me! Kill them, they killed my husband. They burned my house and child."[25]

Sibley tried his prisoners before military courts. In the eyes of most whites, merely being a Santee was proof of guilt. Juries needed, on average, five minutes to convict and sentence each of 307 men to hang for murder. President Lincoln, however, wondered about five-minute jury trials. An experienced lawyer himself, he understood the difference between justice and, as he put it, just "hangin' Injuns."[26] After personally examining the trial records, he set aside all but thirty-eight convictions. These men died on December 28, 1862, in the largest public execution in American history.

Shock waves from the Minnesota uprising rolled westward. Hundreds of Santee, individually or in small groups, slipped across the Missouri River to find safety with their relatives. The Lakota took them in, fed them, and listened to their grievances. Next year, they knew, soldiers would come after the refugees in force. Ash Hollow had shown what soldiers could do. Sitting Bull and the Hunkpapas would have to fight for their lives. Yet they were not afraid. Unlike the Brulés at Ash Hollow, they would be ready. They sent a warrior to an army post with this message: "The whites in this country have been threatening us with soldiers. All we ask of you is to bring men, and not women dressed in soldiers' clothes."[27]

Back east, the land ran with the blood of civil war. More white soldiers died in battle during the spring and summer of 1863 than the population of all the Lakota tribes combined. In May, General Lee halted a Union drive at Chancellorsville, Virginia. Hoping to follow through on his victory, he invaded Pennsylvania, only to meet disaster at Gettysburg early in July. Later that month, out west, General Alfred Sully took the offensive with 2,000 men.

Sully crossed the Missouri into Lakota territory. A veteran of the Union campaigns in northern Virginia, the general had a two-part plan. The first part was simple: Drive the remaining Santee from Minnesota and punish those who had fled to the Lakota. The second part was more complicated.

In 1862, prospectors discovered gold in Montana. Indians called gold "the yellow metal that makes the Wasichus crazy." They observed that the very word seemed to drive the white men out of their minds.[28] Wasichus would do anything, suffer every hardship, to get the yellow metal. Within weeks of the discovery in Montana, prospectors left Minnesota bound for the mines. Although the Lakota killed them on sight, others always took their place. Here is where the second part of Sully's plan came in. He intended to protect the prospectors by building forts at key points along the route to the mining area and driving the Lakota out.

Lakota scouts followed Sully's advance from a safe distance. As his force approached a village, women quickly packed up and moved away. Frustrated at his inability to make contact, the general prayed for his luck to change. It did. On September 3, 1863, he found a large village of Hunkpapas and Santees at Whitestone Hill, Minnesota, near the Missouri River. Fast-moving cavalry killed 150 Indians, captured another 156, and burned the village. Sitting Bull's band was not there; it was hunting buffalo hundreds of miles away. So far, he had not fought whites.

Sully spent the winter of 1863 to 1864 preparing to renew his offensive. In the summer of 1864, as Union armies again battled their way across Virginia, he again invaded Hunkpapa territory. Sitting Bull's band was camped near the Hunting Ground Where They Killed the Deer, now called the Killdeer Mountains in present-day North Dakota. On July 28, the general appeared with 2,000 men and twelve cannons.

True to their boast, the Hunkpapas welcomed battle. Never having fought soldiers, they had no idea what they were letting themselves in for. Hundreds of warriors lined a ridge, daring the white men to attack.

Sully took the dare. As his cavalry advanced, his gunners went into action. Exploding shells raked the ridge, flinging chunks of hot metal in every direction. The defenders began to waver.

One Hunkpapa, however, held firm. The Man Who Never Walked, disabled since birth, wished to die like a warrior. Sitting Bull was watching the battle when the man arrived seated in a basket on a travois, guiding the horse with long reins of rope. "This man has been a cripple all his life," he called to Sitting Bull. "He has never gone to war. Now he asks to be put into the fight and killed. He prefers to die by a bullet, since he cannot be of any use." Sitting Bull agreed. "That is perfectly all right," he cried. "Let him die in battle, if he wants to." Moments later, The Man Who Never Walked lay riddled with bullets. In death, he lost his name. The Hunkpapa always remembered him as Bear Heart.[29]

Meanwhile, the battle raged. In small or large groups, Lakota warriors galloped along the soldiers' front line, making sure to stay out of range. Suddenly, they would dash in to shoot arrows or bullets, then withdraw quickly. Sitting Bull was in the thick of the fight. Hoping to count coup, he galloped close to the soldiers—closer than his uncle, Four Horns, thought wise. As the Wasichus pressed their attack, he saw Four Horns suddenly sit up with a start and fall forward, grasping his horse's neck with both hands. A bullet had entered his back.

"I am shot," Four Horns yelled, trying to keep from falling to the ground.

Sitting Bull came to the rescue with White Bull, the son of his sister, Good Feather. The two men took Four Horns to a clump of trees, where Sitting Bull gave him some water and bandaged his wound. Four Horns bit his lip so as not to cry out in pain. Although the bullet remained inside his body, he later said that it no longer bothered him, because it had dropped into his stomach.[30]

While Sitting Bull was helping his uncle, Sibley's men pushed ahead. They came so fast that the women had to leave most of their family possessions behind. After burning everything—lodges, food, buffalo robes—the soldiers counted the dead. Over a hundred Indian bodies lay on the ground; only two soldiers had been killed. General Sully ordered a sergeant to cut off several Indian heads and hang them on poles as a warning to anyone foolish enough to offer resistance. He then advanced to the junction of the Yellowstone and Missouri rivers, where he began construction on Fort Buford. He also built Fort Rice a few miles upstream on the Missouri. Those forts showed that the Wasichus had come to Hunkpapa country to stay.

Meanwhile, Sitting Bull's band mourned its dead. Men untied their braids and cut off the tails of their warhorses as signs of grief. Women's mourning was more violent. Mrs. Fanny Kelly, a white captive from an earlier raid by another band, described the scene in her book, *My Captivity Among the Sioux Indians.* "Their cries are terribly wild and distressing . . . and the near relations of the deceased indulged in frantic expressions of grief that can not be described." Blood flowed freely as women hacked off finger joints, cut open their legs, and gashed their faces. Sitting Bull took pity on the captive. He saw by her expression that she was homesick, "so I sent her back."[31]

Sitting Bull had suffered a stunning defeat in his first battle with soldiers. Nevertheless the Killdeer Mountain episode made him lose all respect for whites as fighters. He did not consider them worthy opponents, like the Crow. He saw them as heartless, cowardly, dishonorable creatures.

Soldiers did not fight fairly, in Sitting Bull's view. Unlike truly brave men—Indian warriors—they never tried to count coup. Soldiers fought not as free men should, but in organized groups obedient to officers' commands. These officers sent them to certain death, charging directly into enemy fire to capture a piece of ground, something a war chief would never do. Worse, anyone who needed another person to tell him when to stand, charge, halt, and shoot was scarcely human. He was treated as though he had no will of his own or spirit-helpers to guide him. "The white soldiers," Sitting Bull explained, "do not know how to fight. They . . . have no hearts. When an Indian gets killed, the other Indians feel sorry and cry. But when a white soldier gets killed, nobody cries, nobody cares; they go right on shooting and let him lie there. Sometimes they go off and leave their wounded behind them."[32]

Sitting Bull killed his first white man, a mail carrier named MacDonald, during the winter of 1864. By then, the Civil War was drawing to a close. Union victory came on April 9, 1865. On that day, Robert E. Lee surrendered his army to Ulysses S. Grant, the Union's supreme field commander, at Appomattox Court House, Virginia.

America's other war continued. That spring, as the first discharged soldiers began to return to their homes, there were few places west of the Missouri River where white people slept soundly at night.

Four

A TIPI WORD

"The name of Sitting Bull was a 'tipi word' [household word] for all that was generous and great. . . . He would have proved a mighty power among our present-day politicians—a great vote getter with the people—had he been a white man with a congressional ambition."

—FRANK GROUARD, ARMY SCOUT, 1894[1]

WITH THE END OF THE Civil War in 1865, white people struck out for the frontier in ever-growing numbers. Within fifteen years, 3 million heard the call of opportunity and adventure in the "Golden West." In addition, thousands of black people, mostly former slaves, came westward to start new lives.[2]

The Union victory also began a new era for the U.S. Army. On the day General Lee surrendered, the Union army, with 1,034,000 men, was the largest on earth. Since its upkeep cost taxpayers over a million dollars a day, an economy-minded Congress gradually reduced it to 25,000 officers and men. Of these, more than half did occupation duty in the old Confederacy and manned the nation's coastal defenses. The remainder served on the frontier.

Cutbacks forced nearly every officer to choose between demotion and discharge. Hundreds swallowed their pride. Having chosen the army as a career, they decided to stay. Still, demotion was an awful letdown. Major generals became colonels, colonels became majors, and majors became captains or lieutenants. Some officers even stepped back into the ranks. Brigadier General W. H. McCall returned to his prewar rank of sergeant. McCall's men still called him general in honor of the temporary rank he'd won for wartime heroism.

The units that officers led represented the American melting pot in miniature. The majority of men were native-born recruits who had joined seeking adventure or a steady job. Units also contained a sprinkling of criminals hiding from the law and offenders told by judges to enlist or go to jail. Newspapers described them as "human driftwood," "bummers, loafers, and foreign paupers."[3]

"Foreign paupers" referred to European immigrants, the second largest group in the postwar army. The majority hailed from Ireland, Germany, and England. These were poor men who had come to America seeking opportunity, and had joined the army as a first job. Few intended to make it a lifelong career, but to serve their hitch, save some money, and settle down on a small farm or follow some trade. A soldier-poet told how, in certain outfits, you heard almost any language but English.

> Maginnis scowls at Johnny Bull, an' Yawcob
>   Meyer roars
> At Jean Duval; an' I have heard
>   the comp'ny countin' fours
> In seven different languages; on which
>   eventful day
> The captain burst a blood vessel, an'
>   fainted dead away.[4]

Former "Johnny Rebs" enlisted, too. Unable to make a living in the war-torn South, these veterans exchanged Confederate gray for Yankee blue uniforms. Having fought to preserve slavery, they now served in the same army as black men, former Union soldiers who had decided to stay on and become professional soldiers. In the post–Civil War army, blacks made up four segregated regiments. Although there were black corporals and sergeants, the units were led by white officers. Indians called them "Buffalo Soldiers," because to Indian eyes their hair resembled the buffalo's. Indians and white settlers alike admired the blacks' ability and fighting spirit. Eighteen Buffalo Soldiers won the Medal of Honor, the nation's highest award for heroism, during the Indian wars.

Some Native Americans served in the frontier army as "wolves," or scouts. In Sitting Bull's time, hatred among the different Plains Indian tribes ran deeper and was much more personal than hatred of whites. Becoming army wolves allowed Crow, Arikara, Assiniboin, and Hidatsa warriors to fight their traditional enemies and earn money for the pleasure of doing so. These scouts looked forward to settling scores with the Lakota. A Crow chief named White Shield captured their mood. He advised soldiers to crack down on the Lakota. "The Sioux will never listen to the Great Father [the President] until the soldiers stick their bayonets in their ears and make them."[5] It never crossed the chief's mind that he was betraying his own people. There was no such thing as a single "Indian nation," only separate tribes and bands. White Shield assumed that, by helping Uncle Sam against the Lakota, he was helping his tribe.

The cavalry was the backbone of the frontier army. A cavalry private, or "hoss soldier," earned $13 a month, rising to $16 after five years of service. Corporals made $18 and sergeants $26 after the same period. Although army pay was low compared to factory wages, Uncle Sam also provided soldiers with food, clothing, shelter, and medical aid.

Native Americans called cavalrymen "yellowlegs" and "longknives," because their pants had yellow stripes along the seams and they carried swords. Although the cavalryman always displayed his sword during parades, he seldom used it in combat. Its yard-long blade weighed five pounds and could not outreach a warrior's lance. The cavalryman's chief weapons were the Springfield carbine, a short-barreled single-shot rifle, and the Colt revolver, or "six-gun," which fired six shots before it needed reloading. Warriors gladly traded six horses for a six-gun and a fistful of bullets. In some Lakota bands, eleven-year-old

Soldier of the Plains. A cavalry officer drawn by Frederic Remington. Notice his binoculars. These gave him a terrific advantage when it came to spotting enemies at a distance.

A frontier cavalryman going into action with his single-shot carbine. From a drawing by Rufus E. Zogbaum in <u>Harper's Weekly,</u> March 29, 1890.

boys toted revolvers and knew how to use them.

Frontier units were stationed at ninety-three posts, ranging in size from sturdily build forts housing five hundred soldiers and their families to twelve-man details scattered across the Great Plains and the deserts of the Southwest. "We are about 1,000 miles from nowhere excepting it be the verges of hell," a private wrote from his lonely outpost in Montana, "and I think we 'ain't more nor' ten rods from that delightful spot."[6]

When selecting a site for a fort, army engineers looked for level ground, abundant grass for horses, and timber for fuel and construction. If timber was plentiful, the fort would have a stockade, a wall of logs driven upright side by side into the ground. If timber was scarce, no stockade was built. Instead, rows of buildings formed a rectangle around a parade ground. A fort's chief defense was its garrison and their weapons. Although Indian raids took potshots at forts, they never captured one.

Officers had quarters in "the row," a line of cottages each having three or four tiny rooms. Unmarried soldiers lived across the way in barracks, long, single-story buildings with overhanging roofs for shade. Soldiers with families had quarters in "soapsuds row," where their wives did the family washing and earned extra money by doing officers' laundry. The headquarters building, hospital, armory, guardhouse, and mess hall completed the rectangle. Warehouses, stables, corrals, blacksmiths' shops, latrines, and the post cemetery lay beyond the rectangle. Forts were named after famous army officers. Only Fort Abraham Lincoln, Dakota Territory, had the name of a civilian.

Daily life at a frontier outpost was never easy. The inhabitants froze in winter and broiled in summer. Prairie fires turned the night sky orange.

Tornado-like winds blew fine dust under doors and through windows. Buildings swarmed with cockroaches, bedbugs, lice, and chiggers, tiny insects that burrowed under the skin. Wolves prowled at night; some had rabies, and their bite brought a slow, agonizing death. Rattlesnakes often escaped the cold by snuggling up to a warm, sleeping human body. During blizzards, buffalo gathered behind buildings to escape the biting winds. For days on end, the sound of their grunting and their scraping against the walls would make everyone short-tempered. In warm months, clouds of grasshoppers hid the sun at midday. Colonel Philippe Régis de Trobriand, commander of Fort Berthold, Dakota Territory, once saw a "traveling ocean of winged insects. These cursed insects hit us in the face, caught in our eyes and in our beards, got into our clothes, and jumped from the ground in swarms at our every step, like big hail stones bounding on the hard ground."[7]

Soldiering on the frontier required a special brand of courage. War is

When this picture was taken in 1877, officers' quarters at Fort Rawlins, Wyoming, were still fairly basic. Later they became more elaborate.

always frightful, but there are degrees of frightfulness. Although Civil War battles were bloody affairs, enemies fought according to certain well-understood rules. Soldiers knew they must not kill prisoners, let alone mutilate them. The law required them to feed captives and give them the same medical care as their own wounded comrades. Lawbreakers faced death by firing squad. Although these rules were not always followed, a soldier ignored them at his own peril.

Indians fought differently. Warriors killed in ways whites deemed more horrible than their own methods of killing. Frontier soldiers saw things unimaginable on any Civil War battlefield. Their letters, diaries, and official reports tell of incidents that still shock us, though in terms of sheer numbers, we "moderns" have wreaked devastation that would have seemed madness to these Indians.

For example, Lakota raiders once stole some horses from an Arikara village near Fort Berthold. The Arikara chased the thieves and shot one off his horse. "Although the victim was still alive," wrote Colonel de Trobriand, "they began to hack him up. He literally died under the knives with which they were cutting off his hands and feet, opening his stomach and chest to pull out the entrails, the heart, liver, etc., while others were tearing off his extremities. . . . These human scraps were carried to the village in triumph, and dragged around in the mud at the end of cords in the hands of enthusiastic women and children."[8]

The colonel, a newcomer to the Plains, was appalled because he did not understand that these actions were not cruelty for cruelty's sake, but rooted in Indian beliefs about life and the world. General George Crook, a veteran Indian fighter, thought that white people had nothing to feel morally superior about when it came to cruelty in war. Crook told a group of young officers, "With all his faults, and he has many, the American Indian is not half as black as he has been painted. He is cruel in war . . . but so were our forefathers."[9] And so were their descendants. During the Vietnam War, for example, some Americans collected the ears of dead enemy soldiers, which they kept on strings.

Frontier soldiers might fare no better than the poor man Colonel de Trobriand saw. In one incident, raiders butchered Sergeant Frederick Wylyams of the 7th Cavalry regiment. The sergeant had a large tattoo of the British coat of arms on his chest. This the raiders cut away and preserved, along with his scalp. Wylyams's comrades later recaptured both from a Cheyenne camp.

The soldier's worst fear was not of scalping or mutilation, but of torture. Whether Indians tortured prisoners, and who did so, is a complicated matter. Historians agree that certain Eastern Woodland tribes, like the Iroquois and Huron, tortured captured warriors to avenge past wrongs and to test the captive's courage. A family that had lost a son might adopt a man who withstood torture bravely, or a widow take him as a replacement for her late husband. The ability to withstand pain without crying out proved a man had good medicine.[10]

Historians also agree that tribes on the northern Great Plains—Lakota, Cheyenne, Arapaho, Crow—generally did not torture captives. George Bird Grinnell, who interviewed hundreds of warriors on reservations in the early 1900s, said "they never practiced torture, except, possibly, in some cases where they were still very angry over some injury they believed they had received." Although warriors killed captives of any age or sex, they also showed mercy. Not only did they spare captives' lives, as Sitting Bull spared Jumping Bull's, they treated them as honored guests. When, for example, the Lakota captured a small band of Pawnee men, women, and children, they invited them to a feast, later releasing them with gifts of horses. Another time, when some Lakota stole Crow horses, Crow warriors overtook them. After killing a few, they whipped the others and let them go.[11]

The thought of capture terrified soldiers. Like the emigrants, they had read exaggerated accounts of Indian atrocities. Veterans also amused themselves by frightening new recruits with horror stories; they called it "stuffing the tenderfeet." For whatever reason, most soldiers believed that all Indians tortured captives. Preferring suicide to capture, they adopted this motto: "Keep the last bullet for yourself." Soldiers in tight spots made suicide pacts, agreeing to shoot each other to avoid capture. Individuals tied bootlaces together to form a long cord with a small loop at each end. One loop was for hooking over the big toe, the other for hooking onto the trigger of a rifle. The idea was to put the barrel into one's mouth and pull the trigger with the toe.

Soldiers dreaded nothing more than having their loved ones captured. Husbands made their wives understand that falling into Indian hands meant torture. To defend themselves, nearly all wives put in time with a carbine and six-shooter at the fort's target range. Many also carried derringers, or "pocket cannons," tiny, single-shot pistols of the sort John Wilkes Booth used to kill Abraham Lincoln. If capture seemed certain, they were prepared to shoot their children before turning the gun on themselves. If an officer thought his wife might be unable to pull the trigger, he assigned an aide to do it in the event that the officer himself was absent.

The 7th Cavalry regiment commanded by George Armstrong Custer had a standing order to shoot the commander's wife, Elizabeth, if necessary. That order gave her no end of worry. One day, for example, she was riding with a small cavalry escort when her heart sank. "Without the least warning . . . we suddenly came upon a group of young warriors seated in their motionless way in the underbrush. My danger in connection with the Indians was twofold. I was in peril from death or capture from the savages, and liable to be killed by my own friends to prevent my capture."[12] As it happened, the warriors let them pass safely. Her husband would not be so lucky when he met Sitting Bull's warriors.

Sitting Bull viewed forts as deadly spearheads thrust into the Hunkpapa homeland. Once implanted firmly, he feared, they would never be dislodged. To prevent this he began a series of hit-and-run raids in the fall of 1866. He started by attacking Fort Rice at the junction of the Cannonball and Missouri rivers in what is now North Dakota. For several days, he led some three hundred warriors in running off the fort's livestock and shooting up rescue parties. Yet he could not make a dent in the fort's defenses. Every time he gathered a few dozen men in the open, cannons let loose with explosive shells, which sprayed them with fragments of hot iron.

In December 1866, Sitting Bull struck Fort Buford, Montana, and the surrounding countryside. Whites' fears turned to panic as the Hunkpapas sniped at sentries and scalped gold-seekers bound for Montana. In one bold move, Sitting Bull led a war party across the frozen Missouri to capture the sawmill only a few hundred yards from the fort itself. As bullets whipped overhead, the chief beat time on the large circular saw blade and sang to the "tune." During a lull, he bought a bright red shirt from a trader named David Pease; to show his courage, he promised to wear it so the defenders of Fort Buford could easily see him. Pease sent word to the fort, where

Colonel Rankin, the commander, ordered his men to concentrate their fire on the Indian wearing the red shirt. They did—and missed.[13]

Sitting Bull kept up the pressure. During one shootout, according to newspaper reports, things grew so desperate that Colonel Rankin "shot his devoted wife to prevent her from falling captive to the savage fiends."[14]

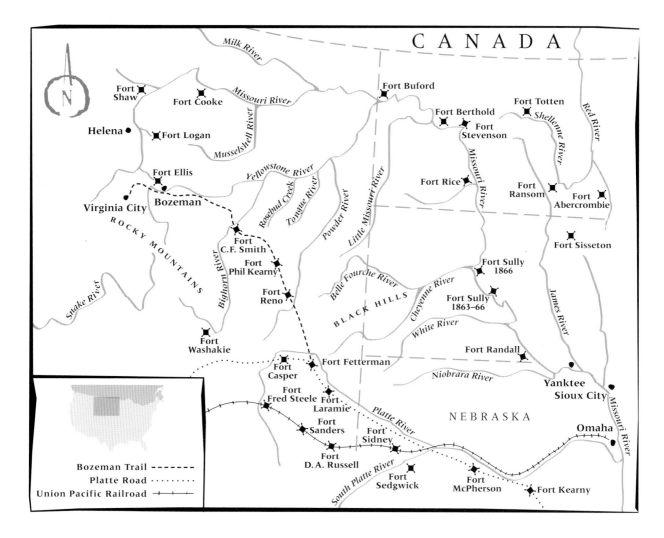

The Northern Plains, 1866–68.

Luckily (for her) the reports were untrue. In the end, however, Sitting Bull failed to take the fort or disrupt its activities for very long. As he had learned at Killdeer Mountain and Fort Rice, mounted warriors were no match for soldiers armed with cannons.

Sitting Bull's attacks on Fort Buford were pinpricks compared to the full-scale war raging to the south, in Wyoming. In the fall of 1865, the government opened the Bozeman Trail, a shorter, easier route to the Montana

A drawing of Fort Phil Kearny, one of the forts protecting the "Bloody" Bozeman Trail.

mining camps than the old one, which led westward across the Dakota and Montana plains. Near Fort Laramie the new route branched north from the Oregon Trail and ran across Wyoming into Montana through the lands of the Oglalas. To guard key points along the trail, soldiers built three forts—Reno, Phil Kearny, C. F. Smith—the following summer. Because the trail cut through the Oglalas' prize hunting grounds along the Powder River in Wyoming and Montana, they felt they had no choice but to fight. Makhpíya-Lúta—Red Cloud—led the resistance. Thanks to him, the trail soon earned the nickname "Bloody Bozeman."

Born about 1822, Red Cloud was a famous Oglala Lakota warrior who had led raids against the Pawnee and Crow. Although not a chief, his reputation as a fighter brought him a large following of warriors who looked to him for leadership. Since the late 1850s, Red Cloud had watched with growing concern as whites passed through the Powder River country. Yet, except for horse-stealing raids, he left them alone. Now, he realized, they had come to stay.

Whites not only threatened the buffalo herds, they insulted the Lakotas' religious beliefs by digging into the sacred body of Mother Earth. "The Great Spirit raised both the white man and the Indian," Red Cloud said. "I think he raised the Indian first. He raised me in this land and it belongs to me. The white man was raised over the waters, and his land is over there. There are now white people all about me. I have but a small spot of land left. The Great Spirit has told me to keep it."[15] Red Cloud meant to fight.

White people call that fight Red Cloud's War or the Powder River War. Sitting Bull did not take part in that war because it was the Oglalas' fight; besides, his band was hunting far to the east, along the Little Missouri River in today's North Dakota.

Red Cloud thought his warriors could handle the soldiers just fine. One of his best fighters was twenty-four-year-old Tashunka Witko—Crazy Horse. Born about 1841, he had received his name from his father, a holy man, after brave exploits against the Oglalas' enemies. The Oglala counted this quiet, thin-faced man with the sad eyes among the bravest of the brave. Crazy Horse never sent men into battle; he led them with all the dash and courage of Sitting Bull himself.

In forcing the removal of the forts on the Bozeman Trail, the Oglala leader Red Cloud became the only Plains Indian to lead his people in a successful war against the United States.

On December 21, 1866, Red Cloud sent Crazy Horse to lure a detachment led by Captain William J. Fetterman into a trap near Fort Phil Kearny. The fight that followed has different names. The Oglala called it the Battle of the One Hundred Slain; soldiers called it the Fetterman Massacre. After twenty minutes, Fetterman's entire command lay dead on a hillside covered by dry grass. Fearing torture, the captain and his aides killed themselves, probably by placing pistols to each other's heads and pulling the triggers at the count of three. Rescuers found their comrades' bodies stripped and mutilated, many beyond recognition. "We walked on top of their internals and did not know it in the high grass," a horrified cavalryman wrote. "Picked them up, that is their internals, did not know what soldier they belonged to, so you see the cavalry man got an infantry man's guts and an infantry man got a cavalry man's guts."[16]

"Fetterman's Massacre" was thus far the army's worst defeat in the West. Amid the shock and outrage that followed, a horrible idea began to form in the minds of many white Americans. We in the twentieth century would call this idea genocide: that is, the systematic killing of entire groups of people.

In 1866, they had different terms for it. While gathering material for this book, it amazed me how often I found whites using words like "extermination," "extinction," and "annihilation" when referring to Native Americans. Colonel de Trobriand said frontiersmen "believed that the only way to settle the Indian question was to exterminate *all this vermin*." Many of his fellow officers agreed, including William Tecumseh Sherman, the army's general in chief. This grim-faced soldier with a scraggly red beard and unruly hair had been one of the Union's top commanders in the Civil War. Sherman always spoke his mind. A week after the Fetterman disaster, he wrote: "We must act with vindictive earnestness against the Sioux, even to their extermination—men, women, and children."[17]

A Civil War hero, General William Tecumseh Sherman later became the army's general-in-chief.

Sherman often spoke of extermination, but never issued the orders for it. Had he done so, he would have raised a storm of protest from reformers back in the East. Not all whites hated Indians or wished to see them wiped out. For over fifty years, educators, clergymen, and people interested in worthy causes had campaigned for the abolition of slavery. After the Civil War, many turned their attention to the plight of the Native American. Calling themselves "Friends of the Indian," they feared that native peoples really did face extermination unless the nation found a humane solution to the "Indian problem."

Congress agreed. The lawmakers formed the Select Peace Commission, a group of civilians and military men, in-

Members of the 1868 Peace Commission posing with a Lakota woman. General William S. ("Mad Bear") Harney is second from the left. General William Tecumseh Sherman faces the woman on the left.

cluding none other than William Tecumseh Sherman. "Uncle Billy," as his men called him, was willing to give peace efforts a chance—at least this once. Sherman's fellow commissioners believed that the key lay in persuading the tribes to settle on reservations far away from the advancing whites. There, guided by sympathetic whites, they might gradually abandon their "savage" ways and become "civilized." During the spring of 1868, the commissioners sent messengers to call the Northern Plains tribes at Fort Laramie to sign a treaty.

Early in May, Father Pierre Jean De Smet, a Catholic missionary, rode into Sitting Bull's camp under a flag bearing the image of the Virgin Mary surrounded by golden stars. Plains Indians trusted this "Blackrobe" more than any living white man. Fearless and straight-talking, he traveled with only an interpreter, treating the sick and preaching goodwill to anyone who would listen. The priest begged Sitting Bull "to bury all your bitterness toward the whites, forget the past, and accept the hand of peace which is extended to you."[18]

For the only time on record, Sitting Bull revealed how deeply the massacre at Sand Creek had affected him. Although the Blackrobe set down his own version of the chief's speech, its meaning is perfectly clear:

Blackrobe, I hardly sustain myself beneath the weight of white men's blood I have shed. The whites provoked the war; their injustices, their indignities to our families, the cruel, unheard of and wholly unprovoked massacre at [Sand Creek] . . . shook all the veins which bind and support me. I rose, tomahawk in hand, and I have done all the hurt to whites that I could. Today . . . I will listen to thy good words, and as bad as I have been to the whites, just so good am I ready to become toward them.[19]

Now Sitting Bull wanted peace with the whites more than anything else. Yet "peace" without justice was merely a hollow word. Everyone, he said, staring into De Smet's eyes, should know that he would never give away "any part of my country." No treaty could last if the whites did not stop cutting timber along the rivers, particularly the little stands of oak. Sitting Bull loved the oaks because they thrived despite winter storms and summer heat—much like the Indian did. Like Red Cloud, Sitting Bull insisted that the soldiers leave their war houses, because "there is no greater source of trouble and grievance to my people."[20] He closed with a promise to send an observer, his friend Pizi—Gall—to the treaty council. If all went well, he would touch the pen along with the other war chiefs.

The Treaty of Fort Laramie is the most important document in the history of Indian-white relations on the Great Plains. It set aside a Great Sioux Reservation on all of present-day South Dakota west of the Missouri River up to and including the Black Hills. It also barred all whites except government officials from the reservation and from a vast "unceded" territory lying between the Black Hills and Bighorn Mountains. These lands belonged to the Lakota "forever," promised the treaty, unless three-quarters of the tribes' men agreed to part with them. Those who settled on the reservation would receive food and clothing while learning to support

The boundaries of the Great Sioux Reservation according to the treaty of 1868.

themselves by farming. They could claim their supplies at central points set up with warehouses and offices called "agencies," so named because each had a government-appointed manager, or agent. Those tribes who did not wish to settle down could hunt in the unceded territory while the buffalo lasted. Finally, the government agreed to close the Bloody Bozeman and abandon the forts.

The Fort Laramie treaty seemed to give the Indians everything they wanted. Yet things are not always what they seem. Captain Albert Barnitz, a cavalry officer who witnessed the signing, said the Indians "*have no idea that* they are giving up . . . the country which they claim as their own." He was right.[21]

White interpreters did not explain that, since the treaty did not close the gold mines, prospectors would keep coming. And if the Indians tried to stop them, the army would not stand by with its hands in its pockets. The interpreters also failed to explain that whites did not expect the buffalo to last very long; indeed, that they would do everything within their power to exterminate the herds. In any case, after a week of discussions, several important Lakota chiefs touched the pen: Spotted Tail of the Brulés; Running Antelope, Bear's Rib, and Man Who Goes in the Middle of the Hunkpapas; and Red Cloud of the Oglalas. No sooner did the soldiers march away than Red Cloud's warriors burned the hated forts to the ground.

Throughout the rest of 1868 and into 1869, most Lakota bands, numbering 17,000 people, moved onto the Great Sioux Reservation. A visit to Washington, D.C., in 1870, convinced Red Cloud that he had been wise to sign the treaty. Government officials liked to have chiefs visit the capital. Such visits were supposed to impress the Indians with the power of the United States and to weaken their resolve to resist its demands. Red Cloud received the grand tour. He saw huge stone buildings lining wide streets lit by lanterns at night. At the National Arsenal he saw more guns than he ever imagined existed. These included a cannon with a barrel wide enough to "swallow" a full-grown man; its crew showed its power by firing a shell two miles down the Potomac River. Above all, he saw swarms of white people in the streets—more people than all the Lakota tribes combined. And Washington was only one town.

Red Cloud left Washington a changed man, and a *sad* man. He was no longer the fearless warrior who led raids against the Crow. Although he had closed the Bozeman Trail, he realized that he had only slowed the whites' advance, not halted it forever. *Nothing* any Indian did could change that, he believed. "When we first had this land we were strong," he told some Friends of the Indian. "Now we are melting like snow on a hillside, while you are growing like spring grass."[22] He now believed it better to yield to white demands in the hope of salvaging something, rather than to lose everything in another war. He encouraged the Oglala to try farming. Some did try, but with little success. Although the government sent supplies, these were nowhere near the amount promised in the treaty.

Not all Lakota people saw things Red Cloud's way. A hard core of about 3,000 Lakota stubbornly resisted government efforts to "civilize" them. Among them was Gall, who had signed the treaty but had soon come to regret it. Rather than try farming, they either stayed away from the reservation or left it after a short time to join the hunting bands in the unceded territory. Others tried to have the best of both worlds. During the hunting season, they led the old free life of the plains. During the winter, they enjoyed the security and rations of the agencies.

Sitting Bull did not sign the treaty; in fact, he wanted nothing to do with it. For him, the whites had no right to ask for, and the Indians no right to give away, one inch of the Great Plains. Worse, he thought the whites had cast a spell over the Oglala chief. "The white people have put bad medicine over Red Cloud's eyes to make him see everything and anything they please," he said.[23] He hated the Fort Laramie treaty and everything it stood for.

A "new" life on a reservation! What did *that* mean? He challenged the very idea of a new life. For him, there was only one life: the life Wakantanka had created for his people. Scorning agency Indians, he called them "coffee-coolers" and "loafers" who had surrendered their birthright. He dared them to think and act like free men and women. "Look at me," he said. "See if I am poor, or my people either. The whites may get me at last . . . but I will have good times until then. You are fools to make yourselves slaves to a piece of fat bacon, some hardtack, and a little sugar and coffee." To show his contempt for the treaty, in 1869 he led another raid on Fort Buford. Joined by 150 warriors, he made off with most of the fort's beef herd and killed three soldiers.[24]

Crazy Horse did not follow Red Cloud onto the reservation, either.

Some time after the Fetterman fight—we do not know when or how—he became friends with Sitting Bull. For him, as for Sitting Bull, living on a reservation was unworthy of the Lakota. Wakantanka did not create Indians to work the land, let alone take handouts from white men. "Now you tell us to work for a living," he told a government official, "but the Great Spirit did not make us to work but to live by hunting. You white men can work if you want to. We do not interfere with you, and again you say, why do you not become civilized? We do not want your civilization. We would live as our fathers lived, and their fathers before them."[25]

As Sitting Bull and Crazy Horse spoke, more trouble was already brewing. Although Sitting Bull did not know it then, that trouble would take him to another milestone in his life.

A treaty similar to Fort Laramie had set aside two reservations for the tribes of the southern Great Plains—Southern Cheyennes, Comanches, Kiowas—in Indian Territory, the future state of Oklahoma. There, as in the north, warriors missed the free-roving life. Hunting and fighting were in their blood, and the freedom to pursue these gave meaning to life. A young warrior expressed this in a dramatic way. He stood up, jerked off his breech-cloth, and stood naked before those who talked peace. "Look at me," he shouted. "I am brave. I want to distinguish myself. I can do anything. Go to war, kill the enemy. I am a man!"[26]

In August 1868, several Cheyenne bands "jumped" the reservation—left without permission. Throughout the summer and into the fall, their war parties attacked settlers as far away as eastern Colorado. Come winter, the bands either returned to the agencies to collect their supplies or huddled in warm lodges beside frozen streams.

The press demanded action. Hadn't the Indians signed a peace treaty? Not only had they broken their promises, they had killed white people to boot. Where was the army? No more "coddling savages"! Headlines grew larger and bolder, editors more insistent that the army "do something at once."

General Sherman was ready. He and his frontier commander, General Philip H. Sheridan, had learned their trade in that great school of killing, the Civil War. Both men believed in "total war": that is, targeting not only the opposing army, but also enemy civilians. The idea was to make civilians so wretched that soldiers would have to quit out of concern for their fami-

General Philip Sheridan planned the army's strategy in its wars with the Plains Indian tribes.

lies. "War is cruelty and you cannot refine it," Sherman had told citizens of Atlanta, Georgia, during the Civil War. "You might as well appeal to the thunderstorm as against these terrible hardships of war."[27] In 1864, while Sitting Bull had fought at Killdeer Mountain, Sherman had been burning Atlanta and other cities in his march across Georgia. In 1865, Sheridan torched hundreds of Virginia farms to prevent them from raising food for the Confederate army. Cruelty, the generals believed, was a sort of kindness—in the sense that it shortened the war, thus saving more lives than it claimed.

Now the generals meant to give all Indians, and not just the Southern Cheyenne, a lesson in total war. In the past, the army had pursued raiders in the spring, summer, and fall. Naturally, Indians on horseback were hardest to catch in good weather. Sherman and Sheridan planned to attack in wintertime, when snow and subzero temperatures kept the enemy close to camp.

They commanded an all-weather army. Soldiers wearing fur-lined clothing, their horses fed from wagons carrying oats, could go farther and stay out longer than any warriors. When they struck, they must do so without pity. Not only must they shoot the warriors, but destroy the band's ability to fight by burning its supplies and leaving it homeless in the dead of winter. Sheridan knew this strategy meant severe hardship, even death, for women and children. So be it. "If a village is attacked and women and children are killed," he wrote Sherman, "the responsibility is not with the soldiers but with the people whose crimes necessitated the attack."[28]

Sheridan gave the mission to Lieutenant-Colonel George Armstrong Custer and his 7th Cavalry. Before daybreak on November 27, 1868, after riding through a howling blizzard, Custer found a Cheyenne village along the Washita River in Indian Territory. Ordering the regimental band to play "Garry Owen," a snappy marching tune, he charged the sleeping village. Custer neither knew nor cared that the villagers had not taken part in any raids. He was out for blood and glory. He got plenty of each. This action established his reputation as an Indian fighter and made him a hero in the newspapers.

Artist Theodore R. Davis drew this "reunion" on the Kansas plains in 1867. Eleven members of George Armstrong Custer's 7th Cavalry had been ambushed weeks earlier and their arrow-riddled bodies left behind.

Awakened by galloping horses, startled villagers ran from their lodges. Custer's men shot them down. Soon 103 Cheyenne lay dead in the snow; 93 were women and children, plus Chief Black Kettle and his wife; 21 troopers lost their lives. The colonel then ordered his men to burn the lot—lodges, tools, clothes, riding gear, lariats, buffalo robes, dried meat—and

A scene from Custer's attack on a Cheyenne village along the Washita River in November 1868. The drawing is by an artist known only as Kappes and appeared in Custer's book, My Life on the Plains.

shoot 875 captured horses. The hungry, exhausted refugees fled northward to Crazy Horse, who gave them food and shelter until they could get back on their feet.

The Hunkpapas were shocked. Coming so soon after the Fort Laramie treaty, the fight on the Washita River convinced them that the hunting bands must unite under a single chief to resist further white aggression. Such a chief had never existed before. Nor would all the bands agree with their decision. Changing times, however, demanded that people change their ways if they hoped to survive.

Those who wanted a supreme chief had no problem finding the right man. Everyone knew Sitting Bull's name and reputation. At age thirty-eight, he had every qualification. Lakota people said that Sitting Bull "owned himself": that is, he knew who he was and had total self-control. A good man to his family and a loyal friend, he possessed sound judgment, a kind heart, generosity, courage, religious devotion, strong spirit-helpers, and an uncanny ability to foretell the future. A brilliant speaker and composer of inspiring songs, he knew how to sway others to his way of thinking. In his day, as in ours, few presidents have had such qualities.

In the spring of 1869, the free Hunkpapa, Blackfeet, Miniconjou, Sans Arc, Oglala, and Cheyenne met to elect their supreme leader. After the chiefs voted, Four Horns rose. Facing his nephew, the old man said: "Because of your bravery on the battlefield, and your reputation as the bravest warrior of all our bands, we have elected you . . . head war chief. When you say 'fight,' we shall fight. When you say 'make peace,' we shall make peace."[29]

Sitting Bull accepted the honor with a song he composed for the occasion:

> *Ye tribes, behold me.*
> *The chiefs of old are gone.*
> *Myself, I shall take courage.*[30]

The world was changing as the chief sang. He would need all the courage and wisdom he could muster to meet the challenges ahead.

Plains Indians and whites got along fairly well during the early 1870s. The reservations kept them apart, as intended, while the hunting tribes ranged over the unceded territory and the lands beyond. The Hunkpapas and their cousins were as aggressive as ever. They pushed the Shoshones farther west, raided the villages of the Three Tribes, and attacked the Pawnees. In 1873, a war party of Oglalas and Brulés rode across southwestern Nebraska. One day, they forced 250 Pawnee men, women, and children to take cover in a ravine. Riding along the edge of the ravine, warriors shot into the people huddled below, killing sixty-nine. Had not a detachment of the 3rd Cavalry arrived in time, there is no telling how many more they would have killed. Things got so bad that the army removed the rest of the Pawnees to Indian Territory for their own good. Hundreds of Pawnee warriors enlisted as army wolves.[31]

As always, the war between the Lakota and Crow followed the seasons. Each spring and summer, war parties fought in the valley of the Yellowstone River and along the Bighorn River. The Crow had hunted these lands for nearly two centuries, but the Lakota did not want to share them with anybody.

Sitting Bull often fought the Crow. In 1869, soon after becoming supreme chief, his band was camping beside the Yellowstone River when Crows stole some of his horses and killed a small boy. A Crow warrior, lagging behind the rest, fell with a bullet in the brain. Sitting Bull was furious. "Cut him to pieces," he shouted, pointing to the body. "They killed one of us." So the warriors cut off the Crow's arms and legs, and carried the bloody trophies back to camp.[32]

Later that year, thirty Crows attacked two Hunkpapa youngsters while they were out hunting. Although the Crows killed one youngster, his friend was able to race back to camp with the news. With Sitting Bull in the lead, warriors galloped after the Crows, caught up to them, and killed them all. Nothing, it seemed, could halt the Lakota advance; nothing, that is, except the arrival of more hairy men from the east. This time they came not as emigrants in wagon trains, but as railroad builders.

Railroads were the fastest, cheapest way of moving people and goods in nineteenth-century America. Starting with 13 miles of track in 1830, the mileage steadily increased: 3,328 miles in 1840, 6,000 in 1848, 30,636 in 1860. Travelers who had once spent three weeks going from New York City to Chicago by stagecoach made the 750-mile journey by rail in three days. Railroads also played a key role in the Union's victory in the Civil War.

After the war, the government gave millions of acres of land to companies willing to build railroads. Before long, the idea of a super railroad, or a transcontinental railroad, gripped the nation's imagination. Americans believed that a railroad spanning the continent from coast to coast would bind the nation together and open the Great Plains to ranchers and farmers. General Sherman went further. He called the railroad an essential part of "a final solution" to "the Indian problem."[33] Nothing, he insisted, moved troops and supplies as efficiently. Except during a massive blizzard, trains pulled by two engines could go through any snowdrift; crews fitted some engines with huge snowplows. Equally important, telegraph wires strung on poles beside the tracks could carry messages hundreds of miles within seconds.

On May 10, 1869, work crews linked the Central Pacific Railroad from the West and the Union Pacific Railroad from the East at Promontory Point, Utah, stretching from St. Louis, Missouri, to San Francisco, California. When linked to the eastern railroads, this formed an entire transcontinental system. In 1871, workers began laying tracks for the Northern Pacific Railroad. Starting at Duluth, Minnesota, this line was to cross present-day North Dakota into Montana, then follow the valley of the Yellowstone River, ending at Seattle, Washington. Surveying parties, escorted by cavalry from Fort Abraham Lincoln, went ahead of the construction crews to map the route. Both soldiers and surveyors earned their pay the hard way.

The Lakota claimed the Yellowstone country as the northern boundary of their lands. They did not look kindly on trespassers. Before long, their war parties were giving the intruders no rest. Again, the army's leaders turned to Colonel Custer.

George Armstrong Custer (1839–1876), the "hero of the Washita," was born in Ohio and attended the United States Military Academy at West Point, New York. A poor student, he once broke into an instructor's office to steal examination questions. After graduating in 1861, last in his class, he joined the army as a cavalry lieutenant. The Civil War had just begun, and Custer loved every minute of it. The danger and the excitement of battle thrilled him as nothing else could. "I cannot but exclaim 'Glorious War!'" he once cried after a battle.[34]

George Armstrong Custer was a daredevil cavalry leader during the Civil War. This picture was taken in May 1865, less than a month after the war's end.

Fearless and reckless, Custer led wild charges against the Confederates. Though successful, those charges cost his division the highest percentage of losses suffered by any outfit in the Union army. No matter. Although men died all around him, "Custer's luck" always got him through without a scratch.

Success boosted Custer's confidence, making him feel as if he led a charmed life. It also won his superiors' admiration, particularly that of General Sheridan. Within three years of leaving West Point, Custer became a major general at twenty-four, the youngest officer to hold such high rank in the Union army. It was Custer, the "boy general," who received Robert E. Lee's surrender flag at Appomattox. As a gift for Custer's wife, Sheridan gave him the table on which Lee signed the surrender. In the end, Custer led the Union army during its triumphal parade in Washington, D.C. Then he gave up his general's rank and became a colonel as the price of staying in the service.

You could never miss Custer in a crowd. He stood six feet tall in his boots and weighed 170 pounds. The colonel had blue eyes set in a thin face, a drooping mustache, and golden-brown hair reaching to his shoulders. Indians called him Pe-hin Hanska, or "Long Hair." Soldiers called him Old Curly.

By any name, Custer was never shy. Like Sitting Bull, he enjoyed drawing attention to himself; he wanted the enemy to know they were facing him and not some ordinary officer. To make himself noticed, Custer invented his own uniform. It consisted of blue flannel pants, a blue velvet jacket with gold embroidery on the sleeves, a blue shirt, and a flaming red bandanna knotted around his neck. "He looked like a circus rider gone mad," a fellow officer noted.[35]

George Armstrong Custer and his wife, Elizabeth ("Libby"), shortly after their marriage in 1864. After his death, she wrote several books describing her life as an army wife in the West.

High-spirited and brimming with energy, Custer could not hide his feelings. When he was down, he sulked and brooded as if he carried the woes of the world on his shoulders. When he was happy, he fairly exploded with joy. He would race around his quarters, shouting and whooping while throwing chairs and overturning tables. "As for me," his wife Elizabeth (Libby) recalled, "I was tossed about the room, and all sorts of jokes played upon me, before the frolic was ended." It always ended with a bear hug and a kiss.[36]

The couple had married in 1864. Custer could not stand being away from "my little durl," as he called her, for any length of time. She went with her darling "Autie" almost everywhere, riding at his side on a cavalry horse. She rode sidesaddle, because ladies never sat a horse "clothespin" style: that is, rode astride. When duty kept them apart, Autie wrote her thirty-page letters each night. They had no children.

Libby recalled that her husband loved any animal he could ride, fondle, cuddle, tickle, or talk to. His pets included a badger, a porcupine, a beaver, a prairie dog, and a wild turkey. He tamed a tiny field mouse and kept it in an empty inkwell on his desk. The mouse grew so fond of him that it ran over his shoulders and through his hair. Once a pet raccoon washed the money in his wallet so energetically that nothing remained but scraps of torn paper. Custer's favorites, however, were his pack of Irish staghounds. The colonel pampered the big, shaggy dogs, allowing them to share his bed during campaigns. Tuck, a large female, liked to sit on his lap while he wrote letters. If she fell asleep, her master set her down "like a little baby deposited in its crib."[37]

Officers and their families at a social gathering, Fort Bridger, Wyoming, about 1880. By then, the army had broken the power of the Lakota and their Cheyenne allies.

Custer had another, less appealing side. A racist, he detested black people and thought Indians little better than wild beasts. A braggart and a bully, for breaking his rules he had soldiers tied in agonizing positions and exposed to swarms of buffalo gnats. Any junior officer who disagreed with him, or questioned his version of a story, got "chewed out" in front of the regiment. They obeyed his orders, like professional soldiers, but despised the man. Troopers called him "Hard Ass" and "Iron Butt" behind his back.[38]

On June 18, 1873, orders arrived at Fort Abraham Lincoln by telegraph. Two days later, Custer and the 7th Cavalry left for the Yellowstone country.

George Armstrong Custer with his military "family," Fort Abraham Lincoln, 1873. Custer is third from the left, and his wife, Elizabeth, is fifth from the left.

Sitting Bull's band had been hunting buffalo in this area for over a month. As Custer's column moved west, Hunkpapa scouts followed its every movement. Sitting Bull knew it was coming—and he was ready, waiting.

On August 4, Custer was riding a few miles ahead of the main column with a ninety-man escort when Sitting Bull struck. Outnumbered better than three to one, Custer ordered everyone to take cover in a clump of trees alongside the Yellowstone River. His men were raring for a fight. "Say, Teddy, I guess the ball's opened," Custer heard a trooper call to a friend. "Yis," the other replied in a thick brogue. "And by the way, thim rid nagurs [red niggers] is openin' wid a grand march."[39]

The "ball" opened with a volley of rifle bullets. Rather than risk lives in a head-on attack, Sitting Bull set fire to the tall grass. The fire made lots of smoke, but no wind rose to drive the flames toward the trees. Even so, the defenders' ammunition began to run dangerously low. By late afternoon, things were looking grim. Yet Custer's luck held. Suddenly, they heard a distant bugle call. The main column had seen the smoke in the distance. Putting two and two together, officers figured Custer needed help. A rescue party saved the day by scattering the Hunkpapa attackers.

A week later, the 7th Cavalry camped at the mouth of Arrow Creek, a tributary of the Yellowstone River. On August 11, the regiment awoke to find the bluffs lined with Hunkpapa and Oglala warriors. Sitting Bull and Crazy Horse had joined forces. They were not only friends, but allies.

Custer reacted swiftly. Posting a screen of riflemen in front of the camp, he ordered them to keep up a steady fire while he prepared the regiment to receive a massed charge.

Instead, the warriors fought as individuals. Young men raced their horses back and forth in front of Custer's riflemen, clinging to their manes while firing from under their necks. This gave them a chance to show courage but provided no battle honors.

As the day wore on, a medicine man named Long Holy described a dream he had the night before. In the dream, his spirit-helpers taught him a song:

> *There is nobody holy besides me.*
> *The Sun said so; the Rock said so;*
> *He gave me this medicine, and said so.*[40]

Long Holy promised that if the warriors sang this song as they approached Custer's position, it would make them bulletproof.

They swept forward, spurred on by Crazy Horse. Before long, however, wounded warriors began tumbling from the saddle. Long Holy insisted they continue. No one had died, he said, and no one would. His medicine was good.

As the supreme war chief, Sitting Bull had a triple responsibility: advise the warriors, lead by example when necessary, and pray to the Great Spirit for victory. Today, he watched the fighting from the bluffs, wanting to see how things developed. After a while, he could not sit and watch any longer.

Riding among the warriors, he shouted, "Wait! Turn back! Too many young men are being wounded! That's enough!"[41]

Long Holy turned on the chief. "I brought these men here to fight," he snapped. "But, of course, if they *want* to quit, they can."

Sitting Bull understood his meaning. Long Holy was suggesting that he had more courage and leadership ability than the Lakotas' supreme war chief.[42]

Sitting Bull could easily have physically overpowered the medicine man. Yet force would not have answered Long Holy's challenge. There was only one way to respond. Sitting Bull must do the bravest thing imaginable.

The chief dismounted. Laying down his weapons, he took his pipe and tobacco pouch from a saddlebag. Armed only with these, he walked past the mounted warriors as if taking a leisurely afternoon stroll. He walked straight toward Custer's firing line and sat down in the grass a hundred yards away, well within rifle range. His easy manner was an insult to the soldiers and a challenge to the warriors.

Riflemen cut loose with everything they had. The chief calmly took out his pipe, struck a spark with a flint and steel "lighter," and started puffing. He smoked slowly, relishing every puff like a favorite dish prepared by his wives. After a while, he turned to the astonished warriors. "Any Indians who wish to smoke with me, come on!"[43]

The warriors looked at one another, puzzled. Most thought *that* too much to ask even of brave men like themselves. They stayed put.

Only four men took the dare. White Bull (Sitting Bull's nephew), Gets the Best of Them, and two visiting Cheyennes seated themselves beside the chief. He handed the pipe to White Bull, who took a few quick puffs, then passed it along. White Bull did not scare easily; he had one of the best coup records in the band. This time, however, he had to use every ounce of willpower to control his instinct to run. Years later, he told an interviewer: "We others wasted no time. Our hearts beat rapidly, and we smoked as fast as we could. All around us the bullets were kicking up the dust, and we could hear bullets whining overhead. But Sitting Bull was not afraid. He just sat there quietly, looking around as if he were at home in his tent, and smoking peacefully."[44]

A warrior named Two Crow rode in front of the "smoking party," as White Bull called the group.

Bang.

Two Crow's horse collapsed in midstride, throwing him to the ground and knocking him senseless.

With the horse killed just an arm's length away, White Bull could only bend his head and shut his eyes—tight.[45]

Sitting Bull saw his companions' fear but refused to hurry. When the pipe came back to him, he continued to smoke as if nothing was happening.

At last the tobacco burned out. Slowly the chief tapped the ashes out of the bowl and cleaned the pipe stem with a twig. Then he stood up, brushed the dust from his clothes, and walked back to the mounted warriors. His companions followed but did not dare to run ahead of him.

"That's enough!" Sitting Bull shouted. "We must stop! That's enough!"[46] No one argued after such a display of courage. No one, that is, except Crazy Horse.

When it came to courage, Crazy Horse yielded to no one. Armed with just a lance, he charged across the length of the soldiers' firing line. Tongues of flame lashed out from the rifles. Crazy Horse did not duck or flop down over the horse's side for protection. He held his head high and looked straight ahead, as if the soldiers did not exist. Talk about showing contempt for the enemy!

Bang.

A bullet hit his mount and sent him tumbling head over heels. Crazy Horse leaped to his feet and ran to safety. So ended the Battle of Arrow Creek. It cost the 7th Cavalry four dead and two wounded. The Lakota probably lost about the same number.

Did Custer know the identity of the smoking party's leader? If so, what did he think of Sitting Bull? The historical record is silent on these questions. Yet this much is certain: The smoking party solidified Sitting Bull's hold on his people's loyalty. From then on, they had complete faith in his medicine. They would follow him anywhere.

Suddenly, everything seemed to change. Within two months of the battle, the railroad surveyors vanished, along with their soldier escorts and construction crews. Sledgehammers stopped beating on steel rails. Whistles stopped tooting. No iron horses came chugging west of Fort Abraham Lincoln. Only birds' calls broke the silence in the valley of the Yellowstone River.

Sitting Bull and Crazy Horse were delighted. Wakantanka had helped them drive the invaders from their country. Back east, however, men in wood-paneled offices had a different explanation. Economic disaster, not Lakota courage, had halted work on the Northern Pacific Railroad.

They called the disaster the "Panic of '73." On September 18, a major New York City bank closed its doors. The effect was like dropping a rock into a still pond. Ripples from the bank failure spread throughout the economy. Within weeks, hundreds of banks and businesses shut down. The stock market crashed. As factories closed, one in five city workers lost their jobs. Unemployed people rioted, threatening to overthrow the government if they did not get work to feed their families. Farmers, unable to repay their loans, lost their land. In the Midwest and Great Plains, clouds of grasshoppers blackened the sky "like coal smoke from a steamer."[47] In some places, grasshoppers covered the ground to a depth of four inches.

A frightened nation looked to its president for guidance. If anyone inspired confidence, it was President Ulysses S. Grant. As General Grant, he had led the Union armies to victory in the Civil War. Generals Sherman and Sheridan had served under him during the darkest days of the war. He had approved Sherman's plan to march through Georgia and ordered Sheridan to burn Virginia farms. Yet winning battles was easy compared to dealing with the Panic of '73.

What to do? The answer came in a single word: Gold! America needed the yellow metal to revive its economy. Grant and his advisers believed that putting more gold into circulation would drive prices upward. Higher prices would encourage factory owners to increase production by hiring more workers and raising wages. The president hoped to get more gold by developing new mines in the West. One place came to mind immediately. Lakota people called it Paha Sapa—the Hills That Are Black. White people called them the Black Hills.

General Ulysses S. Grant led the Union armies to victory in the Civil War. After the war, he became President of the United States. The Great Sioux War grew out of his desire to seize the gold-rich Black Hills.

Five

War for the Black Hills

> "Friends, what are you talking about?
> The Black Hills belong to me.
> Saying this, I take fresh courage."
> —Sitting Bull

SOME SIXTY YEARS AFTER Sitting Bull's ancestors crossed the Missouri River, a Lakota hunting party wandered into the Badlands of what is now the state of South Dakota. Later described by white travelers as "a part of hell with the fires burned out," the Badlands is a jumble of treeless buttes carved into weird shapes by wind and rain. The Lakota found petrified tree trunks and dinosaur bones strewn along the bases of the buttes and projecting from their walls. The Badlands are still among the world's prime fossil-collecting areas.

Other hunting parties, sometimes entire bands, went farther. Continuing southward, they came to an earthly paradise. In 1776, as patriots gathered in Philadelphia to sign the Declaration of Independence, Lakota scouts saw Paha Sapa rising from the sunbaked plains. Located on either side of what is now the South Dakota–Wyoming border, the Black Hills are a rugged mountain range towering above lush valleys. They cover an area of 3,500 square miles. Harney Peak, named for General "Mad Bear" Harney, who led the assault on Ash Hollow in 1855, is the highest point in the United States east of the Rocky Mountains. From a distance, dark green pine forests make the mountainsides appear black.

Bands of Kiowa had lived in and around the Black Hills for generations. The Lakota pushed them aside, as they had pushed aside so many other tribes. These mountains had everything they needed for a happy life: sparkling streams filled with trout, wood for lodge poles, game of every description. Paha Sapa's beauty stirred them so deeply that they imagined the land as a goddess whose breasts overflowed with life-giving food. More, the place seemed to vibrate with *wakan,* or sacred energy. The Lakota thought of Paha Sapa as the center of the world. Old men went there to restore themselves spiritually, young men to seek visions and find spirit-helpers.

The rise of the fur trade brought the first whites to Paha Sapa. In 1823, the explorer Jedediah Smith crossed the hills from east to west, going on to discover South Pass through the Rocky Mountains. Although Smith was not looking for gold, and found none, he thought it might exist in this beautiful land. He was right. According to the Oglala medicine man Black Elk, "Our people knew there was yellow metal in little chunks up there; but they did not bother with it, because it was not good for anything."[1]

Smith's men mentioned his idea to others. They did not have to say very much, since even a little talk of the metal greatly excited the whites. Before long, small groups of adventurers were prowling the Black Hills. Some of them found nuggets of gold in streambeds. Yet none lived to enjoy their new wealth. In 1834, for example, Ezra Kind and six partners struck it rich. After Lakota warriors killed his partners, Kind scratched these words on a flat stone: "Got all the gold we could carry out ponies got by Indians I have lost my gun and nothing to eat and Indians hunting for me."[2] His grammar was poor, but his meaning is clear. No white person ever saw him again.

A few years later, warriors brought a handful of gold nuggets to Father De Smet. The blackrobe's face darkened at the sight. After a long silence, he told them to bury the nuggets and never mention the yellow metal that drove white people crazy. They followed his advice.[3]

At various tribal councils, warriors vowed to kill any Indian who revealed the secret of the Black Hills. We do not know if they ever carried out the threat. What we do know is that things went very hard for anybody, Indian or white, who disobeyed. In 1871, for example, hunters caught an Oglala leaving the hills with some gold nuggets. They took away the gold, whipped him with their bows, killed his horse, and promised to kill him if he ever spoke of the incident. Hercule Lavasseur, a prospector, learned an even harsher lesson. To prevent him from writing or speaking about his discovery, warriors hacked off his hands and cut out his tongue.[4]

These actions only aroused further curiosity. Whites began to ask questions: Why did Indians kill or maim strangers who ventured into the Black Hills? Did they have something to hide? What was it? Could there be any truth to the rumors of gold?

President Grant wanted to find out. As the Panic of '73 spread, the president ordered General Sheridan to send an expedition to the Black Hills. The expedition was to map the area and get to the bottom of the rumors. However, the hills were part of the Great Sioux Reservation according to the terms of the Fort Laramie treaty. Whites could not enter them without their owners' permission. Lacking that permission, the expedition would be a deliberate violation of a solemn promise. That did not bother government officials. Treaty or no treaty, the army must do its job. America needed gold!

A Gatling gun, an early machine gun, of the sort Custer took on his Black Hills expedition.

Colonel Custer, Sheridan's favorite officer, got the assignment to lead the expedition. He left nothing to chance. The "scientific corps," as he called

In line and ready for the signal to start. Custer's expedition prepares to set out for the Black Hills.

it, was really an invading army accompanied by scientists. Custer's force included the 7th Cavalry, two companies of infantry, a sixteen-piece band, one hundred Crow and Arikara scouts, mapmakers, engineers, botanists, geologists, and mining experts. The force had a grand total of twelve hundred men and nearly twice that number of horses and mules. To guarantee that the Lakota kept their distance, Custer took along a quick-firing cannon and three Gatling guns, an early type of machine gun.

On July 2, 1874, at 3:00 A.M. sharp, the band played "Garry Owen" as the expedition left Fort Abraham Lincoln. Its ordeal began the moment the sun slid over the horizon. Temperatures soared to over a hundred degrees. Clouds of dust, churned up by the wheels of 110 wagons, shrouded the column in a gray haze. Sunburned men ate dust, sweated, and cursed. Nevertheless, Custer was enjoying himself. Accompanied by a small escort, he rode ahead of the column in search of adventure. Shooting a grizzly gave him the thrill of a lifetime. "I am gradually forming my menagerie," he wrote Libby. His menagerie included a live rattlesnake, two jackrabbits, an eagle, and four owls. As usual, his dogs shared his bed.[5]

Three weeks later, on July 25, Custer entered the Black Hills from the

Custer proudly views the grizzly bear he shot during his expedition to the Black Hills. Bloody Knife, his favorite scout, is seated at left.

northwest, by way of a Lakota hunting trail. The temperature quickly dropped twenty degrees, much to everyone's relief. Yet at first the hills did not seem special. After a while, however, the soldiers changed their minds. Like Sitting Bull's ancestors, they, too, discovered a beautiful, unspoiled world. A trooper described it as "an Eden in the clouds."[6]

One particular valley took their breath away. These hard-bitten men had never seen anything so magnificent. Nor had their colonel, who named it Floral Valley. "Every step of our march that day," Custer wrote, "was amid flowers of the most exquisite color and perfume."[7] Cavalrymen leaned from the saddle to pluck flowers by the armful. Wagon drivers wove garlands for the heads of their mules. Officers slipped flowers into notebooks to take home to their wives and girlfriends. The only Indians they met were five Lakota families camped beside a creek. Custer invited the chief, One Stab, to bring his people for presents of sugar and coffee. One Stab agreed to come but fled in the night.

July 27 was a red-letter day. After lunch, Horatio N. Ross, a mining ex-

A view of Custer's supply wagons passing through Castle Creek Valley in the Black Hills.

pert, strolled along the bank of what they dubbed French Creek. He was taking it easy, looking at nothing in particular, when he suddenly noticed pinpoints of yellow glinting in the gravel along the bank.

Gold! Ross's news struck the camp like a lightning bolt. Soldiers who had been napping under trees or playing a newly invented game called baseball rushed to the bank with tin pans and cups. They found a few tiny grains of gold and, after a while, left disappointed. But the mining experts refused to give up. Five days later, they found gold nuggets a few miles up-stream and in other places as well. Custer had accomplished his mission!

Custer left the Black Hills on August 15 and camped close by at the foot of Bear Butte, the birthplace of Crazy Horse. There he paused to write his official report. Although scouts found signs of Indians nearby, nothing could dampen the colonel's enthusiasm. "I could whip all the Indians in the northwest with the 7th Cavalry," he boasted.[8] Already the Lakota were calling the route he had followed the "Thieves' Road."

Parts of Custer's report read like an adventure novel. After describing the beauty of the Black Hills, he revealed the discovery. We can imagine him sitting at his camp table, pen in hand, grinning from ear to ear. "I have upon my table," he wrote, "forty or fifty particles of pure gold. . . . In one place . . . a hole was dug eight feet in depth [and] the miners report that they found gold among the roots of the grass, and from that point to the lowest point reached, gold was found in paying quantities. On some of the water courses almost every pan full of earth produced gold in small yet paying quantities. It had not required an expert to find gold in the Black Hills, and men without former experience in mining have discovered it at an expense of but little time or labor."[9] Although finding gold was not as easy as Custer said, there was plenty of it, if you looked in the right places.

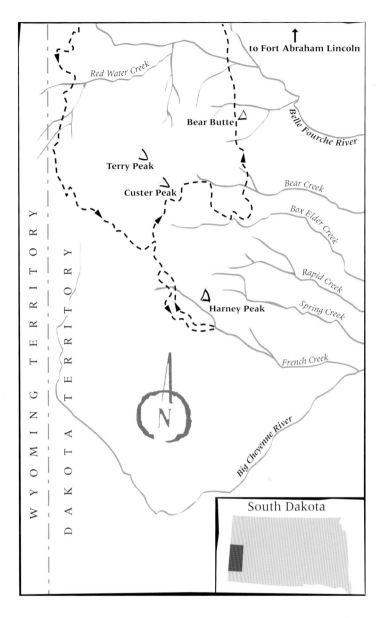

Custer's Black Hills expedition, 1874.

The expedition returned to Fort Abraham Lincoln on August 22, having covered 1,205 miles in sixty days. Custer lost no time in sending a copy of his report to General Sheridan. He gave another copy to newspaper reporters.

Screaming headlines announced the discovery. "EASY MONEY!" "GOLD! THE LAND OF PROMISE." "STIRRING NEWS FROM THE BLACK HILLS." "FROM THE GRASS

ROOTS DOWN IT WAS 'PAY DIRT!'" "PREPARE FOR LIVELY TIMES!" "NATIONAL DEBT TO BE PAID!" Custer's news restored hope to a nation reeling from the Panic of '73. It also triggered a second, civilian, invasion of the Black Hills.[10]

Men ruined by the panic headed westward. The Union Pacific Railroad carried them to jumping-off points in Nebraska; steamboats took them to landing points along the upper Missouri River. Merchants in towns such as Bismarck, the Dakota Territory, and Omaha, Nebraska, charged whatever they pleased for tools, food, wagons, and mule teams.

Calling themselves "pilgrims," prospectors came to the Black Hills singly or in small groups. And the Lakota killed them singly or in small groups. Bodies of nameless men, horribly mutilated, lay across the Thieves' Road as warnings to others. Now and then, pilgrims passed a man's head stuck on a pole set in the ground. A wooden board serving as a grave marker had this epitaph scrawled on it:

> Put away his pick and shovel,
> He will prospect no more;
> Death has sluiced him for his trouble,
> Panned him on the other shore.[11]

Yet there was no shortage of pilgrims, as lust for the crazy-making metal overcame the fear of death. Scores of wagons with "BLACK HILLS OR BUST"

Prospectors panning for gold in a stream in the Black Hills.

These prospectors in the Black Hills have built a sluice to enable them to separate particles of gold from gravel.

painted on their canvas set out for the diggings every week. Upon arriving, some prospectors built dams and sluices, long, inclined troughs for separating gold from sand. Others panned the streams; that is, washed gravel in a pan to separate the tiny gold particles. At a time when a factory worker was glad to earn $4 a week, a prospector might collect gold worth $50 in one day. Before long, mining camps dotted the hillsides and clustered along the streams. The camps had names like Deadwood, Last Chance, Devil's Dream, Poor Man's Gulch, and Go to Hell.

President Grant had ordered the army into the Black Hills. Now he saw the results of his action spinning out of control. Lakota people were in no mood to let miners ravage the sacred soil of Papa Sapa. Rather than risk a full-scale Indian war, Grant ordered Sheridan to enforce the Fort Laramie treaty.

Sheridan sent cavalry patrols to halt trespassers, burn their wagons, and arrest their leaders. The patrols did their best, but it was not good enough. Prospectors simply refused to obey their government. There was gold in those hills. They wanted that gold and would get it, no matter who stood in their way. One prospector spoke for them all. Let the soldiers do as they pleased, he said defiantly. "I have been captured and sent out of the Hills four times. I guess I can stand it as long as they can."[12] Only a soldier's bullet, or a warrior's arrow, would keep him from the golden land.

American public opinion favored the invaders. Members of Congress defended the rights of citizens to go anywhere in their own country. Newspaper editorials blasted the president for putting Indians ahead of the voters who had elected him. They insisted that white people needed the Black Hills more than "a pack of lazy redskins" did. If gaining those hills meant killing every Indian, then so be it. Humanitarians might weep for the "poor" Indian, but the Bismarck *Tribune* dismissed their concerns as childish. "Their prayers, their entreaties, cannot change the law of nature; cannot arrest the causes which are carrying [the Indians] on to their ultimate destiny—extinction. An Indian war would do no harm, for it must come, sooner or later."[13]

President Grant wanted a peaceful solution to this new crisis. That solution, he believed, did not lie in defying the will of the American voter. It lay in buying the Black Hills from their owners. So, in the fall of 1875, he sent a commission to the Great Sioux Reservation. The commissioners invited both the reservation Indians and the hunting bands to a council. As required by the Fort Laramie treaty, they would first have to persuade three-fourths of the adult males to sell.

Grant's action caused a split among the Lakota. Red Cloud, the leading reservation chief, wanted to sell. True, Paha Sapa was holy ground. Nevertheless, his second visit to Washington in 1872 had convinced him that fighting even for something so sacred was useless. With more miners arriving daily, he believed the Black Hills were already lost. Therefore, he argued, the Lakota should try to get the best price they could while the whites still felt like paying. Red Cloud wanted $600,000,000, or one hundred times more than the government's offer. Even at the higher price, it would have been a terrific bargain. The Black Hills had more gold than anyone suspected in 1875. By 1975, the Homestake Mining Company, the largest, had dug out $1.5 billion worth of gold.[14]

Although Red Cloud refused the government's offer, he was not ready to go to war. Sitting Bull, who spoke for the hunting bands, was not about to compromise. The chief refused to sell Paha Sapa at any price—refused even to attend the council. "We want no white men here," he insisted. "The Black Hills belong to me. If the whites try to take them, I will fight."[15]

September 24, 1875, was the day of the council. The commissioners and their interpreters sat on chairs in front of a large army tent. A 120-man cavalry escort waited nearby, in case of trouble. Thousands of reservation Indians sat on the ground before the tent or watched from nearby hillsides.

People were still arriving when, toward noon, a cloud of dust rose from behind the hills. Moments later, two hundred mounted warriors swept down the slopes. Drawn from both the reservation and hunting bands, they had come to deliver a message.

Whooping and waving their rifles above their heads, the warriors circled the tent, then halted before the seated white men. This was just the beginning. Somebody gave a signal, and another group emerged from the hills, repeating the performance. More and more groups came forward until a solid wall of warriors surrounded the tent and its cavalry guard. The commissioners stared at them and at one another, not knowing what to expect.

Suddenly, the lines parted and a lone warrior galloped toward the white men. He was Little Big Man, a warrior from the camp of Crazy Horse up north. Wearing only a breechcloth and a warbonnet, he held a rifle in one hand and bullets in the other. Coming closer, he pulled in the reins, making his horse rear up on its hind legs. As it did, the warrior shouted that he had come to kill the white thieves and any chief who agreed to sell Paha Sapa. His companions roared their approval. Like a cheerleader, he encouraged them by chanting:

> *Black Hills is my land and I love it*
> *And whoever interferes*
> *Will hear this gun.*[16]

Warriors galloped around the tent again. This time, however, cries of *"Ho-ka hey!"*—"Charge!"—rose above the clatter of horses' hooves. Red Cloud's allies sprang into action. These were extremely brave men. Ignoring their own safety, some escorted the commissioners and cavalry to safety, while others demanded that the warriors leave at once. The whites were guests, they said. Killing them would violate the rules of hospitality, angering Wakantanka. The warriors left. Although the commissioners failed in their mission, their failure had achieved an important result. It proved beyond doubt that the Lakota meant to keep the Black Hills.

Ulysses S. Grant faced a dilemma. Now he must choose between two equally bad options. Whatever he did (or did not do) would stain his reputation and damage him politically. As president, he was bound to uphold the laws of the land, including the Fort Laramie treaty. However, no elected official could resist the voters' wishes for long. If he enforced the treaty, they would topple his administration in the upcoming elections. Yet if he seized the Black Hills, the Friends of the Indian, the courts, and many private citizens would condemn him as a treaty-breaker. How to escape this dilemma?

Grant decided to take the "easy" way out. He wanted to take the Black Hills *and* follow the letter of the law. To do this, he must manufacture a war with Sitting Bull and his allies. Once the shooting began, he would blame the reservation people for breaking the Fort Laramie treaty and grab the Black Hills as a war prize. Historian Stephen E. Ambrose puts it this way in his book *Crazy Horse and Custer:* "The government was going to make war on the northern Sioux because their relatives at the agencies would not sell the Black Hills to the United States."[17]

On November 3, the president called a Cabinet meeting in the White House, with General Sheridan present. General Sherman, however, did not get an invitation. Although Sherman despised Indians, he was an honest man; everyone knew he would never support a scheme he thought dishonest or illegal. He and Grant had once been close friends, but they had drifted apart after the Civil War. Sherman came to regard his former chief as just another scheming politician.

Grant's Cabinet devised a three-part plan. First, the government would announce that the army would no longer keep trespassers out of the Black Hills. Second, it would order the hunting bands to report to the reservation by a certain date, a clear violation of the Fort Laramie treaty. Finally, the army would secretly prepare for a campaign against any "hostiles" who disobeyed the order. The idea was to provoke either a fight or an unconditional surrender. Whatever the Indians did, it would allow the President to squirm out of his dilemma.

On December 5, 1875, the government addressed the Hunkpapa chief directly. It ordered "Sitting Bull's band and other wild and lawless bands of Sioux Indians" to move onto the Great Sioux Reservation by January 31, 1876—*or else.* Anyone who refused would be treated as an enemy by the U.S. Army.[18]

The order was impossible to obey even had the hunting bands wished to turn themselves in. The winter of 1875 to 1876 was extremely harsh. Few runners sent to deliver the order got through the snowdrifts and sub-zero winds that lashed the northern Great Plains. Only a lunatic would travel hundreds of miles in that frozen wilderness. Besides, Indian horses fared poorly in winter because they fed not on grain but on patches of dry grass exposed when the wind blew the snow away. These undernourished animals, little more than bags of bones, could not pull a travois through deep snow. Young children and infants, the sick and the elderly, would never have made it to the agencies alive. Even if they had, they would have faced starvation, because most of the supplies the government promised had not arrived. Some reservation people, hoping for a bit more to eat, actually braved the cold to join Sitting Bull's camp along the Platte River in Wyoming.[19]

January 31 came and went. Sitting Bull failed to appear. Nor did any of the hunting bands. As a result, the army received its marching orders. President Grant would have his war for the Black Hills.

General Sheridan planned a winter campaign like the one on the Washita eight years earlier. The job of leading it went to Brigadier General George Crook, an honorable man and a brilliant officer who had fought in the Union army throughout the Civil War. Indians called him Three Stars, because he wore a star on his hat and one on each shoulder strap. Three Stars believed that greedy, stupid whites were to blame for the troubles in the West. Yet he understood political and military realities. Although he always spoke softly, his words had the sting of truth. "The In-

General George Crook was a Civil War hero and a skilled Indian fighter. He believed that whites provoked the Indians into fighting.

dian," he told West Point cadets, "commands respect for his rights only so long as he inspires terror for his rifle."[20] A professional soldier cannot choose his wars. Politicians start wars; soldiers fight them. And George Crook knew how to fight, having recently defeated the Apaches in Arizona. Now he turned his energies to the Lakota and Cheyenne.

Crook left Fort Fetterman, Wyoming, on March 1, 1876, with 900 troopers and a wagon train loaded with grain for their horses. Following the old Bozeman Trail, he led the column past the ruins of Forts Reno and Phil Kearny. Each trooper wore layers of wool and fur from head to toe. This outfit, an officer recalled, made them look like a column of Santa Clauses bound for the North Pole with "gifts" of guns and bullets.[21]

While they marched, the temperature dropped steadily. One morning, the thermometer froze at −22° Fahrenheit. Men's breath formed icicles on their mustaches and beards. Before cooks could fry the bacon, they had to split it with an ax. Three Stars tried to cheer his men, saying: "The worse it gets, the better; always hunt Indians in bad weather."[22] The men just gritted their teeth and trudged on, too cold even to complain.

Two weeks later, on March 16, scouts located the village of Two Moons's Cheyennes and He Dog's Oglalas near the mouth of the Little Powder River close to what is now Moorhead, Montana. At sundown, Crook sent Colonel Joseph J. Reynolds ahead with a 300-man strike force; Three Stars himself stayed with the main column.

Reynolds struck at dawn the next day. In the half-light, his troopers charged into the sleeping village with bugles blaring and guns blazing. Taken by surprise, villagers struggled to escape from lodges laced tightly against the cold. Women and children, most clad only in sleeping robes, ran for cover in the brush along the river. Two Moons's and He Dog's warriors grabbed their weapons. In no time, from the bluffs nearby, they were pouring a steady fire into the attackers, shattering Reynolds's self-confidence. Although only four troopers had fallen, he ordered a hasty retreat. Before leaving, however, his men burned the village.

Crook was furious; he later had Reynolds put on trial for his failure. Yet, with supplies running low and his men exhausted from marching, Crook had to call off the campaign.

Meanwhile, the refugees searched for help. After incredible suffering, they reached Sitting Bull's winter camp sixty miles to the north at the mouth of the Tongue River, where they were made immediately welcome. "Oh, what good hearts they had!" a Cheyenne warrior named Wooden Leg recalled. "I can never forget the generosity of Sitting Bull's Hunkpapa that day."[23] Women brought steaming pots of buffalo meat one after another, until their guests could not swallow another morsel. Others came with clothes, blankets, cooking utensils, lodges, riding gear, and horses.

Although Crook's campaign was a failure, the meaning of it was clear to the Indians of the Great Plains. It convinced the hunting bands that the whites had marked them for extermination. Their only hope of survival lay in unity. "We are an island of Indians in a lake of whites," Sitting Bull told a tribal council. "We must stand together, or they will rub us out separately. These soldiers have come shooting. They want war. All right, we'll give it to them!"[24]

Snow still lay deep on the ground when the first messengers left Sitting Bull's camp. These Hunkpapas headed to winter camps scattered along the tributaries of the Yellowstone River and to every agency on the Great Sioux Reservation. They pushed their winter-weakened horses to the limits of their endurance. Wherever they stopped, they gave Sitting Bull's rallying cry: "It is war. Come to my camp at the Big Bend of the Rosebud. Let's all get together and have one big fight with the soldiers!"[25] Everyone knew the place. Rosebud Creek, a tributary of the Yellowstone River in eastern Montana, had always been a favorite warm-weather campsite. Bands came there to socialize, do the Sun Dance, and hunt. Come spring, they would gather to fight the Wasichus.

Sitting Bull's words burned in people's hearts. Veteran warriors, furious over the violation of Paha Sapa, traded for guns and ammunition. Restless youngsters, eager to go on their first war party, yearned for action. So, when the new grass grew high enough to feed their horses, they left for the Rosebud. Red Cloud urged people to ignore Sitting Bull's call, because it could lead only to disaster. Yet even his own son, Jack Red Cloud, eighteen, rode off with the others. He took his father's warbonnet and Winchester repeating rifle, a gift from the "Great White Father," President Grant. By May 1876, the agencies had lost more than half their Indian population.

Sitting Bull's camp grew steadily. It did not attract only Indians. White men were there, too. We do not know their exact number; ten seems like a fair estimate. Some had married Lakota women and were living with their families. Others were renegades from white society. Only one of these men ever gave his name or told his story. Frank Huston, a Confederate veteran, had hated the "damn Yankees" ever since drunken Union soldiers beat his mother to death in the closing days of the Civil War. Instead of surrendering in 1865, Huston made his way west without taking the oath of allegiance to the United States. For the next sixteen years, he lived as an Indian. Huston never admitted to killing any frontier soldiers. "Would you, *then* or *now,* acknowledge it?" he later asked. Nevertheless, he saluted those who had killed them.[26]

As his camp grew, Sitting Bull called the chiefs to another council. The first thing they must do, he said, was to choose leaders for the coming war. That was easy. Although each tribe chose its own chiefs, they elected Sitting Bull supreme war chief. Even those who had not voted for him in 1869 now voted for him unanimously. Once elected, he was everywhere, doing everything. To stiffen the people's determination, he rode from band to band singing this song:

> *You tribes, what are you saying?*
> *I have been a war chief.*
> *All the same, I'm still alive.*[27]

The chief advised warriors (he could not command them) to bring the war to the enemy before he brought it to them. They must attack trading posts, settlers' cabins, and ranches. "Go in small parties—two or three or four in a bunch. Then the soldiers cannot catch you; they will not chase you. Listen, young men. Spare nobody. If you meet anyone, kill him and take his horse. Let no one live. Save *nothing*!"[28] And so they did.

Most Americans knew little, and cared less, about events in the "Wild West." The economy had recovered on its own, without the help of Black Hills gold. That spring of 1876 found the nation preparing for its first centennial. It was to be a gala event, a national party in praise of what the advertising men called "the greatest nation on the face of the earth." In Philadelphia, city leaders organized a fair around the theme "A Century of Independence and Progress." When it opened on May 10, visitors crowded into the exhibition halls to marvel at Alexander Graham Bell's telephone and Thomas A. Edison's duplicating machine, called a mimeograph. They also saw a mowing machine, a typewriter, and a device for mass-producing cigarettes.

General Sheridan was in no mood to celebrate anything. With quick, nervous steps, he paced the floor of his Chicago office. A map of the West covered a large oak table. Piles of reports lay on his desk. All that centennial hoopla might distract others, but he had a war to win. How? That was the big question. General Crook's failure proved that a single column of troops could never deliver a decisive blow. Although a detachment might capture a village or force a small battle, it could not trap horse Indians who could scatter across thousands of square miles of open country.

Sheridan knew he must change tactics. Rather than send one column, he would use three at once. The idea was simple: The columns would converge from different directions on an area favored by the hunting bands. Although he did not know the bands' exact whereabouts, he felt that at least one column would find and destroy them.

Again Sheridan ordered Crook to move up from the south. Meanwhile, Colonel John "Red Nose" Gibbon got orders to march eastward along the Yellowstone River from Montana. Finally, Major General Alfred H. Terry began moving westward along the river from Dakota Territory, a few days ahead of his main striking force. That force was the famed 7th Cavalry under George Armstrong Custer.

Rosebud Creek lived up to its name that spring. By early May, wild roses grew in thick patches along its banks, their sweetness filling the air for miles around. Every seven days or so, the camp criers announced a move to a different site along the stream. It took about a week for the hunters to kill most of the game, and the horse herds to eat most of the grass near a campground. There were so many Indians (about eight thousand so far) that the first arrivals at a new campsite raised their lodges and ate supper before the last group arrived.

The size of the camp filled Sitting Bull with pride. Yet something troubled him, too, a strange feeling he could not put into words. As usual, at such times, he asked his spirit-helpers for guidance. On May 21, he climbed to the top of a hill. Seated on a buffalo robe, the chief prayed long and hard, losing all track of time. Eventually, he fell asleep and dreamed. He saw a black cloud drifting across the sky from the east. A fluffy white cloud glided toward it from the west. The two clouds met directly over his head. Lightning bolts zigzagged. Thunder crashed. Wind-driven rain fell in sheets. When the storm passed, the black cloud had vanished. Only the white cloud remained.[29]

Sitting Bull described the dream to his fellow chiefs and holy men. All agreed that the black cloud represented soldiers. Clearly, the soldiers were coming to engulf their village in black, the color of death. Yet Wakantanka, the white cloud, would not let them. Again Sitting Bull had glimpsed the future. Even as he dreamed, soldiers were on the march.

He received a similar message two weeks later. On June 14, the tribes held a Sun Dance at Deer Medicine Rocks, a group of freestanding boulders beside Rosebud Creek. Sitting Bull took a leading role in the ceremony. Those present that day carried the scene with them for the rest of their lives. White Bull and the warrior Wooden Leg later told the story to white interviewers.[30]

After spending a night without food or sleep, Sitting Bull stepped into the dance circle. Naked except for a strip of buckskin around the waist, he had blue stripes painted across his shoulders. These represented the sky. His hands and feet were stained bloodred. This color symbolized his offering to Wakantanka.

Sitting Bull sat on the ground with his back to the dance pole, his legs fully extended and his arms resting on his thighs. His adopted brother, Jumping Bull, knelt at his side. Jumping Bull took an awl and a knife from a beaded pouch. Raising the chief's right arm, he stuck the awl into the skin at the base of the wrist. Slowly, carefully, he raised the skin and cut off a piece the size of pinhead. Then he withdrew the awl and inserted it higher up. He continued this way until he cut fifty pieces of flesh in a straight line ending at the shoulder blade. Jumping Bull then cut another fifty pieces of flesh from the left arm. Each lifting and cutting sent flashes of pain through Sitting Bull's body. Blood flowed freely, staining the ground. The chief neither flinched, nor let out a sound, nor showed any sign of fear. He just lay under the awl and blade, begging Wakantanka to have mercy upon his people.

After sacrificing his flesh, Sitting Bull danced around the pole. He danced looking directly into the sun, keeping time to the drums and blowing an eagle-bone whistle. Hour after hour, he followed the radiant disk in its passage across the sky. When the sun set, he kept dancing, never pausing to eat, drink, or catch his breath. He danced continuously for a day and a half. Then, suddenly, he stopped and stood rigid as a pole, staring wide-eyed into the sun. Bystanders sensed powerful medicine. Gently laying him on the ground, they sprinkled his face with cold water. Moments later, he motioned for a medicine man named Black Moon to come close. Black Moon put his ear near Sitting Bull's lips, and Sitting Bull whispered his message.

Black Moon walked to the center of the dance circle. Sitting Bull, he said, wished to share his experience with everyone. A voice had come to him from above. "I give you these because they have no ears," the voice had said. Sitting Bull had seen soldiers without ears hurtling through the sky. They were upside down, their feet pointing to the clouds, their heads toward the earth, and their hats falling off. They were falling right into the Indian camps.[31]

Sitting Bull's vision foretold an attack by soldiers. Yet it also promised that Wakantanka would protect his children. Those earless ones, those men deaf to cries for justice, would find death when they fell into the village. The people believed in Sitting Bull's medicine; his vision made them excited and confident. Frank Huston, an eyewitness, recalled: "Not an Indian there but was confident that Bull's prophecy would be fulfilled and that they could lick all hell and creation."[32]

The test came soon enough. Three days after the Sun Dance, scouts sighted a cloud of dust rising in the south. Three Stars Crook had arrived.

He brought 1,200 soldiers and 388 Crow and Shoshone wolves. During their advance through the valley of the Rosebud, the column passed a large herd of buffalo. Three Stars ordered his men to ignore the animals; he did not want to waste time or ammunition. His Indian allies, however, had other plans. They charged the herd, slaughtering hundreds and leaving their carcasses to rot.

Three Stars protested. Old Crow, the leading chief of the Crow tribe, brushed the protest aside. His warriors, he explained, would do anything to prevent the hated Lakota from hunting. "The great white chief will hear his Indian brother," the old man added.

These are our lands by inheritance. The Great Spirit gave them to our fathers, but the Sioux stole them from us. They hunt upon our mountains. They fish in our streams. They have stolen our horses. They have murdered our squaws, our children. What white man has done these things to us? The face of the Sioux is red, but his heart is black. . . . The great white chief will lead us against no other tribe of red men. Our war is with the Sioux and only them. We want back our lands. We want their women for our slaves—to work for us as our women have had to work for them. . . . The Sioux have trampled upon our hearts. We shall spit on their scalps.[33]

Over 1,500 Lakota and Cheyenne warriors rode to the attack. Sitting Bull went with them, but his swollen arms and blurred vision kept him from fighting. Instead, he urged the warriors onward. "Steady, men!" he cried. "Remember how to hold a gun! Brave up, now! Brave up!"[34]

Crazy Horse took command. *Command* is the proper word. That day, Crazy Horse broke with custom. He had the strength of character to get what he wanted from the warriors, and he knew what he wanted. He asked them not to attack in small groups or circle around the soldiers on their horses; that only spoiled their aim. They should strike home white-man style. Waves of mounted warriors should charge straight into the soldiers and break their lines. They should hit hard, and keep on hitting, without pausing to count coup or take scalps.

For six hours, each side charged and countercharged. In some places, where the fighting was most intense, soldiers grew terrified at the idea of capture and, they imagined, torture. They passed the word: "No surrender." Reporter John F. Finerty was there with his notebook. "Each one of us," he wrote, "would have blown out his own brains rather than fall alive into Indian hands."[35]

Jack Red Cloud disgraced himself. During a charge, a bullet killed the young man's horse. Normally, to show contempt for the enemy, a warrior took off his horse's bridle and slowly walked away. Jack Red Cloud panicked. Seeing him run for his life, three Crows chased him on horseback. One snatched his father's warbonnet off his head. Another yanked his father's Winchester out of his hands. All three beat him with their riding whips. Jack fell to his knees, burst into tears, and begged for mercy. Such a coward was not worth killing, so the Crows rode away, laughing. Jack Red Cloud returned to the reservation in disgrace.

A Cheyenne performed the bravest deed that day. Comes in Sight, a respected warrior, was turning away after a charge when a bullet killed his horse. As he sprang to his feet, some Crows and Shoshones rode in to kill him. But quickly another horse and rider dashed between them. A hand reached down and in a split second Comes in Sight was behind the rider, galloping out of harm's way. His rescuer was his sister, Buffalo Calf Road Woman, as good a rider as any warrior. That is why the Cheyenne named the fight with Crook's column "Where the Girl Saved Her Brother."

Three Stars Crook called it the Battle of the Rosebud, claiming victory because the enemy withdrew at sunset. His soldiers knew better. They had nine men killed and twenty-three wounded, about the same as the enemy. Moreover, Crazy Horse's tactics had stopped a major American offensive. General Crook, recognizing that he hadn't really won, could only bury his dead and attend to his wounded. Next morning, as Sitting Bull moved camp again, Three Stars began his retreat.

Sitting Bull led the bands to a new campground fifty miles to the west, over the next ridgeline, along the banks of a stream the Indians called the Greasy Grass. Whites called it the Little Bighorn River.

The war for the Black Hills had only just begun. This encounter, Sitting Bull knew, had not fulfilled his vision. He had still to see, literally, soldiers falling into camp.

SIX

SOLDIERS FALLING INTO CAMP

"They tell me I murdered Custer. It is a lie. He was a fool who rode to his death."

—SITTING BULL, 1877

THE INDIAN ENCAMPMENT sprawled for three miles along the south bank of the Greasy Grass and a half mile inland. At its northern end lay the Cheyenne camp under Dull Knife, Two Moons, and Little Wolf, eminent chiefs who remembered the Washita. Moving southward, a visitor would have passed through the camps of Lakota tribes: the Miniconjous of Hump and Black Moon; the Sans Arcs of Spotted Eagle; the Oglalas of Crazy Horse, Big Road, and Low Dog. Bands of Blackfeet, Brulé, Two-Kettle, and Arapaho formed smaller camp circles, joined by scores of Santee refugees from Minnesota. The Hunkpapa of Gall, Crow King, and Sitting Bull guarded the extreme southern end of the encampment, near a clump of trees just a few hundred yards from the riverbank.

Sitting Bull's lodge stood at the southern end of the Hunkpapa camp circle. Eleven people lived with the chief: his two wives (Four Robes and Seen by Her Nation); his mother, Her Holy Door; his two daughters; and a son from his earlier marriages; two stepsons; his widowed sister Good

Feather; and twin sons born to Four Robes just a few weeks earlier. His two nephews, Good Feather's sons One Bull and White Bull, lived nearby with their own families.

Each morning, before dawn, Sitting Bull and Crazy Horse sent scouting parties in all directions. Their plan was simple—and deadly. When the scouts sighted the enemy, they would not set out to attack him. If the enemy force was very large, they would immediately break camp, scattering in small groups to avoid capture. If the enemy force was manageable, they would watch it carefully. Then, when it drew near, they would strike with their full force. Even if it attacked by surprise, they expected the warriors to react quickly—within minutes to cover the escape of the women and children and then to destroy the attackers.

Meanwhile, on May 17, 1876, the day dawned crisp and cool at Fort Abraham Lincoln. An early-morning fog hovered close to the ground.

The 7th Cavalry stood at attention on the parade ground, awaiting its marching orders. Besides its 750 officers and men, the regiment counted thirty-five Indian scouts, including an Arikara named Bloody Knife, Colonel Custer's favorite. Two interpreters, Mitch Bouyer and Isaiah Dor-

Seated before his tent, Custer confers with his favorite scout, Bloody Knife, while his dogs relax.

man, also rode with it. Bouyer, a rugged frontiersman, was the son of a French father and a Santee mother. All we know about Dorman is that he was a black man who had married a Lakota woman and lived among her people for several years before leaving to serve their enemies. The Lakota hated Dorman, calling him Wasicun Sapa, or Black White Man. Both Bouyer and Dorman spoke the Lakota language fluently.

The Custer family—Long Hair's soldiers called it the "royal family"—was also well represented that day. Captain Tom Custer, the colonel's younger brother, was a Civil War hero. Shot through the face and neck during a cavalry charge, he had kept on fighting until his brother put him under arrest, forcing him to go to a surgeon for treatment. His bravery won him the Congressional Medal of Honor—his first. Tom won his second medal three days later, for a similar charge. The rest of the royal family consisted of Boston Custer, nineteen, its youngest member; Autie Reed, sixteen, a nephew who had come out for the "fun"; and Lieutenant James Calhoun, a brother-in-law.

Captain Thomas Custer died with his elder brother at the Battle of the Little Bighorn.

Colonel Custer sat on his horse, brimming with pride. Suddenly he took off his hat, waved it over his head, and pointed westward. Instantly, the band struck up "The Girl I Left Behind Me," a sentimental marching song. Soldiers' families lined the dirt road that wound throughout the fort's grounds. When the column began to move, wives waved handkerchiefs and blew kisses to their husbands. Children tied handkerchief "flags" to sticks and, pounding tin-pan "drums," marched beside their fathers. How many of them noticed their mothers' tears, or could imagine why they should cry during this exciting spectacle?

The fog was burning off as the regiment left the fort. Suddenly, a change in the temperature created a mirage, or optical illusion. Libby Custer described it in her book *Boots and Saddles* as "a scene of wonder and beauty." It was perhaps the strangest thing any of the families had ever seen. As the 7th Cavalry set out across the plain, another regiment, its reflection, alike in every detail, marched across the sky to meet its fate. Although Libby knew nothing about Sitting Bull's vision, "a premonition of disaster that I had never known before weighed me down," she recalled. That premonition grew stronger with each passing day.[1]

On June 16, deep in Lakota territory, the 7th Cavalry came upon the body of a warrior on a burial scaffold. The royal family pulled down the scaffold and took the funeral gear—a buckskin shirt, beaded moccasins, an elaborately carved bow and arrows—for souvenirs. Isaiah Dorman threw the naked corpse into the Yellowstone River. Arikara scouts later saw Dorman fishing nearby, apparently using the flesh for bait.

Next morning, June 17, Colonel Custer joined forces with General Terry and Colonel Gibbon at the junction of the Yellowstone River and Rosebud Creek. The general made his headquarters aboard the supply steamboat *Far West*, a large vessel with comfortable cabins that had traveled upriver from Fort Buford. Nobody knew General Crook's whereabouts, or of his defeat that same day. Nor would they know about it for another two weeks.

Custer's scouts soon picked up a wide trail leading westward from the Rosebud. Officers knew that such a trail could only have been made by Sitting Bull's "hostiles" moving to a fresh campsite. Nobody worried about how to defeat them; victory, they believed, was certain once they caught the enemy. Catching them and holding them long enough for a battle was the real problem. The army had to strike before the enemy realized his danger and scattered.

Terry outlined his plan, a simple "hammer-and-anvil" scheme, at a meeting aboard the *Far West*. It called for Gibbon's and Terry's own troops to march up the valley of the Bighorn River from the north and then to the valley of its tributary, the Little Bighorn River. Since they had a mixed force of cavalry and infantry—mostly infantry—they would have to move slowly. Meanwhile, the fast-moving 7th Cavalry would push up Rosebud Creek until it found Sitting Bull's trail. To increase its speed further, a mule train rather than wagons would carry its supplies. The general advised, but did not order, Custer not to follow the trail over the ridge between the Rosebud and the Little Bighorn. Instead, he should keep going and enter the valley of the Little Bighorn from the south. Custer's "hammer" would then strike the Indian camp, crushing any fugitives against the northern "anvil." Terry set the attack for June 26.

Custer prepared for the expedition with his usual energy. He ordered his men to travel lightly, without tents; they would have to sleep on the bare ground, covered by their saddle blankets. He also made them leave their swords behind; each man would carry one hundred rounds of carbine ammunition and twenty-five pistol bullets in his saddle bags. Terry, knowing Custer's reputation for daredevil stunts, offered him three Gatling guns in case he ran into trouble. Custer refused, knowing the heavy weapons would slow him down. Terry then offered him a detachment from the 2nd Cavalry. Again Custer refused, not wanting to share the glory with any other regiment.

At noon on June 22, the 7th Cavalry was ready. As it began to move out, Gibbon called: "Now, Custer, don't be greedy, but wait for us."[2] That was no joke. Gibbon feared Custer might try to take on the enemy by himself.

Custer turned in the saddle, waved his hand, and called back, "No, I won't."

What did he mean by that? No, I won't be greedy? Or no, I won't wait?

For two days, the 7th Cavalry moved south along Rosebud Creek. Custer drove his men hard, pushing ahead with only brief rest stops. So far, everything proceeded according to plan. It must have seemed like the old Civil War days, when he led his outfit deep inside Confederate lines. He alone seemed not to mind the pace. A bundle of nervous energy, he rode all day, grabbed a catnap when he had the chance, and sprang into the saddle as fresh as ever.

On the third day, June 24, things took an ominous turn. That morning, the men found the Sun Dance enclosure where Sitting Bull had had his vision. Custer's Indian scouts grew agitated. They could read the signs clearly. Everywhere they saw evidence that the Lakota had recently made medicine—strong medicine.

The floor of the dance enclosure had a drawing of two sets of hoofprints facing each other. Between the hoofprints lay drawings of dead soldiers with their heads pointed toward the Little Bighorn River. The scouts knew what that meant: The Lakota had no fear of soldiers. Moreover, three stones lay in a row near the drawing, each painted red. This meant that the Lakota trusted Wakantanka's promise of victory. Scouts also noticed the skull of a buffalo bull set on the ground opposite the skull of a cow, an arrow pointing to the cow's skull. This meant that the Lakota would fight like bulls, while the Wasichus ran like frightened women.[3] Yet the scouts were brave, loyal men. Ignoring the medicine, and their own feelings of imminent doom, they stayed with the regiment.

Toward evening, scouts found the trail. It had grown considerably in the last few days. Thousands of travois poles had scored the ground, making it look like a plowed field a mile wide. The marks pointed west, over the ridge separating the valleys of the Rosebud and Little Bighorn. Now even the greenest recruit knew that a huge camp of "hostiles" lay ahead. No matter. Custer did not care about how many Indians he might face. His only concern was preventing their escape. He believed in himself and his regiment. Together, he felt, they were invincible. "There are not Indians enough in the country to whip the 7th Cavalry," he boasted.[4]

At 9:30 P.M., Custer called an officers' meeting. While they sat on the ground, huddled around a flickering candle, he gave his orders. They were not going to attack from the south after all. The regiment would cross the ridge under cover of darkness, hide in the hills overlooking the Little Bighorn, and rest there for a day. The hammer would strike, as planned, at sunrise on June 26. Custer had already sent Crow scouts ahead to locate the enemy camp.

The 7th Cavalry set out in darkness, with only the palest moonlight to show the way. Meanwhile, as it climbed the ridge, Sitting Bull set out on a different sort of mission. Although the Lakota and their friends had beaten Three Stars Crook, the chief sensed a greater danger looming. So he untied his braids, painted his body in sacred patterns, and crossed the Little Bighorn River with his nephew One Bull. It was a swift stream twenty to forty yards wide, two to five feet deep. After reaching the other side, the two men rode to the top of a low hill. Nowadays, thousands of tourists visit that hill every year. Most have no idea of its place in Lakota history. They come to see the monument dedicated to Custer and his "gallant band."

One Bull stood a little distance away, watching his uncle. When Sitting Bull looked down, he saw the river, a silvery ribbon curving in the moonlight. All was quiet, save for crickets chirping and grass rustling in the gen-

Monument to the members of the 7th Cavalry who died at the Battle of the Little Bighorn. The picture was taken in 1881.

tle breeze. Raising his pipe to the heavens, Sitting Bull cried out to the Everywhere Spirit. The words came from the depths of the man's soul. "Wakantanka, pity me. In the name of the nation, I offer You this pipe. Wherever the Sun, Moon, Earth, Four Winds, there You are always. Father, save the people, I beg You. *We wish to live!* Guard us against all misfortunes and calamities. Take pity!" Before going back to camp to sleep, Sitting Bull left tiny buckskin bags of tobacco tied to twigs stuck in the ground. He had already offered his flesh and blood to Wakantanka. Now, with these sacred gifts, he appealed to his god for the last time before battle.[5]

For the 7th Cavalry the night march became an ordeal. Unable to see even their hands in front of their faces when clouds hid the moon, troopers banged tin cups and frying pans to keep contact with one another. Many stopped trying to stay in touch. Groggy with fatigue, they wrapped their arms around their horses' necks and dozed off until the animals stumbled or ran into low branches.

Shortly before daybreak on Sunday, June 25, 1876, Custer halted the regiment to await his scouts' report. The scouts reached the Crow's Nest, a rock ledge overlooking the valley of the Little Bighorn. In the dim light of dawn, they found a ridge blocking their view of the valley. Nevertheless, they saw brown specks swarming "like worms" over hillsides about fifteen miles away. The enemy's horse herds! They also saw countless wisps of smoke curling above the treetops. There it was—the largest encampment ever made by Plains Indians. On that day it numbered, overall, between 12,000 and 15,000 people, among them 3,000 to 4,000 warriors. There were also 20,000 horses.[6]

Custer's troops reached the Crow's Nest by midmorning. He could see nothing, even with the aid of a good pair of field glasses. By then, perhaps, the sun's glare made it difficult to spot even herds of horses at that distance. Nevertheless, the scouts knew what *they* had seen. "More Sioux in that village than all of Son of the Morning Star's soldiers have bullets," murmured a Crow named White Man Runs Him. (The Crow called Custer Son of the Morning Star.)[7]

Custer turned away without answering. Mitch Bouyer, however, refused to let the matter drop. "If you don't find more Indians in that valley than you ever saw together before," he said, "you can hang me!"

The colonel did not appreciate that remark. "It would do a damned sight of good to hang you, wouldn't it?" he said sarcastically. If Bouyer was afraid, let him leave the regiment!

That hurt Bouyer's pride. "I am not afraid to go in with you anywhere," he snapped, "but if we go into that valley, we will both wake up in hell!" Custer's reply—if he made one—is lost to history.[8]

When Custer returned to the regiment, his brother Tom reported that a patrol had seen Indians on a back trail, near the mule train. "They've spotted us!" he blurted out. "The Sioux know we're marching against them!"[9]

The words had scarcely left his lips when Mitch Bouyer reined in his mount after a dash from the Crow's Nest. His scouts had seen six Lakota warriors crossing a patch of open ground. They suddenly stopped, and one began to ride his horse in a tight circle. Surely it was a signal to other, unseen warriors that the cavalry was near.

For the second time, Custer decided to scrap his plan. He would attack without delay. True, he was a full day ahead of schedule and would have to fight without the support of Terry and Gibbon. Well, that was just fine. The colonel's decision was that of a gambler risking everything on a single throw of the dice. Yet it seemed a good bet. His worst fear was not fighting against heavy odds, but the enemy's escaping without a fight. Besides, he felt nothing had ever stopped George Armstrong Custer! Nor would it today.

Back at Fort Abraham Lincoln, one early riser was deeply troubled. The sun came up red, like a ball of fire. A scorching wind spawned dust devils, tiny whirlwinds of dust that swirled across the parade ground. Libby Custer stood at a window of the commander's house, looking out at the post's shabby buildings. Suddenly, tears welled up in her eyes, and she sobbed as if her heart were breaking. In her mind's eye, she had seen a dreadful sight. A naked warrior had galloped across the parade ground. Halting outside her window, he had raised his arm and given a triumphant shout. In his hand, the warrior held a clump of yellow hair. Her husband's scalp. Despite the suffocating heat, Libby shivered uncontrollably.[10]

Back on the ridge, others shared similar feelings of doom. *"Otoe Sioux! Otoe Sioux!"* murmured the Arikara scouts, "Plenty Sioux! Plenty Sioux!"[11] Half Yellow Face, a Crow, led his friends in a solemn ceremony, one strange to Custer. As the warrior offered tobacco smoke to the four winds, his companions painted white stripes on their faces. When Custer asked about the ceremony's purpose, Mitch Bouyer translated the reply: "Because you and I are going home today—by a trail that is strange to both of us." For a moment, the color drained out of the colonel's face.[12]

Captain Frederick Benteen could not return in time to help Custer's column fight a combined attack by Gall and Crazy Horse.

Yet nothing seemed to shake Custer's determination to fight. Around noon, he divided his command into four battalions, or combat units made up of several smaller units. He sent Captain Frederick W. Benteen with the 125 troopers of Companies D, H, and K to investigate a line of bluffs to the southwest. Custer himself followed Upper Ash Creek (later called Reno Creek), a stream that flowed into the Little Bighorn near Sitting Bull's encampment. The colonel moved along the creek's right bank with Companies C, E, F, I, and L—225 troopers and Crow scouts. Major Marcus A. Reno rode along the creek's left bank with companies A, G, and M, a total of 140 troopers. Captain Thomas M. McDougall stayed behind with 129 men to guard the pack mules and supplies. Custer had violated a basic military principle: Never divide your force without knowing your opponent's strength and position. His action robbed the 7th Cavalry of any safety it might have had in numbers.

Custer and Reno had proceeded ten miles when an officer rode ahead to the top of a knoll. From there, he saw several warriors galloping toward the camp on the Little Bighorn four miles away. Cupping his hands to his mouth, the officer shouted to Custer, "Here are your Indians, running like devils!"[13]

Running like devils! Custer's worst nightmare seemed about to come true. If he did not attack instantly, the enemy would escape.

"After them, boys!" Custer cried, jabbing his spurs into his horse's sides. "Charge!"

As his mount lurched forward, Custer sent an order to Reno. The major must continue along Ash Creek, cross the Little Bighorn, and strike the enemy camp. Custer promised to support him with the whole outfit. The time was 2:30 P.M.

Custer followed Reno, but only for a few minutes. While Reno's battalion advanced, Custer's battalion suddenly changed direction. The major had no idea that his backup had left.

It took Reno and his men twenty minutes to reach the Little Bighorn and cross at a shallow spot. On the opposite bank, they formed a battle line; Reno assumed Custer would support him once the shooting began.

Major Marcus Reno struck the first blow in the Battle of the Little Bighorn. When Custer did not support him as promised, he retreated across the river and took a defensive position on a hilltop.

The temperature was over a hundred degrees in the shade, making the air shimmer. Yet everyone was too busy to notice the heat. Troopers tightened belts and checked harnesses for the last time. Sweaty hands patted carbines and six-guns for comfort. Mouths went dry. Stomachs knotted with anxiety. Eyes squinted in the sun's glare.

Now!

Reno gave the signal to advance at a quick trot. With two miles to go, the trot became a charge. The sound of hoofbeats shattered the afternoon calm. A pillar of dust rose above the battalion. A guidon, or fork-tailed flag, with a large 7 on it, snapped in the hot breeze. As the Hunkpapa tipis came into view, Reno's battalion fired from the saddle as one man. So began what whites call the Battle of the Little Bighorn and what Indians know as the Battle of the Greasy Grass.

The Indians were enjoying a gorgeous day. Theirs was a happy encampment, an old-time encampment, busy yet filled with good times. Women chatted with one another as they combed the hillsides for wild turnips or tanned buffalo hides outside their lodges. Young men slept late after a night of singing, dancing, and courting. Young women gossiped and spoke of marriage. Naked children splashed in the swift river, paying little attention when teenage sisters told them to be careful.

The chiefs, however, expected trouble. For the last two days, scouts had kept them informed of the cavalry's movements. An attack was coming: That they knew. To be sure, they wanted an attack to fulfill Wakantanka's promise of soldiers falling into camp. Sitting Bull and Crazy Horse had agreed to play it safe, to hold back until the critical moment. Like good generals they refused to commit their forces until they knew exactly when and where the enemy would strike. The answer came a few minutes past three o'clock that afternoon of June 25.

Years later, any Indians old enough to remember knew exactly what they had been doing in the encampment when Reno's forces struck. The experience of Black Elk, age thirteen, was typical. His father had sent him to water the family horses at the river. After a while, the future Lakota medicine man left them with a cousin and went swimming with some friends to escape the heat. They were splashing and having fun when they heard a shout from the Hunkpapa camp. "The chargers are coming! They are charging! The chargers are coming!"[14] Looking up, Black Elk saw a pillar of dust rising in the south. It was Reno's column, advancing.

"The chargers are coming!" Each camp circle took up the cry, passing it to its neighbor. The effect was like a bolt of lightning streaking across the sky. Within minutes, the entire encampment exploded into action. Old men shouted advice and encouragement to the warriors. Boys caught their fathers' and older brothers' warhorses. Women abandoned their lodges, grabbed their children, and ran. The widow of Chief Spotted Horn Bull recalled that some women just stood frozen to one spot and "tore their hair and wept." Kate Bighead, a Cheyenne, saw a Lakota woman "jumping up and down and screaming, because she could not find her little son."[15]

Black Elk, left, fought at the Little Bighorn as a boy and later became a famous medicine man. He is shown here with a friend during a European tour with Buffalo Bill's Wild West Show.

After losing several family members, Gall joined Crazy Horse to crush Custer's column in the Battle of the Little Bighorn.

By then, bullets were crackling overhead and bursting through lodge walls. "I heard a terrific volley of carbines," recalled Moving Robe Woman, the daughter of Sitting Bull's boyhood friend Crawler. "The bullets shattered the tipi poles. Women and children were running away from the gunfire. In the tumult I heard old men and women singing death songs for their warriors who were now ready to attack the soldiers." Bullets found the two wives and three children of the Hunkpapa war chief Gall, killing them instantly. "It made my heart bad," he later told an interviewer. "After that I killed all my enemies with the hatchet."[16]

When Reno struck, Sitting Bull put his mother and sisters on horseback and led them to safety in the hills nearby, then hurried back to camp. Meanwhile, his wives fled with their children. In the excitement, Four Robes grabbed only one of her infant sons. After reaching the hills, she discovered her mistake and rushed back to the lodge to rescue his brother. Both survived.

Although Sitting Bull's arms were still damaged from the Sun Dance, he encouraged others to fight in his place. Finding his nephew One Bull, he placed his own shield over his shoulder and gave him his bow and arrows. The shield's design, which Sitting Bull's spirit-helpers had given him in a dream, would protect the young man with its magical power. In return, One Bull gave his uncle his rifle and pistol.[17]

"Go right ahead," Sitting Bull cried. "Don't be afraid, go right on!" One Bull leaped onto the back of his horse and raced toward the sound of the gunfire.[18]

Moments later, Sitting Bull mounted his coal-black stallion and, joined by his other nephew, White Bull, rode toward the action, too. As warriors gathered around the chief, he shouted, "Brave up! We have everything to fight for. If we're defeated, we'll have nothing to live for. It'll be a hard time, but fight like brave men! Brave up!"[19]

Reno saw mounted warriors pounding toward his battalion. At first, they came by twos and threes, then by scores and hundreds. "The very earth seemed to grow Indians," was the way he put it later.[20]

A half mile from the camp, Reno ordered his men to dismount, except every fourth trooper who held the reins of three horses. The dismounted riders formed a thin defense line, firing as fast as they could reload their carbines. The carbine barrels grew hot, burning their hands. Now and then, men looked over their shoulders, expecting to see Custer charging to the rescue. But there was no dust, no men, nothing. "What's the matter with Custer?" they asked one another. "Why are we staying here?"[21]

Warriors began working their way around Reno's defense line and toward its rear. Fearing encirclement, the major ordered a retreat to a stand of cottonwoods beside the river. It was no help. Warriors fired from all directions at once. Bullets whipped through the branches, showering the troopers with chunks of bark and leaves.

After fifteen minutes, the shady cottonwood was a bedlam of screaming, dying troopers. One dropped, then another and another. Isaiah Dorman fell, mortally wounded. "Oh, my God! I have got it," someone cried nearby, his hands clutching his belly.[22] Bloody Knife, the Arikara scout, turned to say something to Reno. As he did, a bullet hit him between the eyes. Bloody Knife's head blew apart, splattering the major's face with blood and brains. Reno, horrified, shook all over. Red Bear, another scout, noticed Reno's mouth and beard dripping with white foam, his eyes wild and rolling. Finally regaining control of himself, Reno ordered a retreat across the river.

What followed was not an orderly withdrawal, but a wild stampede. Reno's men remounted and headed for the riverbank. As they burst from the tree line, the thunder of hoofbeats and shriek of eagle-bone whistles overtook them from behind. Crazy Horse had joined forces with Sitting Bull.

The warriors let out an ear-splitting shout: "Crazy Horse is coming! Crazy Horse is coming!"[23]

Scene from Major Reno's retreat, drawn from memory in 1895 by a warrior named White Bird. Isaiah Dorman, the only black man present that day, lies dead at the right.

The Oglala chief, mounted on his yellow pinto, came like a whirlwind. He was wearing only a breechcloth, his body painted with his war medicine: white hailstone marks and streaks of blue lightning across his face. *"Ho-ka hey! Ho-ka hey!"* he shouted at the top of his voice. "It is a good day to fight! It is a good day to die! Strong hearts, brave hearts, to the front! Weak hearts and cowards to the rear!"[24]

"Ho-ka hey! Ho-ka hey!" "It is a good day to fight! It is a good day to die!" warriors shouted in reply. Nobody went to the rear.

The night march had exhausted Reno's troopers and their mounts. Now only fear and the excitement of battle kept them going. Their opponents were fresh, angry, and sure of victory. Wakantanka had spoken to Sitting Bull, and the chief's predictions had always come true.

Warriors rode among the fleeing troopers, calling, "You are only boys. You ought not to be fighting. We whipped you on the Rosebud. You should have brought more Crows and Shoshones with you to do your fighting."[25] A bullet or an arrow followed each taunt.

When Reno's men got to the riverbank, they found a six-foot drop at the crossing point. Horses teetered on the edge, afraid to jump. Troopers furiously spurred them on. Although the terrified animals jumped, several riders could not escape. Warriors shot them from the riverbank or chased them into the water. Troopers and warriors wrestled on horseback, as in the Throwing-Them-off-Their-Horses game. Warriors knocked their opponents into the water, dismounted, and held them under until they stopped struggling.

A trooper was writhing in pain when a warrior rode up to Black Elk. "Boy," he ordered, "get off and scalp him." Black Elk obeyed. The trooper, he recalled, "had short hair and my knife was not very sharp. He ground his teeth. Then I shot him in the forehead and got his scalp." Eager to show his mother his first scalp, the boy rode to a hill where a crowd of women and children had gathered. She was so proud that she sang for joy.[26]

Thirty-four members of Reno's battalion lay dead by the time it recrossed the Little Bighorn. Breathless, their hearts pounding, the survivors scrambled up the nearest hillside, now called Reno Hill. Reaching the top, they dismounted and formed a defense line. Hundreds of warriors had also crossed and were preparing to finish them off. Then, as if by magic, they vanished. Save for a few snipers that had stayed behind, the battalion found itself alone on Reno Hill. Little did it know that it owed its salvation to Sitting Bull.

The moment Sitting Bull reached the riverbank, he saw that the warriors meant to wipe them out. "Let them go!" he shouted. "Let them go! Let them live to tell the truth about this battle!"[27]

Saving the enemy was more than an act of mercy. The attackers' behavior puzzled Sitting Bull. A handful of troopers had charged a huge encampment. Why should they do such a silly thing? *Was* it so silly? The answers came to him in a flash: Those Wasichus were not alone! They expected others to back them up! Only after the battle did he learn the others' identity: Custer and his battalion.

We will never know what passed through Custer's mind that afternoon. Yet, if we try to see things through his eyes, his actions seemed logical. With the sound of gunfire echoing in the valley below, the colonel decided not to follow Reno into battle. Instead, he veered off to the right and galloped along the bluffs that run parallel to the Little Bighorn. Custer did not inform Reno of the unexpected change of plan, probably because it came as a split-second decision. In his mind, we suppose, he still meant to support Reno, only from a different direction.

Custer soon reached the head of Medicine Tail Coulee, a dry ravine leading down to a river crossing. On the opposite bank, he saw the encampment for the first time. Its size astonished him, but also stirred his fighting spirit. Slapping his leg with his hat, he called out, "Custer's luck, boys! We've got them! Come on!"[28]

He did "have" them—almost. With Reno keeping most of the warriors busy at the southern end of the encampment, he almost certainly meant to strike the Cheyenne village at its northern end. Scores of burning lodges and thousands of fleeing women and children would have spread panic in the warriors' rear. Terry and Gibbon were still far away. Yet he might pull off a miniature version of the hammer-and-anvil scheme by himself.

Custer paused long enough to send orders to Captains Benteen and Mc-Dougall to come on the double. Yet it was not to be. Neither Benteen or McDougall could reach Custer in time; instead, they joined forces with Reno on the hilltop. That action saved the command from annihilation by increasing its numbers and bringing much-needed ammunition.

Down in the valley, One Bull had rejoined his uncle and brother. Suddenly One Bull pointed to the bluffs. Wasichus! Other warriors saw them, too, and reacted to the threat at once. Crazy Horse and Gall led their warriors back along the riverbank, toward the Cheyenne camp.

We do not know if they met to plan that move, or if it was a natural reaction by experienced warriors who saw a chance to head off the enemy. In any case, Sitting Bull did not follow them. One Bull recalled that he sat on horseback "on the edge of the battlefield sort of directing things, though he himself did not go into the fight at all."[29] Sitting Bull knew he could not add much to the actual fighting. As a holy man and a war chief, he knew his duty was to pray to Wakantanka for victory and to encourage the warriors. Later, he led scores of Hunkpapa women and children to a safe spot across the valley. There, guarded by a handful of warriors, they watched the next stage of the battle unfold.

Custer led his battalion down Medicine Tail Coulee, toward a ford, a shallow spot where the river could be crossed easily. The time was about 3:45 P.M.

Mitch Bouyer expected the worst. He turned to Curley, the youngest of the Crow scouts. "Curley," he said, "you are very young. You do not know much about fighting. I am going to advise you to leave us. . . . That man [Custer] will stop at nothing. He is going to take us right into the village where there are many more warriors than we have. We have no chance at all." They shook hands and Curley left.[30]

Moments later, Custer dismissed the other scouts; they had served him well, and he no longer needed them. Bouyer, however, never wavered. Although he knew that Sitting Bull had offered one hundred horses for his head, he stayed with the battalion to the end. Curley and his comrades were the only survivors of the Custer fight. Thanks to them, historians have at least some idea of what the battalion experienced before the final blow fell.

Custer would have crossed the river had it not been for five warriors who returned from hunting too late to join in the Reno fight.[31] When they came to the Cheyenne encampment, they

Curley left Custer's column with several other Crow scouts shortly before it was wiped out.

found it nearly deserted. Yet they did not flee with the other villagers but hid behind some fallen logs along the riverbank. As Custer's battalion moved toward the crossing, the warriors opened fire from across the way. The troopers could easily have ridden them down, had they known their true strength. Suspecting an ambush, Custer halted, turned back up Medicine Tail Coulee, and continued to ride along the bluffs. Two of his officers, Captain Myles Keogh and Lieutenant James Calhoun, halted their companies to serve as a rear guard, covering the colonel's retreat.

The five warriors had bought precious time for their friends coming from the Reno fight. Gall rode through the village and crossed the river near the fallen logs. Crazy Horse rode entirely through the village and crossed the river further upstream. While Gall meant to hit Custer's force from the right, left, and rear, Crazy Horse meant to block it in front.

Gall struck first. As his men splashed across the river, they dismounted and left their horses out of range. Taking cover in gullies and behind rocks on either side of the coulee, they darted from place to place, shooting at Custer's rear guard as they went.

Keogh's and Calhoun's men dismounted, too. It was no use. Their own horses turned against them. Each trooper had to fire from the knee to steady his aim, holding his horse's reins over an arm. The terrified animals reared, broke loose, and ran away. Wounded horses whinnied in pain, scaring others into stampeding. The defense collapsed. Troopers fled in panic, only to be cut down by their pursuers.

Custer may have known that Keogh and Calhoun were getting the brunt of Gall's attack; soon they and their commands would all be dead. Yet nothing could halt Gall's angry warriors, who kept pressing their attack

Custer's Last Fight, an 1896 painting by Otto Becker, hung in taverns throughout the United States. Although it shows Custer fighting bravely to the end, nobody knows for sure when he died or who killed him.

from the sides and rear. Custer must have grown desperate. He had never been in such a scrape, not even during the worst days of the Civil War.

A hill loomed ahead of him. If they could reach the top and dig in, they might hold out until Terry and Gibbon arrived. We call the place Custer Hill. It is where the monument to the Battle of the Little Bighorn stands today.

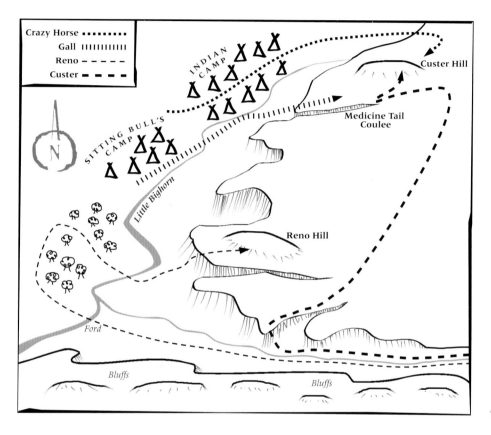

The Battle of the Little Bighorn.

With troopers dropping every step of the way, Custer kept pointing to the hilltop and shouting orders. By the time they reached the base of the hill, he led only his relatives, headquarters staff, and the remnants of his three companies. Up they went, under a hail of arrows and bullets. Men spurred their horses without mercy. The exhausted animals needed plenty of urging to keep going. They reared and plunged, trampling tiny packets of tobacco dangling from twigs stuck into the ground.

The troopers had almost reached their goal when their hearts sank. Crazy Horse rode over the crest of the hill. After breaking off his attack on Reno, the Oglala chief had led his warriors clear through the encampment. Crossing the river at a shallow point above the Cheyenne village, he swept up the ridge from the north. At the same time, Gall pressed in from the south. Each group of warriors formed the jaw of a trap with Custer in the middle. Then the jaws snapped shut.

Somehow, White Bull had joined Crazy Horse. The Oglala knew Sitting Bull's nephew well and respected him as a warrior. Crazy Horse now de-

Painting on a buffalo-hide lodge cover showing a battle with soldiers.

cided to hold a contest to set an example for his own men. He challenged White Bull to join him in a dash through a group of Custer's men. White Bull accepted the challenge. With Crazy Horse in the lead, the two galloped forward. An Oglala named Red Feather could not take his eyes off Crazy Horse. "The soldiers fired at once," he recalled, "but didn't hit him. The [other] Indians got the idea the soldiers' guns were empty and charged immediately on the soldiers."[32]

Although none of them survived to tell the tale, it is not difficult to imagine the battalion's last moments of life. Screams and war whoops, the whine of bullets, and the screech of eagle-bone whistles mingled in the air. The dust rose like smoke, turning the fighters into shadowy, ghostly figures. Custer's men did not know which way to turn. They coughed. Gunsmoke stung their eyes. Seeking shelter, if only momentarily, they shot their horses and dropped down behind the carcasses. Nothing helped. Simultaneously attacked from front and rear, their numbers dwindled steadily.

Not all died at the warriors' hands. We do not know exactly how many killed themselves. Yet it is certain that some, fearing torture if captured, took their own lives. Gall's men saw them put pistols to their heads and pull the triggers.

A group of forty-five men tried to escape the hill of death by making a run for the river. Nobody made it. Kate Bighead told an interviewer years later:

> There were hundreds of warriors, many more than one might have thought could hide themselves in those small gullies. I think there were about twenty Indians to every soldier there. The soldier horses got scared, and all of them broke loose and ran towards the river. Just then I saw a soldier shoot himself by holding his revolver to his head. Then another one did the same, and another. Right away, all of them began shooting themselves or shooting each other. I saw several different pairs of them fire their guns at the same time and shoot one another in the breast. For a short time the Indians just stayed where they were and looked. Then they rushed forward. But not many of them got to strike coup blows on living enemies. Before they could get to them, all the white men were dead. . . . The Indians believe that the Everywhere Spirit made all of them go crazy and do this, in punishment for having attacked a peaceful Indian camp.[33]

Soon afterward, Crazy Horse's men killed the last soldier on the hillside. The final encounter with Custer's command had taken no more than fifty minutes.

Victorious warriors did not take prisoners. They raced their horses over the hillside, killing any wounded trooper they saw. Those who could, took the troopers' weapons and clothing, leaving only naked bodies behind. Some found strange objects that went *tick-tick-tick-tick-tick-tick* or had needles that always pointed north. They also found green picture paper in the soldiers' pockets. Thinking the paper useless, they flung it into the air or gave it to children to decorate their toys. When Sitting Bull arrived, he became angry. Stealing from dead soldiers, he said, was bad medicine and offended Wakantanka. He feared that in the future the Lakota would become

Custer's dead as drawn by a warrior named Red Horse. Notice that many of the bodies have been stripped and mutilated.

slaves to the white man's things. He did not know that the picture paper was money, or that the soldiers had received a month's pay the day after leaving Fort Abraham Lincoln.

After finishing with Custer, warriors returned to Reno Hill. Troopers fought there for the rest of the day from behind dead horses and a barricade of saddles. Despite a hail of bullets, men had to pinch themselves to stay awake. Fear and loneliness tortured their spirits. "Where is Custer?" they kept asking. "Why has he abandoned us?" No one knew the answer. "We felt terribly alone on that terrible hilltop," recalled Sergeant Charles Windolph. "We were a million miles from nowhere. And death was all around us."[34]

Night brought no relief. Bonfires circled the base of the hill, casting an eerie orange glow. Sounds of people shouting and drums throbbing rose from the vast encampment. Troopers imagined painted warriors whirling around fires, waving their comrades' scalps. They were wrong.

Sitting Bull set the tone. He was calm, lacking any bitterness toward those who had attacked his people. Custer, in defeat, had changed the chief's opinion of white soldiers. True, they were killing machines. Yet, put to the test, some could fight as bravely as any Indian. The battle with Custer had claimed the lives of 246 whites; historians believe that 38 warriors died. "My heart is full of sorrow that so many were killed on each side," Sitting Bull said, "but when they compel us to fight, we must fight. Tonight we shall mourn for our own dead, and for those brave white men lying up yonder on the hillside."[35]

Sitting Bull had struck the right note. Although excited, people were not happy; there would be no victory dances until after they broke camp and left the banks of the Greasy Grass. Years later, Standing Bear, a Miniconjou, recalled how, as a teenager, he spent that night. "We built fires all over the camp, and everybody was excited. I couldn't sleep because when I shut my eyes I could see all those horrible sights again. I think nobody slept."[36]

Daylight on June 26 brought renewed fighting. Conditions on the hilltop grew steadily worse as the day wore on. Bullets and arrows kept the troopers pinned down, unable to hide from the blazing sun. Dead horses swarming with maggots swelled in the heat. Whenever a bullet struck a carcass, it exploded, sending chunks of putrid flesh flying in all directions. The hillside had no water, and men's tongues swelled, making talking painful. Desperate, the men chewed grass for the moisture. One fellow drank his urine. Moments later, he went crazy, leaped up, and ran toward the river. A bullet dropped him in his tracks. At one point, a few volunteers managed to sneak down to the river to fill enough canteens to give everyone a swallow of warm water.

Had the warriors attacked from all sides at once, they would surely have annihilated the rest of the 7th Cavalry. Yet they did not attack. Around noontime, the shooting slackened, then stopped completely.

That was no accident. Sitting Bull had arrived at the base of Reno Hill just as the troopers were starting to lose hope. "Let them go now so some can go home and spread the news," he cried. "I just saw some more soldiers coming."[37] He meant that Lakota scouts had seen the Terry-Gibbon column advancing from the north, less than a day's march away. He also wanted the survivors to tell the whites about the fate of those who had invaded the Lakotas' country.

Indian dead at the Little Bighorn as depicted by the warrior Red Horse.

The quiet was deafening. "A trick! Watch out!" troopers told each other. Time passed. One inquisitive fellow stood up. No guns fired at him. Others joined him. Before long, the whole command stood at the edge of Reno Hill.

No man present that day ever forgot the scene. Grass fires sent clouds of smoke striking up from the valley floor. Warriors had set fire to the dry grass not to screen their movements, but to burn forage for the horses of any pursuers, and to announce their victory. A group of Crow scouts saw the smoke fifty miles away and knew there was no point in going farther. They returned to their camp.

Breaks in the smoke revealed a huge procession stretching for two miles and reminding Sergeant Windolph of "some Biblical exodus."[38] Thousands of Indians rode horses dragging travois loaded with their belongings. Other thousands of horses followed the procession, driven ahead by youngsters waving blankets. As the sun set, the troopers cheered, realizing that the Battle of the Little Bighorn was over, and they were still alive.

At daybreak on June 27, 1876, lookouts on Reno Hill heard a distant bugle call. Peering into the valley below, they saw a column of blue-clad men moving along the bank of the Little Bighorn. General Terry and Colonel Gibbon had arrived. "Thank God!" men said, turning to one another. Whooping and hollering, they ran down the hill to greet their comrades. Veterans embraced. Some wept.

After a while, the column came to the site of the Indian encampment. It found the place strewn with abandoned gear of every type. Officers believed the occupants had fled in panic, leaving their belongings behind. But it wasn't so. Grieving families had discarded their loved ones' possessions; often they killed a warrior's horse so its spirit could speed its master's spirit into the next world. Troopers also found bloodstained pants, shirts, and underwear. Many items had labels with familiar names written in indelible ink. "Where are they?" men asked. "Are they dead or alive?"

The answers came soon enough. A member of a patrol that had crossed the river at the Cheyenne campsite rode up to General Terry. "I have a very sad report to make," he said grimly.[39] The patrol had just discovered the bodies of Custer and his command. Its only survivor was Captain Myles Keogh's horse, Comanche, found wandering among the dead. An army surgeon dressed the animal's wounds and he became the regimental mascot. Later, an official order directed that no one should ever ride Comanche or put him to work.

Terry, Reno, and their staffs inspected the battlefield. "I shall never forget the sight!" wrote Lieutenant Edward Godfrey. "The naked, mutilated bodies, with their bloody fatal wounds, were nearly all unrecognizable and

A survivor of the Custer disaster. Captain Miles Keogh's horse, Comanche, became the mascot of the 7th Cavalry Regiment.

presented a scene of sickening, ghastly horror!"[40] Burial squads gathered the remains and laid them in shallow graves. Today, a stone marker stands above each grave.

Searchers found Custer's body leaning against the bodies of two troopers. The colonel had a bullet hole in the left side of his head and one in his chest, near the heart. All three men were naked. Unlike the troopers' heads, however, Custer's had its scalp intact. It seems that he was getting bald; besides, he had cut his hair short before leaving Fort Abraham Lincoln. Warriors probably did not think his scalp worth taking.[41]

The *Far West* steamed down the Yellowstone River toward Fort Buford with news of the disaster. "Moccasin telegraph," however, spread it faster than any boat. Fort Abraham Lincoln learned the truth on July 2, nearly a week before the *Far West* arrived. That morning, two Crow scouts, Horned Toad and Speckled Cock, galloped across the parade ground. Moments later, wives found themselves widows and their children without fathers.

Tears flowed freely but not for long. "There was no fuss," Libby Custer recalled. "We were soldiers' wives."[42] Widows went to their houses to pack their belongings. In defeat as in victory, they knew that the life of the army must go on. Replacements were coming. They needed places to live, so the grieving families had to leave quickly. The Northern Pacific Railroad, which the 7th Cavalry had fought to protect, gave them free tickets to their home-towns.

Libby's fellow citizens made plenty of "fuss." If her husband wanted fame, he had it now. News of the Little Bighorn arrived just as the United States' centennial celebrations were getting into full swing. Immediately, a stunned nation went into mourning. Americans, some said, had not grieved so deeply since the assassination of Abraham Lincoln. Even Confederate veterans mourned the Union's "boy general."

Newspapers played a key role in shaping the public's view of the disaster. The Bismarck *Tribune* of July 6 set the tone. Its "extra" led the way with bold, black headlines: "MASSACRED. GEN. CUSTER AND 261 MEN VICTIMS. NO OFFICER OR MAN OF 5 COMPANIES LEFT TO TELL THE TALE. SQUAWS MUTILATE AND ROB THE DEAD. VICTIMS CAPTURED ALIVE AND TORTURED IN THE MOST FIENDISH MANNER."[43] Other newspapers took the *Tribune*'s lead article, the first to come from anywhere near the scene of action, and reprinted it from coast to coast, adding their own comments.

Yet the press failed in its duty to give readers the truth, and only the truth. Few details about the disaster were available when the story first broke. No reporter had interviewed any survivor of Reno Hill, let alone the Crow scouts Custer had sent away at the last moment. Nobody knew (or knows) when Custer died or who killed him. Ignorance, however, did not prevent editors from rushing into print. They knew a good story when they saw it. And good stories sold lots of newspapers, putting hard cash into their pockets. So, whatever information editors lacked, they simply made up—created out of thin air.

Press accounts often reveal more about white racism than about the Battle of the Little Bighorn. Nobody imagined that "Indian savages" could ever whip the "invincible" 7th Cavalry. But they had, and badly. Why?

Newspapers blamed one man: Sitting Bull. They retold any rumor, any piece of foolishness, as fact. No mere savage could have destroyed Custer, the all-American hero, reporters reasoned. Therefore, "Custer's murderer" must have been an equal: that is, a white man. Articles described Sitting Bull as a white renegade who despised his own people. They pictured him as an evil genius who spoke English, German, French, and Chinese fluently. Some reports made him a graduate of West Point, where he had studied the campaigns of Napoleon Bonaparte, Europe's greatest soldier. In other words, the Lakota chief could only have beaten the army at its own game, by using its own strategy.

Custer was no pushover, reporters said. They turned the fact of his defeat into the legend of "Custer's Last Stand." Their version of the battle soon became part of American folklore, and it still is. Outnumbered and surrounded, the legend goes, Custer fought to the last bullet and the last man. A typical article, appearing in the New York *Herald* on July 13, 1876, presented a scene of horror and glory. The author had no firsthand knowledge of the events he described so graphically. Yet he portrayed "wild, swarming horsemen" circling the doomed battalion "like shrieking vultures." Defying the odds, "the Seventh fought like tigers" and died like heroes.[44]

The nation's three top soldiers knew better. Its most decorated soldier, President Grant, viewed "Custer's Massacre as a sacrifice of troops, brought on by Custer himself." Generals Sherman and Sheridan agreed in condemning his reckless attack in the face of overwhelming odds. Obviously, they said, he had more courage than brains. As more information became available, the press also blamed the "disaster" on Custer's recklessness.[45]

They were wrong, however, on one count. "Custer's Massacre" never took place. A massacre, we recall, is the slaughter of helpless, unarmed people. Custer's force was anything but helpless and unarmed. Their colonel had led his troops against a peaceful village, whose inhabitants killed them and treated their remains according to their own traditions. Captain Benteen knew that the Indians had fought in self-defense. "We were at their hearths and homes," he said later, "and they were fighting for all the good God gives anyone to fight for."[46] Nobody has ever said it better.

Similarly, "Custer's Last Stand" is not history but fiction. Experts studied the battlefield twice. The first time, Terry's and Reno's officers went over it before the burial squads did their job. The second time, in 1984, scientists combed it with metal detectors. Both groups noted the position of the dead in relation to the empty shell casings found nearby. Since soldiers and warriors usually had different types of guns, and therefore different ammunition, one could easily tell which side fired from any given spot. Many shell casings of a certain type at one spot suggest a strong defense. Few shell casings scattered here and there suggest a total collapse.

Scientific findings supported the officers' original verdict. Officers saw only a few army-issue shell casings. Apart from Lieutenant Calhoun's company, they said, no unit held its ground for more than a few minutes. Captain Benteen likened the dead to a handful of grain flung across a barn floor. "I went over the battlefield carefully," he told an investigating committee. "I arrived at the conclusion that . . . it was a rout, a panic, till the last man was killed; that there was no [defense] line formed." Thus, there was no heroic last stand.[47]

The newspapers' use of words like *massacre, mutilate,* and *torture* helped create a national hysteria. Grief turned to outrage, and outrage to cries for vengeance. Editors suggested that the government find a way to spread smallpox among the hostiles. Newspapers readers demanded that the hunting bands, "wild beasts," be "caged" on reservations or exterminated "like vermin." Miners in the Black Hills offered bounty hunters $50 for each Indian head brought into Deadwood. A gunman named Texas Jack showed off a head in the saloons of Deadwood; the town board of health gave him a commendation, since killing Indians was "conductive to the health of the community." In Custer's hometown of New Rumley, Ohio, first-graders swore to kill Sitting Bull on sight.[48] Already Sitting Bull was becoming for whites not a man, but a terrible legend.

Seven

A HARD TIME

"A warrior
I have been
Now
It is all over
A hard time
I have."
—SITTING BULL

AGAIN, GENERAL PHILIP SHERIDAN pored over his maps. He had no idea of Sitting Bull's whereabouts, only that the united bands were growing less dangerous by the day. Such a large camp, he knew, consumed all the game and grass for miles around, making it impossible for the bands to hold together for any length of time. Before long, they must separate.

He was right. Sitting Bull's people had no plans for a prolonged war. After destroying Custer, they headed south, toward the Bighorn Mountains, where they celebrated with a victory dance. Then, one by one, the bands struck out on their own. By August, most had returned to the Great Sioux Reservation. From then on everything would be downhill for the tribes of the northern Great Plains.

Sheridan decided to place soldiers in the Yellowstone River valley, the Lakotas' prized hunting ground. Columns of soldiers would then pursue the "hostile" bands constantly, keeping them moving and preventing them from gathering food for the winter. Eventually, cold, hunger, and exhaus-

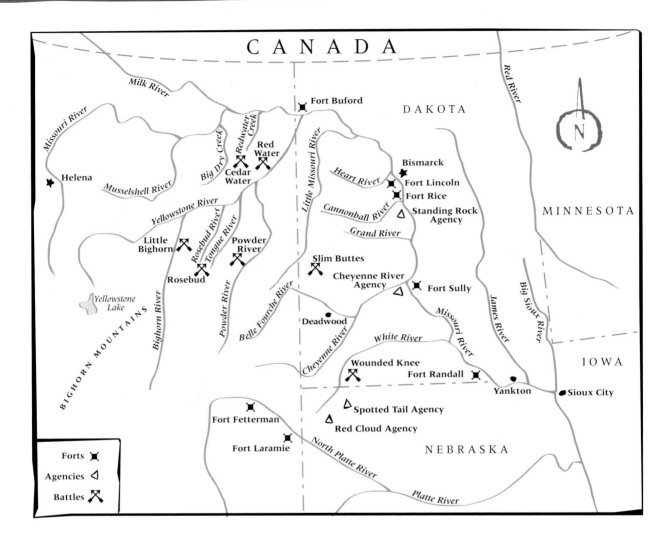

The Great Sioux War, 1876–77

tion would force them onto the reservation. There soldiers would seize their guns and horses, requiring them to live on government handouts. Thus, Sheridan demanded total war—war without letup or mercy. He had no qualms about inflicting hardship upon those who continued to resist the government. As he once put it, "The only good Indians I ever saw were dead."[1]

President Grant liked the general's plan. On his orders, telegraph keys began to clatter at military outposts across the country. Throughout the summer and fall of 1876, reinforcements poured into forts on the northern Great Plains. By late autumn, Sheridan had 9,077 men, or nearly half the total strength of the U.S. Army, available for the approaching campaign. Calling themselves "Custer's avengers," his men were out for blood. The result was a dozen widely scattered actions, all tiny compared to the Battle of the Little Bighorn, but crushing in their total effect.

George Crook led off from Wyoming. "Rosebud George," as soldiers called him, had scores to settle with Sitting Bull. Despite drenching rainstorms and seas of mud, he kept going. Nothing could make him turn back this time. Crook had vowed to teach the "hostiles" a lesson. He meant to show that neither distance nor bad weather nor short rations could prevent the army from chasing them down. To keep up their spirits, his men sang:

> We're marching off for Sitting Bull!
> And this is the way we go—
> Forty miles a day on beans and hay,
> In the regular army, O!

Crook's persistence paid off. On September 9, 1876, he struck a Miniconjou village in a dawn attack near Slim Buttes in northwestern South Dakota. Surprised by the swift attack, the warriors fled to a bluff overlooking the village. After getting their families out of harm's way, they opened fire on the soldiers below. Meanwhile, they sent messengers to the Hunkpapas and Oglalas, who were camping nearby. "The soldiers are killing all the children," the messengers cried as they rode through the villages. Their words stabbed into Sitting Bull's heart. He was mourning the loss of a son, kicked in the head by a horse a week earlier.[2]

Sitting Bull and Crazy Horse hurried to the rescue with their warriors. Crook's men withdrew, but not before burning the Miniconjou village. Sitting Bull rode among the smoking ruins, tears streaming down his cheeks. Wherever he turned, he saw saw death and misery.

"Are you living?" he asked a woman sitting with a blanket over her head. She was dead. Nearby, he found the bodies of a little girl, a young mother holding her baby, and a woman with her skull smashed by a bullet.[3] Just then, he met several captives freed by Three Stars to deliver a warning. The general wanted them to say that the army would keep pounding away until those who refused to go to the Great Sioux Reservation were either dead or captured. The Lakota, he added, should be sensible and surrender, instead of "exposing their wives and children to accidents."[4] To Sitting Bull, the deaths of those women and children had not been "accidental." They were murder.

Yet Crook could not carry out his threat. With food running low, he turned toward Deadwood in the Black Hills. Cavalrymen called that part of the campaign the "Horsemeat March." After a week of slogging through mud, they began to eat their mounts. At first they ate horses that had died, or were about to die, of natural causes. Then they shot healthy animals. Although eating their mounts made some feel like "cannibals," most troopers developed a taste for the stringy, sweet-smelling horsemeat. Relief came on September 16, when the citizens of Deadwood met them with wagons loaded with food.

By 1876, the Black Hills town of Deadwood had become a center of the gold-mining industry.

The soldiers found Deadwood a bustling, brawling boomtown. People from everywhere jostled one another along the main street, a muddy path lined with shabby buildings. There were German shopkeepers and Chinese with long pigtails, former railway builders who had started small restaurants and laundries. Saloons, dance halls, and gambling dens stayed open around the clock. Women dealers ran the card and dice tables. "I observed one of them with some attention," said reporter John Finerty. "She had a once-handsome face, which crime had hardened into an expression of cruelty. Her eye glittered like that of a rattlesnake and she raked in the gold dust . . . with hands whose long white fingers, sharp at the ends, reminded one of a harpy's talons."[5] Money in Deadwood was gold dust weighed on a scale after each transaction. Men broke their backs for it in the mines, then drank and gambled it away in a wild "fling." Others killed them for it. Scarcely a day went by without one or two men shot dead in a robbery or a gambler's quarrel.

While Crook's men were taking in the sights of Deadwood, another commission reached the Great Sioux Reservation. Its instructions were to complete the theft of the Black Hills. The commissioners were brutally frank. They had not come to negotiate, or even to win the approval of three-quarters of adult Indians as required by the treaty of 1868. Congress, they told tribal leaders, had refused to vote money for food unless they gave up all claims to the Black Hills and the unceded territory. In short: Sign or starve.

Major General Nelson A. Miles took a leading role in driving Sitting Bull's band into Canada after the Battle of the Little Bighorn.

Red Cloud and his allies signed. However, the agreement was illegal, and remains so to this day. It even embarrassed the commissioners. "Our cheeks crimsoned with shame," they wrote in their official report.[6]

Meanwhile, Sitting Bull faced a new opponent. No sooner had Three Stars ended his campaign than Colonel Nelson A. Miles took the field. Nicknamed "Bear Coat" by the Lakota, because of his winter outfit, Miles was a big, handsome fellow with an iron will and a keen mind. During the fall of 1876, he invaded the Yellowstone country with a mixed force of cavalry and infantry. Constantly on the move, his columns scoured the lands north and south of the river.

Colonel Miles found Sitting Bull camped near the mouth of the Tongue River. The chief did not want to fight, but he did not want to give up, either. When scouts reported soldiers nearby, he ordered a mixed-blood man who had joined his band to write their commander a note. "I want to know what you are doing traveling this road," he demanded. "You scare all the buffalo away. I want to hunt in this place. I want you to turn back from here. If you don't, I will fight you."[7] Bear Coat did not scare easily. Instead of leaving, he asked to meet Sitting Bull in person. The chief agreed.

The leaders sat on horseback between the lines of their fighting men. It was a tense meeting, as Miles later described it in his *Personal Memoirs*. Sitting Bull impressed him more than any other Indian he had ever met, or would meet. "He was a strong, sturdy looking man of about five feet eleven inches in height, well built, with strongly marked features, high cheekbones, prominent nose, straight, thin lips, and a strong under-jaw, indicating determination and force. He had a wide, large, well-developed head and low forehead. He was a man of few words and cautious in his expressions, evidently thinking twice before speaking."[8]

We do not know what Sitting Bull thought of Miles. The chief came straight to the point. White people were bad, and he wanted nothing to do with them, he said. All he wanted—all he had *ever* wanted—was to live in his own country in his own way. Miles brushed this aside, demanding that the Hunkpapa give up their weapons and go to the reservation. That was too much! Miles recalled that the corners of Sitting Bull's mouth tightened with anger. The colonel also recalled the chief's pride and dignity. "He declared that God Almighty made him an Indian and did not make him an agency Indian either, and he did not intend to be one." There was nothing else to say.[9]

Both men returned to their lines. Fifteen minutes later, Miles opened fire. Sitting Bull managed to escape this time, but he knew he was helpless against artillery and Gatling guns. So did his followers. Within a week, two thousand of them left for the reservation.

Miles kept after Sitting Bull. On December 18, a detachment led by Lieutenant Frank Baldwin found the chief's village beside Red Water Creek in northeastern Montana. With most of the warriors out hunting buffalo, Baldwin attacked. Although nearly all the women and children escaped with the horses, Baldwin burned scores of lodges and tons of dried meat. The raid left Sitting Bull heartbroken but still determined to hold on at any cost. "Friends, hardships pursue me," he sang. "Fearless of them, I live. . . . Love of my country is the reason I am doing this."[10]

So it went throughout that awful winter of 1876 to 1877. Columns of soldiers invaded the Lakota hunting grounds along the Yellowstone and kept the war going even when snow fell and temperatures plummeted to −30° Fahrenheit. Run, run, run. It took all a person's strength just to keep body and soul together. Hungry and exhausted, the Lakota bands wandered the windswept plains, searching for food and safety. "Wherever we went," Black Elk recalled, "the soldiers came to kill us, and it was all in our own country."[11]

Old people died; some asked to be left behind so as not to burden their families. Children cried out in the night, haunted by nightmares of charging soldiers. Mothers in Crazy Horse's band comforted them with a song:

> *Sleep, my little owl, no soldiers come shooting.*
> *This is a good place.*
> *The medicine of the Strange Man*
> *Covers all the people.*
> *Sleep, my little owl.[12]*

Still, there was no "good place." One by one, worn down by lack of food, cold, constant moving, the remnants of the hunting tribes surrendered. Bands of Cheyenne, the Lakotas' best friends, settled on reservations in Oklahoma and Dakota Territory. The Miniconjou, Sans Arc, and Brulé reported to agencies on the Great Sioux Reservation. The Oglala held out until the spring of 1877.

Crazy Horse realized that further resistance was useless. On May 6, he led 889 people and 12,000 horses into captivity at Camp Robinson, Nebraska. That same day, Sitting Bull halted at some mounds of stone arranged in a straight line. These marked a boundary that Lakota people had always called the *chanku wakan,* or Medicine Line. The Hunkpapa had run out of places to hide in their own land. Looking back sadly, they crossed the Medicine Line into Canada. It is impossible to say exactly how many crossed the line and when. The bands did not travel together, and so did not cross at once or at the same place. Two months earlier, in March, about

1,500 crossed with Black Moon and other chiefs. Sitting Bull brought another 300, more or less.

When the Hunkpapa entered Canada, traders told them it was ruled by Queen Victoria, Queen of England and ruler of the British Empire. Since they also learned that she was a kindly grandmother, they called Canada "Grandmother's Land." Canada, like the United States, had its "Wild West." There, too, native peoples—Blackfeet, Crees, Assiniboins—hunted buffalo and fought white intruders. To make matters worse, for nearly twenty years Americans had operated trading posts called "whiskey forts." At places with names like Whoop-Up, Spitzee, and Robbers' Roost, they encouraged tribesmen to exchange furs for "white lightning." As a result, hundreds died each year in drunken brawls. Warriors, driven crazy by whiskey, sometimes murdered their own families.

Major James Morrow Walsh befriended Sitting Bull during his exile in Canada.

Canada had neither the money nor the desire to use military power against the Indians. The government in Ottawa saw the frontier not as a problem for an army, but for a special type of police force. That force, created in 1873, was the Royal Northwest Mounted Police. Like the British redcoats during the American Revolution, police officers, or Mounties, wore scarlet jackets with blue breeches, blue hats, and brown boots. The Mounties set out to tame the frontier with three hundred men sworn to uphold the law. Yet they were more than a police force; they were a complete legal system on horseback. Not only did they close the whiskey forts and arrest lawbreakers, they acted as judges, passing sentences and exacting punishment. Above all, they kept their word. Having made a promise, they strove never to break it. Then came the Lakota.

Sitting Bull's uncle, Four Horns, led the first refugees across the Medicine Line in March 1877, near Fort Walsh in the province of Saskatchewan. Before long, a unique man rode into his village with a small escort. Major James Morrow Walsh, the fort's commander, had left the army to join the Mounties. At thirty-one, Walsh was a stubborn, domineering man. Always impatient, he could swear a blue streak and make even hardened frontiersmen cringe. Yet "Long Lance," as the Canadian Indians called him, had an equally strong sense of honor and justice. He despised the way Americans treated their native peoples. If Indians made trouble, he insisted, the blame lay not with them, but with the shameful policies of the U.S. government.[13]

Walsh lectured Four Horns. He used no soft words, no sweet talk, no glittering promises. Though surrounded by warriors who could have killed him in an instant, he spoke his mind. The major said firmly:

> All right. You must know there are laws here and everybody—whites, reds and blacks—must obey. . . . They govern the conduct of every person who stands on British ground and every Britisher defends them with his life. What they demand of you is that you will not kill either man, woman or child, no matter what their color or tribe may be. You will not steal. . . . You will not do any injury of any kind to either persons or property. . . . If you obey these laws, you and your families can sleep soundly here, safe as if walled around by ten thousand warriors. But if you think you cannot conform to these laws, return to your own land because you cannot live on British soil any more than fish can live without water.[14]

Four Horns understood. Grasping the major's hand, he promised to obey the Grandmother's laws. Walsh believed the old man. To show his trust, he allowed traders to sell the Lakota ammunition for hunting.

Sitting Bull's arrival two months later came as no surprise to the Mounties. Nevertheless, there were some tense moments when they first met. Walsh calmly rode into the Hunkpapa camp with five police officers and an interpreter. He came unannounced, as if it was his right to go wherever he wished.

Wasichus! Wasichus! The warriors grabbed their weapons. No white man had ever come into their camp like this before, and they suspected a trick. Walsh noticed that several rode horses branded "7 CAV"; he passed lodges with scalps dangling over the doorways. They were the scalps of white men.[15]

Sitting Bull laughed at the white leader's boldness—or stupidity. First impressions are lasting ones, and Walsh sized up the chief right away. Although Sitting Bull had a fearsome reputation in the States, he seemed like a decent fellow. Clearly, his people respected him, and he radiated self-confidence. As with Four Horns, the major explained the law. "There is no place here for lawless men who think it fun to shoot and kill Indians," he said finally. "And Indians must learn to respect the property of others." Sitting Bull nodded in agreement. Yet Walsh wondered if he really meant it.[16]

The test came sooner than either man expected. Next morning, as Walsh was saddling up to leave, three Assiniboins rode into the village trailing ten horses. Their leader was White Dog, a warrior admired even by Sitting Bull. Walsh's interpreter, however, recognized the horses as stolen from Canadian Indians. Walsh arrested White Dog on the spot.

White Dog, expecting help from the Hunkpapas, sneered at the arrest order. When Walsh waved a pair of leg irons in front of him, he admitted to "finding" the horses wandering on the prairie. Walsh sent him away with a warning to leave "lost" animals alone. But as the warrior turned to leave, he muttered, "I will see you again." The major ordered him to repeat the threat in front of everyone or go straight to the Fort Walsh lockup. White Dog backed down, explaining that he meant no harm. Humiliated, he left the village in disgrace. Sitting Bull was so impressed that he asked the Mountie to tell him more about the Grandmother's laws.[17]

Living without stealing horses seemed so contrary to the Lakota way of life. Warriors were supposed to steal horses; it was part of being a man. However, Sitting Bull meant to obey the law because his people needed a refuge and he believed the Canadians really would allow them to live in peace. When his brother-in-law, Gray Eagle, led a horse raid on a Canadian tribe, the chief used him as an example. Warriors made Gray Eagle mount a fast horse. Sitting Bull ordered them to chase him to the top of a high bluff while shooting bullets over his head. If he stopped or fell off, they must shoot him dead. Gray Eagle stayed on only barely. Later, the chief made him turn in his accomplices. Sitting Bull had them tied up naked and exposed to swarms of gnats for a week.[18]

For the first time in years, the Hunkpapa enjoyed a feeling of peace and safety. There were still plenty of buffalo to hunt, so nobody went hungry. The chief had more time for his children. Villagers saw him bouncing them on his knee and carrying them piggyback. If a child could not fall asleep, he sang lullabies of his own composition. Sitting Bull "buried the hatchet"— made friends—with old enemies like the Blackfeet. "Be cheerful," he told his people. "Be friends with everybody."[19] It was good to make peace, good not to think about awakening to the sound of gunshots. The owner of a trading post even taught Sitting Bull to sign his name.

Sitting Bull and Walsh grew to admire each other. For the first time, the chief dealt with a white man who did not try to outsmart him or make empty promises. For his part, Walsh praised Sitting Bull's influence and character. "In my opinion," he wrote his superiors, "he is the shrewdest and most intelligent Indian living . . . and is brave to a fault. He is respected, as well as feared, by every Indian on the plains. In war he has no equals; in council he is superior to all. Every word said by him carries weight, is quoted and passed from camp to camp." Walsh also found the Lakota "the most noble, moral, hospitable and tractable red men I have ever come in contact with. The character of their women would do credit to any nation. As a people they are affectionate, and family ties among them are stronger than they are among white people."[20]

Walsh, however, did not make policy for the Canadian government. The coming of the Lakota put the government in a difficult position. On the one hand, it was justly proud of its Indian policy. On the other hand, it could not afford to antagonize its powerful neighbor to the south.

Americans had long memories. They remembered that Great Britain had favored the Confederacy during the Civil War. They also remembered how Confederate agents used Canada as a base of operations against the United States. Acting individually or in small groups, agents crossed the border to spy on Union troop movements, blow up bridges, and derail troop trains. Now Canada was sheltering those "red devils" who had "massacred" Custer's command.

Washington gave the Canadians two choices. They could drive out the refugees—straight into the arms of the U.S. Army. Or they could adopt the Lakota, support them, and guarantee that they never ventured south of the border. If Canada accepted the second choice, and the Lakota caused trou-

Colonel Ranald S. Mackenzie led his 4th Cavalry into Mexico to punish the Kickapoos and Mescalero Apaches for their raids into Texas.

The killing of Crazy Horse as depicted by an unidentified Oglala artist.

ble anyhow, Washington would know who to blame and what to do. Army officers had no qualms about crossing foreign borders to attack Indians. In 1873, for example, General Sheridan sent a large force into Mexico to punish the Kickapoos and Mescalero Apaches for raids into Texas. Colonel Ranald S. Mackenzie carried out this illegal attack with the 4th Cavalry, a topnotch outfit. When Mexico protested, President Grant backed Mackenzie and the crisis blew over. Mackenzie or Bear Coat Miles would have jumped at the chance to cross the Medicine Line to go after Sitting Bull.

The Canadian government adopted a middle course. During the summer of 1877, it ordered Walsh to tell the refugees they could stay if they obeyed the law, but must not expect any help from their hosts. Meanwhile, Canadian officials asked the Americans to send a delegation to persuade Sitting Bull to return to the States. Washington agreed. The delegation's leader was none other than General Alfred Terry, who had sent Custer on his doomed mission.

The year 1877 was a bad time to visit the Lakota refugees. Late that summer, they learned that Crazy Horse was dead. On September 5, a soldier had stabbed the chief with a bayonet during an "escape" attempt. Word of his death stunned the Lakota. "They could not kill him in battle," said a bitter Black Elk. "They had to lie to him and kill him that way. I cried all night, and so did my father."[21] Lakota people still believe the escape story was merely an excuse for murder. Nobody can prove—or disprove—the charge. The army, however, never held an official inquiry.

Early in October, as Terry neared Fort Walsh, another tragedy occurred. This time it involved the Nez Percé tribe, or "Pierced Noses," so called from their custom of wearing nose rings as ornaments. The Nez Percé lived in the Wallawa Valley of what is now eastern Oregon, where they cultivated vegetable gardens, hunted deer, and caught salmon in the rivers. Each spring, their young men crossed the Rocky Mountains to hunt buffalo in Montana, where they also fought the Lakota.

Lewis and Clark, who had met the Nez Percé during their expedition early in the century, had praised their honesty and kindness. Tribesmen prided themselves on never having robbed or killed a white person. Unfortunately, settlers wanted their land, and the government agreed they should have it. Thirty days: That is all the time officials gave the Nez Percé to pack up and go to a reservation in Idaho. If they did not leave on time, the army had orders to evict them by force.

The Nez Percé refused to leave. When soldiers came, warriors opened fire, killing several. They had no choice now: Either they fled at once, or the army would deal with them as it had dealt with so many other tribes.

On June 13, under their leader, Chief Joseph, the Nez Percé set out for Grandmother's Land. Ahead lay hundreds of miles of country patrolled by

Chief Joseph led the Nez Percé in their effort to escape to Canada after the U.S. government seized their lands.

Bear Coat Miles's cavalry. During a four-month march, they fought thirteen battles, winning all but the last. Finally, Miles cut them off only forty miles from the Medicine Line. Some two hundred people, however, managed to slip out of the trap and cross into Canada. After wandering for a few days, on September 28 they saw a cluster of lodges in the distance. It was the village of Sitting Bull, their enemy.

Major Walsh had arrived that morning to ask Sitting Bull to meet General Terry. The sudden appearance of the Nez Percé surprised and sickened the Mountie. "Many of them were wounded—men, women, and children," he reported. "Some were shot badly through the body, legs and arms."[22] Walsh saw wounded children tied to horses' backs. Drops of blood went *pat, pat, pat* as they hit the ground, leaving a trail behind the horses. Wretched women, clothed in rags, wept for their children or from their own wounds. Warriors, worn-out men with glazed eyes, walked like zombies. Every warrior had at least one fresh wound on his body.

As the Nez Percé stumbled into the village, they said, "We want to be friends with the Sioux." Those words had an almost magical effect. All traces of animosity vanished like smoke in the wind. The villagers' hearts went out to their old enemies. For a moment, Sitting Bull lost his composure. Visibly shaken, with tears welling up in his eyes, he said, "I am sorry indeed your skin is like mine, that your hair is like mine, and that every one around you is a pure red man like myself. We, too, have lost our country by falsehood and theft." He welcomed the Nez Percé, inviting them to stay as long as they wished.[23]

The fugitives begged the chief to rescue their relatives across the border. Sitting Bull would have gone immediately had Walsh not protested. Canada, he said bluntly, would order the Lakota to leave if they took to the warpath.

Walsh's warning set off a terrible struggle within Sitting Bull. Compassion told him to save those whose only "crime" was defending their homeland. Yet reason told him that, as a chief, he must put his own people's safety above all else. Although it hurt, he decided to hold back.

That decision sealed the fate of the encircled Nez Percé. On October 5, Chief Joseph surrendered. The army packed him and his followers into railroad cars and sent them to a reservation in Oklahoma. There, in a hot, dusty country so different from their beloved northwest valley, many sickened and died, among them all of Joseph's children.

First Crazy Horse, and now the Nez Percé. Why, Sitting Bull asked, should he talk to the Americans? "I will do anything for you, but I can't do this," he told Walsh. The Mountie insisted that he must see the Americans. General Terry and the others were guests of the Grandmother. By refusing to see them, he would be insulting her. Sitting Bull agreed to do as his friend asked.[24]

On October 17, the two sides met in the mess hall at Fort Walsh. The Americans, having arrived first, sat on chairs placed at a long table. Sitting Bull swept into the room a few minutes later, together with the tribal headmen. Ignoring the Americans, he greeted the Mounties warmly. "How, kola!"—"Greetings, friend!"—he said, shaking each man's hand.

The Indians sat cross-legged on the bare floor, facing the table, and lit their pipes. Walsh could tell that Sitting Bull meant to take a hard line. Next to him sat Spotted Eagle; over six feet tall, the warrior held a club studded with three knife blades. A woman, The One Who Speaks Once, entered the room last. Since women never attended tribal councils, Sitting Bull intended her presence as an insult to the Americans.

General Terry stood and read an official message, pausing after each sentence to allow an interpreter to translate it. The U.S. government offered the fugitives "a full pardon" for all hostile acts committed in the past. In return, it expected them to settle on the reservation, where they would have to give up their horses and weapons. There they would live on the white man's charity until they learned to support themselves in the white man's way; that is, by farming and raising cattle.[25]

Terry finished reading and sat down. The chiefs just sat there, puffing their pipes and filling the room with smoke. Five minutes. Ten minutes. The smokers sat silently, showing no emotion at all. What now? the Americans wondered.

At last Sitting Bull rose to speak. He spoke angry words, bitter words, words with the sting of truth. The Americans, he said, had always treated his people badly.

> What have we done that you should want us to stop? We have done nothing. It is all the people on your side that have started us to making trouble. . . . I did not give you my country, but you followed me from place to place, and I had to come here. Look at me. I have ears, I have eyes to see with. If you think me a fool, you are a bigger fool than I am. . . . Go back home where you came from. . . . The country that belonged to us, you ran me out of it. I have come here, and I intend to stay. I want you to go back.[26]

When Sitting Bull finished, he introduced the other chiefs, who gave speeches very much like his own. Finally, The One Who Speaks Once had her say. She complained that the cavalry always pursued her people, so she had no time to raise a family. When Terry said he did not understand her point, the interpreter replied: "She says, General, you won't give her time to breed!"[27] So ended the council.

That evening, Colonel James Macleod, head of the Royal Northwest

Mounted Police, met with Sitting Bull and his chiefs. Macleod reminded them that, although they could stay in Canada if they behaved, they should not expect help from the Canadian government. They must hunt only the buffalo north of the Medicine Line. However, fewer and fewer of these were migrating from the south. Indeed, the buffalo were facing extinction. When they disappeared, the Lakota must either return to the States or starve in Grandmother's Land.

The colonel was right. Sitting Bull faced an impossible choice—reservation or starvation. Even as Macleod spoke, a vast tragedy was unfolding on the Great Plains. Like the tragedy of the Indian, it, too, is part of the American story.

Whites, at first, had little use for the buffalo. Leather made from its hide was too soft for most purposes. Although there was a market for its robes and tongues, these were luxury items lacking wide appeal. Buffalo robes, used as blankets in buggies during the winter, cost twenty dollars in the

An 1876 advertisement for buffalo robes. By then, the campaign to destroy the immense herds was well underway.

East; a really fine robe, decorated with dyed porcupine quills, brought fifty dollars. Big-city restaurants served slices of roasted buffalo tongue as a delicacy. By the 1850s, the northern Great Plains tribes were trading a hundred thousand robes a year and about an equal number of tongues.

Things began to change after the Civil War. The first transcontinental railroad, completed in 1869, separated the buffalo into two main herds, the northern and the southern, which never rejoined each other again. Meanwhile, railroad construction crews built up healthy appetites during their twelve-hour workdays. Since buffalo were everywhere, companies hired professional hunters to supply fresh meat.

The best of these hunters was William F. Cody, a former army scout down on his luck. Armed with his trusty rifle, Lucretia Borgia, he would ride alongside a stampeding herd, firing as he went. Cody killed 4,280 animals within eighteen months, a feat that earned him the nickname Buffalo Bill. Dime novels glorified his exploits, as did a popular jingle:

> Buffalo Bill, Buffalo Bill,
> Never missed and never will;
> Always aims and shoots to kill
> And the company pays his buffalo bill.[28]

At least Buffalo Bill killed for food. His employers, however, opened the buffalo range to any thrill-seeker with a gun in his hands and money in his pockets. For ten dollars, the price of a round-trip ticket, railroad companies offered heart-pounding excitement combined with total safety. Excursions left twice a week from Cincinnati, Chicago, St. Louis, and other cities. As the trains rolled westward across Kansas, they came to the southern herd. The buffalo had not yet learned to flee at the approach of the steam-puffing monsters. Their curiosity aroused, they would run alongside the trains, often so close that passengers could reach out and touch them with their hands.

Then the engineer would slow to eight miles an hour and the "fun" would begin. Suddenly windows flew open, rifle barrels appeared, and a hail of bullets pelted the herd. Scores of buffalo fell dead or lay on the ground, kicking and bellowing in pain. Occasionally, the train stopped to allow "sportsmen" to collect choice morsels like tongues and hump ribs.

Title page of W.E. Webb's 1872 book, *Buffalo Land*. Books like this encouraged white people to come West to hunt buffalo, go into ranching, and build new cities.

In this drawing by Albert Berghaus, "sportsmen" slaughter buffalo from a train.

Randolph Keim, a newspaper reporter, described a typical hunting experience in his 1870 book, *Sheridan's Troopers on the Borders*. He wrote:

The train stopped to afford time to bring in a few "rumps." While this was going on, a party of six or eight of us started down the track to dispatch [an injured] buffalo. . . . Repeated shots were fired into his body. Thug, thug, the bullets could be heard penetrating his thick hide. As each ball entered, a slight turn of the head and switch of the tail were all the external indications of the effect of the bullet. At last after having been literally "peppered" with lead, a sudden quiver passed over the animal's entire frame, he staggered and fell. One deep gasp, a convulsive motion of the jaws, one sudden flash of the eye, a quantity of dark clotted blood ejected from the nostrils, and the buffalo was dead.

Western tourists could buy buffalo-head trophies for a few dollars each.

As the hunters returned to the train, a strange feeling came over the reporter. "I must say that I felt a pang of shame as I left the inanimate carcass a useless waste."[29]

Scenes like this were repeated countless times. Both sides of the tracks, reaching from horizon to horizon, became lined with rotting carcasses and whitened skeletons. Yet, despite the senseless killing, nothing seemed to make a dent in the herds. Some said they would last forever, and that there were more buffalo than bullets.

The real slaughter began in 1871, after a Pennsylvania tannery found a way to turn buffalo hide into high-quality leather. Leather for shoes, furniture, harnesses, and machine drive belts was always in demand. Suddenly, Americans had access to a limitless supply of leather. The price of a "flint" (untanned) buffalo hide went from zero to $3.50, roughly half the weekly wages of a factory worker. Hide hunters flocked to Dodge City, Kansas. With its railroad sidings and warehouses, Dodge City was an ideal base for shooting buffalo. A team of hunters could buy supplies there, kill until it ran out of ammunition, and sell its hides to the traders who had set up shop beside the tracks.

"Hidemen," as they called themselves, killed more efficiently than any Indian or railroad hunter. Hunting, for them, was not a source of food or a

A mountain of buffalo hides awaiting shipment in Dodge City, Kansas, 1873.

test of courage. They did not consider the buffalo a "brother," much less a sacred creature. It was merely a *thing* to slaughter for profit.

A typical hunting team consisted of a shooter and his assistants, who skinned the carcasses and prepared the hides for sale. The shooter was a "sharpshooter," because he used a Sharps rifle. Specially designed for big-game hunting, the Sharps fired a shell two and a half inches in length. A rifle cost one hundred dollars and a bullet twenty-five cents. Yet they were cheap at the price. Their terrific power could drop a buffalo at fifteen hundred yards. Plains Indians were in awe of the Sharps, saying it "shoots today and kills tomorrow."[30]

At sunrise, the sharpshooter set out with his rifle. He went on foot, making sure to stay downwind of a herd; the slightest hint of a man's scent always sent herds pounding in the opposite direction. If he found a herd peacefully grazing, he tried to make a stand, his favorite tactic. The idea was to keep it in one place while he killed its members one at a time. He knew that the crack of a rifle would not alarm the shaggy beasts if they did not see him or the smoke from his gun.

He studied the herd, searching for the leader, usually an old cow. *BANG.* A shot to the lungs brought her down; often a bullet in the heart did not kill instantly, and she might run a quarter of a mile before dropping. Her companions, drawn by the smell of blood, milled around the body, not knowing what to make of this odd behavior.

BANG. Another bullet, and another victim fell bleeding. If, for any reason, a buffalo began to move away, it became the next victim. If several started off at once, the sharpshooter killed each new leader in turn. Then he calmly picked off the others, firing carefully and slowly. It was not uncommon for a hunter to kill 50 or 60 animals in a stand. Some chalked up fantastic records. Tom Nixon, for example, killed 204 in a single stand and 2,173 in a one-month period. Orlando Bond downed 300 in a day. Josiah Wright Mooar held the all-time record of 20,500 kills in less than nine years.[31]

Between 1872 and 1873, the herds vanished from the Kansas plains. Colonel Richard I. Dodge toured the area with friends in the fall of 1873. He could scarcely believe his eyes. "Where there were myriads of buffalo the

Dead buffalo awaiting the skinner, Montana, 1879.

year before," he reported, "there were now myriads of carcasses. The air was foul with sickening stench, and the vast plain . . . was a dead, solitary, putrid desert."[32] The hidemen moved into Texas, where they finished off the rest of the southern herd. When the Comanches and Kiowas fought the hunters, the army forced the Indians onto reservations in Oklahoma.

Reports of the slaughter horrified people across the land. Some Americans had already begun to think about animal rights. Animals, they felt, were as much God's creatures as human beings. Organizations like the Society for the Prevention of Cruelty to Animals (SPCA), formed in 1866, worked for laws to save animals from inhumane treatment. To win public support, they helped build zoos and museums of natural history in the major eastern cities.

The SPCA and its allies took a keen interest in the buffalo. They argued that killing these "noble beasts" just for their skins was "wantonly wicked" and an affront to God.[33] Arizona, Idaho, Wyoming, Montana, and Colorado responded by passing conservation laws. Nevertheless, these laws were born dead—that is, incapable of enforcement. Greed, of course, was the main reason for this. Yet greed is only part of the story. An equally important part involves the U.S. Army.

The buffalo could not vanish fast enough to suit army leaders. Extermination made sense from a military point of view. The Civil War had shown that attacking the enemy's commissary, or food supplies, was as important as defeating its armies in the field. It followed, therefore, that wiping out the buffalo was the ultimate weapon in the struggle against the Plains Indians. Having lost their main source of food, the tribes must surrender or starve. It was that simple.

Halting the slaughter, General Sheridan believed, was silly. When the Texas legislature debated a bill outlawing buffalo hunting, the general asked to speak against it. Praising the hidemen as patriots, he said they deserved a medal in the name of American civilization. "These men," he continued, "have done more in the last two years . . . to settle the . . . Indian question than the entire regular army has done in the last thirty years. They are destroying the Indians' commissary; and it is a well-known fact that an army losing its base of supplies is placed at a great disadvantage. Send them powder and lead, if you will; but, for the sake of a lasting peace, let them kill, skin, and sell until the buffaloes are exterminated."[34] The legislators agreed.

So did President Grant. When Congress passed a conservation bill, he vetoed it.

Apart from a few stray buffalo, by 1877 the southern herd had vanished. During the next year, the hidemen moved into the northern Great Plains. True to his word, Sheridan gave them every encouragement. He ordered fort commanders to hand over, free of charge, all the supplies they needed, including ammunition. They soon turned the triangle of land formed by the Missouri, Yellowstone, and Mussellshell rivers into a killing ground. About five thousand men hunted the buffalo full-time.

These men were a key element in Sheridan's plan to deal with Sitting Bull. The general meant to use the extermination of the buffalo to starve the Lakota refugees out of Canada. Without buffalo to hunt, and with the Canadian government unwilling to feed them, they would have to return on American terms. To that end, Sheridan tried to prevent the herds from migrating into Canada. Whenever they approached the Medicine Line, army patrols set grass fires to drive them back. Soldiers, Indian scouts, and hidemen joined in the slaughter.

The Mounties knew exactly what was happening, and why. Early in the twentieth century, Colonel Lawrence W. Herchmer, a former head of the Royal Northwest Mounted Police, gave a historian the facts as he had learned them from experience. The U.S. government "deliberately destroyed the buffalo in order to force the Sioux . . . to sue for peace and mercy because of starvation."[35]

In the spring of 1879, immense flocks of migratory birds returned to Canada from the south, as they had always done. Again the grass turned green, and the wildflowers blossomed on schedule. Only the buffalo herds failed to appear. It was as if the earth had swallowed the lords of the Great Plains.

Sitting Bull sent scouts across the border to search for buffalo. Instead of buffalo herds, they found rotting carcasses. In certain places, they could walk on carcasses for a quarter of a mile without stepping on the ground. Occasionally, they saw the killers. "Are these men?" the scouts asked one another. Although they had human form, they seemed like evil spirits, their hair and clothing matted with clotted blood.

The slaughter left the refugees dazed. Killing the buffalo, to them, was not only senseless. It was filthy and ungodly, a sin against Wakantanka. Sitting Bull came to despise his former homeland. He told a visiting New York newspaper reporter:

> We know that on the other side [of the Medicine Line] the buffalo will not last very long. Why? Because the country there is poisoned with blood—the poison that kills all the buffaloes or drives them away. . . . We [Indians] kill buffaloes, as we kill other animals, for food and clothing, and to make our lodges warm. They [the Americans] kill buffaloes—for what? Go through your country. See the thousands of carcasses rotting on the Plains. Your young men shoot for pleasure. All they take from [the] dead buffalo is his tail, or his head, or his horns, perhaps, to show that they have killed a buffalo. What is this? Is it robbery? You call us savages. What are they?[36]

Obviously, the Americans had lost their minds. They were not killing the buffalo for food, or clothing, or shelter. No. They killed for the yellow metal that made them crazy. And the more gold they got, the crazier they got.

Killing the buffalo gave General Sheridan exactly what he wanted. It made life harder for everyone north of the Medicine Line. Canadian tribes competed with the refugees for dwindling food supplies. Competition between the tribes made it more difficult for the Mounties to keep order on the frontier. Inevitably, Major Walsh feared, the tribes would go to war with one another and with the Mounties.

Hunkpapa women urged their men to do anything to save their children from starvation. Men ignored the Mounties' warnings and crossed into Montana. Sitting Bull seldom joined them; he feared that getting caught by either the Americans or the Canadians would harm all his people. So he usually camped just north of the Medicine Line to await the return of the hunting parties. Once a newspaper reporter, a friend of Major Walsh's, interviewed Sitting Bull for an article. Although they spoke of many things, the chief made one thing clear: The Hunkpapa must hunt to live. "I am a hunter," he said, "and will hunt so long as there is wild game on the prairie. When the buffalo are gone, I will send my children on the prairie to hunt mice."[37]

General Sheridan ordered Colonel Miles to drive Sitting Bull's hunting

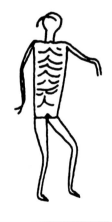

Starvation as depicted in an Oglala winter count. With the buffalo gone, the Plains tribes faced the grim choice of going to a reservation or starving to death.

parties back into Canada. Early in July 1879, Miles caught some Hunkpapas butchering their kill near the Milk River in Montana. This time, the chief had come along for the hunt.

Magpie, a famous Crow warrior, led Miles's scouts. Somehow he learned that Sitting Bull was nearby. Now, for Magpie, just speaking the chief's name brought a bitter taste to his mouth. Before the troopers arrived, he challenged him to personal combat. Sitting Bull accepted.

The two men galloped toward each other, each armed with a rifle. Magpie's gun misfired. Sitting Bull's did not. A bullet blew the top off the Crow's head, killing him instantly. Moments later, Miles arrived with his main force. Sitting Bull led the hunters back over the border, leaving behind tons of precious meat. He could easily have called hundreds of warriors to retrieve the meat, but he kept his promise not to use Canada as a base for attacking the Americans.

The winter of 1879 to 1880 was brutal. Sitting Bull's people ate spoiled horsemeat; indeed, they ate anything they could get their hands on. The Mounties could not bear to see such suffering. These hard-boiled lawmen gladly shared their rations, particularly with the women and children. Even so, there was never enough.

In desperation, Sitting Bull turned to Major Walsh for help. One day, he rode over to Fort Walsh with several chiefs. Without realizing it, he had come at the worst possible time. Walsh was suffering from a skin disease, possibly eczema, that turned his body into a mass of painful, itching sores. These made his famous short temper shorter than ever. When he got like that, his men avoided him like the plague.

"Find out what they want," Walsh growled at his interpreter.

Sitting Bull explained the situation, softly.

"They want provisions, Major."

Walsh reacted as if the chief had tossed a match into a keg of gunpowder buried deep inside his soul. The Mountie exploded. He leaped up, his fists clenched, his face red as his coat. His words hit the chiefs like a hurricane of hot iron.

"Have you forgotten you are American Indians? You haven't any right to be in Canada. You've cost us police God knows how much trouble. You've . . . been a goddamn, bloody nuisance."

Sitting Bull's companions recalled that he did not move a muscle. He just stood there, following Walsh with smoldering eyes. The major stamped about the room, his body shaking with rage.

"You seem to think all white men are afraid of you, you bastard," Walsh snarled. "You're wrong. We've got plenty of our own Indians to look after without being bothered by you."

Nobody had ever treated Sitting Bull with such disrespect. "Be careful," he warned, meeting anger with anger. "You are speaking to the head of the Lakota nation!"[38]

Suddenly, the chief reached for the six-shooter in his belt. Just as suddenly Walsh grabbed him by the shoulders, spun him around, and kicked him in the backside.

Sitting Bull reached for the pistol again. His companions caught the chief's hand and hustled him out the door. He would certainly have shot Walsh had they not interfered. For one of the few times in his life, the chief allowed his emotions to get in the way of his wisdom and good sense. Seething with anger, he rode back to camp.

Each man's anger quickly cooled. Deep down, they understood and respected each other. When Sitting Bull regained his composure, he saw Walsh's insult in its true light: an outburst by a good man tormented beyond endurance. Walsh regretted the incident, too. He realized that his first impression of Sitting Bull was the correct one. This man was a true leader. Whatever he did, he did from concern for his people's welfare, never from any private motive. Without saying it in so many words, both men agreed to forgive and forget.

Respect, however, could not fill empty stomachs. Things grew worse for the refugees. Around the time of the scuffle with Walsh, Sitting Bull's followers began to lose hope. For them, it was no longer a question of loyalty to their chief, or even to their way of life. Their families were starving to death.

One family group after another crossed the Medicine Line and surrendered to Colonel Miles. Gall, Rain in the Face, Crow King, Iron Dog, Hairy Chin, Low Dog, Spotted Eagle: all left in 1880. Some of Sitting Bull's own family joined them. Hunger drove Gray Eagle, his brother-in-law, and Has Many Horses, his daughter, to the reservation. Even Sitting Bull's adopted brother, the ever-faithful Jumping Bull, left with his wife and children. By Christmas, only forty lodges, about two hundred people, remained with the chief.

Walsh knew that the Hunkpapa had come to the end of the line. One day, he confronted Sitting Bull in the harshest terms he could muster. "Bull," said the Mountie, "you know damned well that you can't continue to live by the buffalo and you can't live by mice. Now, what's left? Don't you realize that the sooner you and your people begin to plow and cultivate some ground and grow your own crops and livestock, the better it will be for you?"

Sitting Bull replied, as always, "I will die a hunter. . . . I will remain what I am until I die, a hunter."[39]

Sitting Bull often prayed to Wakantanka to send the buffalo herds. By the summer of 1881, he knew they would never come. One day in July, he put on his feathered warbonnet and paid Major Walsh a final visit. It was his most prized possession, a relic of better days—happier days.

"I won't forget you, Bull, and I hope I'll see you again," said Walsh, grasping the chief's hand.

As Walsh watched in disbelief, Sitting Bull removed the warbonnet. "Take it, my friend, and keep it," he said, handing it to the Mountie. "I'm through with fighting."[40]

Then Sitting Bull returned to camp and prepared to lead his followers into captivity in the United States.

Eight

After the Buffalo Went Away

"The sooner the Indian loses all his Indian ways, even his language, the better it will be for him and the government."

—Richard H. Pratt,
Principal of Carlisle Indian School, 1883

TUESDAY, JULY 19, 1881. It was a morning to remember, a morning for the history books.

Hundreds of armed soldiers ringed the parade ground of Fort Buford, Montana. Although it was brutally hot, this time they did not mind turning out in full battle gear. They knew they would soon be witnessing the surrender of the most famous of all the Plains Indian leaders.

Sitting Bull arrived with the remnants of his band—187 men, women, and children. Soldiers gasped in dismay, hardly able to believe their eyes. Were *these* the dreaded Hunkpapas? Were *these* the victors of the Little Bighorn? They looked so shabby, so wretched, so sad. All but the chief and a handful of mounted warriors rode in borrowed wagons or walked. Sitting Bull wore a torn calico shirt and a dirty, threadbare blanket draped around his waist. Because he was suffering from an eye infection, he had tied a large handkerchief around his head and drew it partly across his eyes. "They are some of them literally naked, and with most of them the clothing is falling off from pure rottenness," Major David H. Brotherton, the fort's commander, wrote his superiors.[1]

An officer directed them to a prepared campsite stocked with army rations. Everyone, he said through an interpreter, should eat their fill and rest up for the next leg of their journey. Solemnly, the warriors dismounted and gave their rifles to a guard detail. Only Sitting Bull kept his weapon, explaining that he wished to surrender it at a formal ceremony later.

Next morning he appeared at the commander's office. Sitting Bull sat next to Major Brotherton and placed his rifle on the floor between his feet. The major explained that, in a week or so, a steamboat would come to take the Hunkpapas down the Missouri River. Their destination was Standing Rock Agency on the Great Sioux Reservation. There they would rejoin their relatives, who had already turned themselves in and were doing just fine. If they behaved themselves, the army would not harm them.

When Brotherton finished, Sitting Bull motioned to his eight-year-old son, Crow Foot. The boy picked up the rifle, a Winchester repeater, and handed it to the major. As he did, his father said: "I wish it to be remembered that I was the last man of my tribe to surrender my rifle."[2]

On July 29, they boarded the steamboat *General Sherman*. Few, if any, knew the significance of that name, or the role its owner had played in their lives.

A whistle blew. Smoke billowed from the twin stacks and the vessel pulled away from the dock. Sitting Bull had seen "fire canoes" before, but had never ridden in one. Now he felt as if he had crossed another kind of "medicine line." He had not simply left one country for another but had entered a different world—one he did not understand. This noisy, shaking, spark-spitting creature of wood and iron had a magical power. Big as it was, it churned its way down the muddy river with ease, obedient to its white masters.

Three days later, *General Sherman* made an overnight stop at Bismarck, North Dakota. Never before had Sitting Bull entered a white-man town. As he walked down the gangplank, he saw his first railroad train at a siding. When an official of the Northern Pacific Railroad invited him to go for a ride, he asked to see it move first. But when the engineer released the brake, and it rolled a few feet, he backed away in fear.

An army ambulance wagon took the chief and his hosts to the dining room of the Sheridan House, the town's best hotel; we do not know whether he had heard that name, either. There he sat on an overstuffed chair, ate an elegant meal, and had ice cream for dessert. That puzzled him. What medicine, he wondered, allowed the Wasichus to make things freeze in midsummer?

Sitting Bull was glad when the steamboat reached Standing Rock on August 2. For the next month, he camped outside the gates of Fort Yates, the agency's army post, named for an officer killed at the Little Bighorn. There he greeted relatives, renewed friendships, and made plans for the future. The government, however, had other plans.

Orders came to move the chief and those who had come with him to Fort Randall two hundred miles farther downstream. Sitting Bull was now a prisoner of war. When told of the order, he demanded to stay with his tribe. In reply, an officer snapped an order. Guards fixed bayonets, and that was that.

Sitting Bull at Fort Randall during the bitter winter of 1882.

Sitting Bull lived at Ford Randall from September 1881 to May 1883. Those twenty months were a learning experience for him. Back in Canada, he had visited Fort Walsh often, but never stayed overnight, let alone lived surrounded by whites. Now he saw them everywhere, always.

White people amazed him. Stanley Vestal learned from the chief's old friends that while some called him a "red savage," others sent letters asking "Big Chief Sitting Bull" for his autograph.[3] Then there were those people who took their teeth out of their mouths and put them back again. He did not know what to make of this odd behavior. Nor did he understand why they needed a device they called a watch. This device, he learned, divided the day into seconds, minutes, and hours.

Sitting Bull learned to sign his name during his exile in Canada. He later sold his autographs for a dollar each.

Sitting Bull

Indians never thought in such small units of time. Sunrise, noon, and sunset were all the divisions of the day they needed. When they traveled, they measured time and distance in sleeps.

Visitors came from the agencies to ask Sitting Bull's advice and describe their new lives to him. Some may have retold a familiar tale. In the long-ago time, before the memory of any grandfather's grandfather, a holy man named Drinks Water fell into a deep sleep. When he awoke, he described the future as it appeared to him in a dream. He said that strangers from the sunrise would weave a spider's web around the Lakota. Although made of fine silken threads, the web was stronger than any cord of buffalo sinew. "When this happens, you shall live in square gray houses, in a barren land, and beside those square houses you shall starve."[4] And so it was.

Life on the Great Sioux Reservation was harder and bleaker than anything the Lakota experienced in Canada. Each band had settled in a cluster of log cabins, usually beside a creek. These clusters were permanent settlements, joined by roads to one another and to the agency, which might be forty or fifty miles away. Although cabins were roomier than lodges, women found them harder to keep clean. In the old days, when a lodge got dirty, the wife simply moved it to another patch of ground; wind and rain cleaned the spot. Another thing: The solid walls of a cabin cut you off from the sun, moon, and fresh air, all gifts of Wakantanka.

Those who managed to leave the reservation for whatever reason were amazed at what they found. Where buffalo herds once roamed in their millions, herds of cattle now dotted the northern Great Plains. Where once a person could walk for weeks across a sea of grass, barbed-wire fences cut the countryside into immense pastures. As the rancher and the cowboy replaced the Indian hunter, the "Wild West" was becoming a fading memory.

Once self-sufficient, the Lakota now depended on Uncle Sam for the necessities of life. They collected these twice a month at an agency warehouse. On "issue day," each woman, holding her family's ration ticket, filed past rows of shelves. As she passed, clerks punched the ticket and gave her packages of sugar, coffee, and salt. Twice a year, each man and boy over fourteen received a hat, a shirt, a pair of pants, and a pair of socks. Females over twelve got a woolen skirt, a pair of woolen stockings, and twelve yards of cotton cloth. This cheap, shoddy stuff quickly wore out. Men hated the pants, because they crowded them at the crotch and hips. Everyone com-

The end of the buffalo opened the great age of the American cowboy. These sketches of cowboy life were made by Charles M. Russell and Jerome H. Smith.

plained that leather boots, unlike moccasins, pinched their feet. Yet there was nothing they could do about it. The end of the buffalo also meant the end of their traditional clothing.

Government beef replaced buffalo meat. The Lakota called cattle *wohaw*—from hearing wagon drivers yell "whoa" and "haw" to their oxen. On issue day, a clerk turned live cattle loose from the agency corral. As the terrified animals ran out, mounted warriors staged a mock buffalo hunt with pistols. Yet it was different. Cattle were not as fast or dangerous as buffalo, and killing them was almost too easy. Moreover, beef seemed tasteless compared to buffalo meat. The sweetish smell of the cattle made some people vomit. Although the government issued tools and seeds, few tried farming and fewer succeeded at it. Warriors saw farming as women's work, unworthy of men.

Sitting Bull begged the army to send him back to Standing Rock. Secretary of War Robert T. Lincoln, the late president's eldest son, decided to give him a chance. Mr. Lincoln approved the request and issued the necessary orders. In May 1883, the chief and his fellow prisoners boarded another steamboat.

Sitting Bull arrived at Standing Rock in an upbeat mood, bubbling with ideas to help his people. Nothing would ever come of those ideas. From the

Major James McLaughlin disliked Sitting Bull and did everything he could to undermine the chief's authority with his people.

moment he stepped ashore, he ran into a stone wall in the shape of the agent Major James McLaughlin.

McLaughlin was forty-one when they met. Called "White Hair" by the Lakota, he had a mop of curly white hair and a bushy white mustache. A Canadian by birth, he had become an American citizen, married a Santee woman, and learned to speak her language fluently. McLaughlin told his story in his 1910 autobiography, *My Friend the Indian*. He honestly saw himself as the Indian's friend. For more than fifty years, he worked for the Indian's "true" welfare. Many, if not most, Indians regarded him as a friend.

In certain ways, McLaughlin resembled his fellow Canadian, James Morrow Walsh. Like Walsh, he was stubborn, quick-tempered, and totally honest. Unlike Walsh, however, he despised "untamed" Indians and their "wild" ways. That should not surprise us. No agency official anywhere in the United States thought differently. Had he, the government would never have given him a job.

Although agents were not soldiers, they held the rank of major as a courtesy. That title, however, reveals a lot about white attitudes and plans. As men of the gun and the bullet, army majors had one mission: destroy the enemy's will to resist by killing people and destroying property. Majors in the Indian service, a civilian post, waged a different kind of war. Theirs was a kindlier, gentler war, but a war just the same. And they waged it on all fronts, always.

According to historian Stanley Vestal, "Major James McLaughlin was sent to Standing Rock to destroy Sioux civilization."[5] That is true. Today we use the word "ethnocide" to describe government policy not only toward the Lakota, but toward all Native Americans. Ethnocide differs from genocide in that it does not aim at killing people physically. Instead, its goal is to destroy their heritage, beliefs, customs, and language—that is, the very things that give meaning and direction to human life.

Ethnocide was not a war waged by brutal enemies, but by white people with good intentions. We have already seen in Chapter 3 how, in the 1860s, Friends of the Indian demanded humane treatment for Native Americans. Their influence grew during the presidency of Ulysses S. Grant and his successors: Rutherford B. Hayes, James A. Garfield, Chester A. Arthur. Believing Native Americans, like the buffalo, to be doomed to extinction, they called them "the vanishing race." However, they also believed that history is the story of human "progress." Native Americans' only hope of survival, therefore, lay in progressing—that is, becoming white in mind, heart, and spirit.

Whites, they claimed, had a God-given duty to raise native peoples from "savagery to civilization." It never occurred to them to consult "red savages" about their own welfare and happiness. Whites knew best. President Grant once told Lakota visitors, "We know what is for your good better than you can know yourselves." Whether they liked it or not, the government would force them to become civilized—that is, to walk "the white man's road." Unlike white citizens, Native Americans could not take their grievances to a court of law. In effect, they had no rights.[6]

Major McLaughlin strove to "civilize" the Lakota. Naturally, that put him at odds with Sitting Bull. The same qualities that had brought Sitting Bull fame as a holy man, warrior, and chief now made the agent despise him as an enemy of progress.

At their first meeting, McLaughlin refused to listen to anything the chief had to say. As Sitting Bull spoke, he did not try to hide his contempt for this man and his ideas. He stood with his arms folded, scowling. When the chief finished, he gave him what he called "some sound advice." All Indians, he said, were equal—none better and none worse than any other. All must forget the past and become farmers.

That outraged Sitting Bull. And, to make matters worse, this arrogant Wasichu treated him as a nobody. From then on, he refused to set foot in the agency offices. "Under the roof of a white man's tipi are lies and intrigue," he explained. "I wish to remain out in the open air. The air outside is pure, inside impure."[7]

Indian agents carried out a detailed set of orders from Washington. McLaughlin, like all his fellow agents, had to prevent warriors from attacking their tribal enemies, taking their scalps, and stealing their horses. To make sure his charges behaved, McLaughlin formed a police force of young Lakota men. Known as Ceska Maza, or Metal Breasts, they wore shiny tin badges on their blue uniforms. Each Metal Breast received between five and eight dollars a month, according to his rank, and better rations and living quarters than ordinary tribesmen.

Serving as a police officer, however, meant more than just getting material possessions. When Sitting Bull handed over his rifle at Fort Buford, he had told his son, Crow Foot: "My boy, if you live, you will never be a man in this world, because you can never have a gun or pony."[8] He understood that the younger generation could never grow to manhood in the traditional Lakota way, by hunting and gaining war honors. Being a Ceska Maza, therefore, fulfilled an important psychological need. While their elders might boast of their feats, young men could gain pride and authority by joining the Metal Breasts; even chiefs had to obey them. Gray Eagle, Sitting Bull's own brother-in-law, joined the force.

In return for his service, a Metal Breast prevented fights, caught thieves, and spied on possible troublemakers. A "troublemaker" was anyone who followed what the government defined as "demoralizing and barbarous customs." These included polygamy, "buying" wives with horses, "pagan feasts," and the willful destruction of property, the usual way of showing grief over a loved one's death. Although a Metal Breast might still respect a man like Sitting Bull, he no longer saw him as a great leader; indeed, he might consider him a troublemaker who clung to the old, now useless, ways. Since only a Christian could become a Metal Breast, these young warriors also came to share the white man's view that a *wichasha wakan* was not a true holy man, but a fraud.

Like his fellow agents, McLaughlin ignored the Constitution's guarantee of religious freedom for all Americans. That freedom, clearly, did not belong to native peoples, who believed in many gods and supposedly worshiped them in a beastly, unclean, and unchristian manner.

Acting on Washington's orders to "root out paganism," McLaughlin banned the Lakota's traditional dances, particularly the Sun Dance. This sacred dance had always brought the tribal bands together for a unifying religious ceremony. Now they could no longer appeal directly to Wakantanka or seek spiritual power in nature. Instead, the agent invited Roman Catholic and Protestant missionaries to convert tribesmen to Christianity. Their task, according to an official, was to save the Indians' souls by rescuing "these benighted children of nature from the darkness of their superstition and ignorance."[9] Many Lakotas did become Christians but also kept some of their traditional beliefs "just in case." Gradually, however, youngsters stopped going on vision quests. As the medicine men died off, fewer and fewer young people took their places.

Finally, the government turned education into a tool for ethnocide. Officials reasoned that, by educating native children as whites, they would forget their own heritage or never learn it in the first place. Once that happened, children would become, in effect, white in all but skin color.

McLaughlin built several day schools and staffed them with white teachers, mostly women. If parents refused to send their children, he, like his fellow agents, refused to issue rations to their families or threw the parents into the agency jail.[10] He also urged parents to send youngsters to boarding schools hundreds of miles from their homes. Separating parents and children, he knew, was painful for everyone. Yet it was necessary. A fellow agent described the separation as "kindly cruel surgery which hurts that it may save, and would in good time cure the Indian race of savagery."[11]

Boarding schools were modeled on the Carlisle Indian School, the first and largest of its kind. Housed in former army barracks at Carlisle, Pennsylvania, the school had this motto: "Kill the Indian to save the man."[12]

Upon arriving at Carlisle, students took their first steps along the white man's road. The moment they entered the gate, teachers stripped them and burned their clothes. Then they got a Christian first name, a scalding-hot bath, and a scratchy woolen uniform. This included a puzzling item called a handkerchief. Students could not understand why anyone should want to blow snot into a piece of rag and then carry it around in their pocket; Indians blew their noses toward the ground and kept walking. In addition, boys got a haircut, which meant losing their long braids. A Lakota male's braids,

Boys at the Carlisle Indian School. The idea behind this school and those like it was to destroy Indian culture by turning youngsters into little white people.

we recall, were symbols of his manhood. Now white women cut off, symbolically, that badge of manhood.

The clock ruled the students' day. There was a time for everything, and everything had its own time. Most of the school day consisted of learning reading, writing, Bible study, arithmetic, and useful trades: farming, carpentry, and blacksmith work for males; homemaking skills for females.

In class, teachers demanded absolute silence and total obedience. When a teacher called on a student, he or she had to recite in English or remain quiet until having learned it. Disobedience brought severe punishment. Teachers or principals beat rule breakers, shaved their heads, and (with boys) made them wear dresses. Any boy who wet his bed had to parade around the school grounds with the urine-soaked mattress on his back. For relaxation, students played white children's games: baseball, hopscotch, croquet, marbles, dominoes, checkers. These were tame, compared to traditional games like Throwing-Them-off-Their-Horses.

Above all, youngsters learned to despise their heritage. Teachers never discussed Native American history, because "savages" had no history. Children learned that there were no Indian heroes, thinkers, or holy people—only Indian murderers, fools, and fanatics. They studied the Pilgrims, who had come to American to find religious freedom. On examinations, they had to describe the voyages of Christopher Columbus, give the details of the Stamp Act, and explain the causes of the American Revolution. A youngster summarized his lessons this way: "The red people they big savages; they don't know anything." Graduates usually returned to the reservation after a period of four to eight years. They returned as misfits, alienated from their families and with little opportunity to use their new skills. A few disappeared into the teeming Eastern cities, losing their identity entirely.[13]

Hard as McLaughlin tried, nothing he said or did persuaded Sitting Bull to walk the white man's road. True, the chief no longer had the right to go wherever he pleased whenever he pleased. However, he still owned his own mind and spirit. After a run-in with McLaughlin, he announced, "I would rather die an Indian than live a white man."[14]

He meant it. When asked to divorce one of his wives, Sitting Bull refused, saying that he loved them both equally. When a missionary urged him to become a Christian, Sitting Bull said it did not matter how a person prayed, if God answered his prayers. Besides, he insisted, the Lakota were better Christians before they ever heard of Christ than nearly any Wasichu he had met. White people preached Jesus' teachings about charity and goodwill but seldom followed them. Lakota people, however, made them part of their everyday lives. Sitting Bull still prayed in the old way, still spoke to his beloved birds, and still made the rain come. During a drought, with not a cloud in the sky, he decided to bring the rain. According to Mary Collins, a Protestant missionary, "He took a buffalo skin, waved it around in the air, made some signs, placed it upon the ground and—IT RAINED."[15]

McLaughlin called him a "non-progressive"—that is, someone who resisted all change. Yet Sitting Bull was not trapped in the past. He saw the world changing and knew that the Lakota had to adapt or die out. Adapting meant learning as much as possible from white people. Although he resented them, he admired their mastery of material things. Anyone who could make ice, build fire canoes, and send words over wires had strong medicine. It was all right, therefore, to borrow the white man's things if they benefited the Lakota. Otherwise they were evil and should be left alone.

Sitting Bull refused to let his children attend the Carlisle school, saying he loved them too much to put them into such a cruel place. Nevertheless, he gladly sent them to an agency day school. During a school visit, he sat in on a reading lesson. After the lesson, he asked to speak to the students and the principal gave him permission. In his talk, Sitting Bull revealed two things: that he knew the Lakota faced difficult times and that the future lay with their children. Here is part of his speech:

> My dear grandchildren. All of your folks are my relatives, because I am a [Lakota], and so are they. . . . You are living in a new path. When I was your age, things were entirely different. I had no teachers but my parents and relatives. . . . I was eager to learn and to do things, and therefore I learned quickly, and that made it easier for my teachers. Now I often pick up papers and books which have all kinds of pictures and marks on them, but I cannot understand them as a white person does. . . . In future your . . . dealings with the whites are going to be very hard, and it behooves you to learn well what you are taught here. But that is not all. *We older people need you.* In our dealings with the white men, we are just the same as blind men, because we do not understand them. We need you to help us understand what the white men are up to. My grandchildren, be good. Try and make a mark for yourselves. Learn all you can.[16]

McLaughlin allowed Sitting Bull to leave Standing Rock for only a short time. He did it as a favor to Buffalo Bill Cody and to get rid of his troublesome prisoner. Cody had given up hunting and had formed Buffalo Bill's Wild West Show to give "tenderfeet" a taste of the old West. Eastern audiences thrilled to scenes of Plains Indians—Lakotas, Cheyennes, Pawnees—racing their horses, doing war dances, and chasing a small herd of buffalo. Each performance also featured warriors attacking the Deadwood mail

This poster shows Buffalo Bill's re-enactment of Custer's defeat.

coach, and its rescue by Buffalo Bill and his posse of hard-riding, straight-shooting cowboys. What better way to boost attendance than to feature the most famous chief of all?

Sitting Bull joined for the summer season of 1885, touring the cities of New York, Philadelphia, and Washington, D.C. During the three-day visit to the nation's capital, Buffalo Bill took the chief and fourteen other Lakotas to see their old enemy, General Sheridan, who now commanded the U.S. Army. When they entered Sheridan's office at the War Department, he came from behind his desk to greet them. If they expected to see a dynamic warrior, they were mistaken. Time had turned Sheridan into a fat, balding man who seemed uncomfortable in his tight-fitting uniform. The visitors found the paintings of western scenes on the office wall more interesting than their host. Sitting Bull admired the scenes but pointedly ignored the man who had brought so much misery to his people. Sheridan died three years later.

Buffalo Bill gave Sitting Bull a good deal: $50 a week for eight weeks, a bonus of $125, and the right to sell his autographed pictures for $1.50 apiece. In return, the chief had to lead the parades and greet visitors in his lodge. To his credit, the showman did not use him in daredevil exploits he staged before sellout crowds. The *Washington Post* (June 24, 1885) described

Sitting Bull and Buffalo Bill in 1885. The showman respected the chief and never presented him to audiences as a savage or murderer.

one performance under the headline: "A Group of Howling Savages Pursue a Defenseless Stage Coach."[17] Buffalo Bill never presented the chief as "Custer's killer." Instead, he declared that Custer's defeat was no massacre but an act of self-defense. Sitting Bull appreciated Buffalo Bill's honesty, and they became friends.

Even so, Sitting Bull became the villain audiences loved to hate. Each time he appeared, audiences burst into catcalls and shouts of "hang him!" After each performance, however, whites stood in line to buy his picture. When a drunken show-goer attacked the chief in his lodge, he knocked out three of the fellow's teeth.[18]

Travel did not improve Sitting Bull's opinion of white people. Cities like New York and Philadelphia swarmed with desperately poor people. That puzzled the chief. He knew from experience that a tribe might go hungry; in bad times, everyone suffered equally. Yet if there was any food, no Lakota would send anyone, let alone a child, away empty-handed. White people, however, seemed incredibly selfish. The sight of crowds brushing past beggars in the streets offended him deeply. He once told Annie Oakley, the famous sharpshooter, that he could not understand how white folks could be so cruel to their own kind. Sitting Bull gave most of the money he earned to the small, ragged boys who hung around his lodge. Finally he decided that "the white man knows how to make everything, but he does not know how to distribute it."[19]

Sitting Bull ended his career as a circus performer after one season. The bustle and noise of big-city America made him long for the West. He returned to Standing Rock with a few dollars and two gifts from Buffalo Bill:

a white sombrero and a gray horse trained to sit and raise a hoof at the sound of a gunshot. Whatever happened, Sitting Bull vowed never to leave home again.

The chief lived with his Hunkpapa band on the northern bank of the Grand River, directly across from his birthplace on the other bank. The Grand River enters the Missouri River a few miles south of Standing Rock Agency. There he worked a small farm with a log barn and three square gray cabins. He kept one cabin for general living, one for his wives Four Robes and Seen by Her Nation, and the last for his daughter Standing Holy. Gradually, he swallowed his pride and tried farming. Within three years, he owned forty-five cows, eighty chickens, and fields of oats, corn, and potatoes. He also had ten horses. Used for drawing a plow and pulling a wagon, these were nothing like the finely trained war-horses he had ridden in his youth.

Sitting Bull and his family at Fort Randall. Left to right: Her Holy Door (mother), Good Feather (sister), Sitting Bull, Walks Looking (daughter), Has Many Horses (daughter), and Tom Fly (grandson).

Meanwhile, the chief mourned the passing of loved ones. His mother, Her Holy Door, died in 1884; his daughter Walks Along and uncle Four Horns died in 1887. Their loss made him love life more than ever. In 1887 he fathered a son and in 1888 a daughter; he also adopted and raised eleven orphans. Always open-handed, he gave to any needy person who came to his place.

White people continued to puzzle him—and none more than the Friends of the Indian. Led by Senator Henry L. Dawes of Massachusetts, they decided that Native Americans were not becoming civilized quickly enough. The reason, they thought, was that Indians clung to their old ways because their community ties remained strong. The solution was obvious: break up the communities by turning their members into independent landowners. That would force them into the mainstream of American society and give more land to white settlers, who were pouring into Dakota Territory. In 1870, it had fewer than 5,000 whites. By 1880, 134,000 whites lived outside the Great Sioux Reservation. Whether they lived on isolated farms and ranches, or in small towns, whites agreed that reservation Indians had more land than they needed.

Senator Dawes wanted to help everyone. In 1887, he proposed, and Congress passed, the General Allotment Act. To speed Native Americans along the white man's road, the act ordered the breakup of the western reservations. The Great Sioux Reservation, for example, would become six

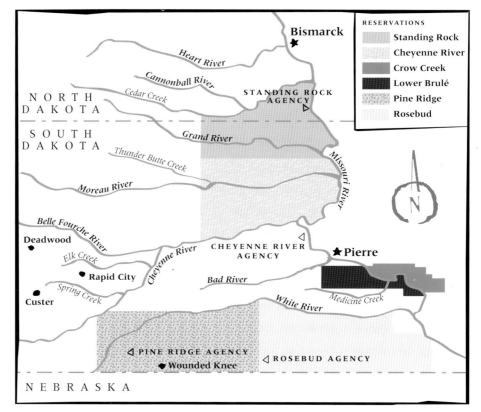

The Lakota Reservations in 1890.

separate reservations: Standing Rock, Pine Ridge, Rosebud, Cheyenne River, Crow Creek, and Lower Brulé. When three-quarters of a reservation's male residents agreed to the act's terms, the President would allot (distribute) 160-acre plots to heads of families. The government would then buy the "surplus" land and sell it to whites. Native Americans, however, would not get any of the money from these sales. Instead, the government would use it for their benefit as it saw fit. Dawes and his allies believed that Indians would not know how to manage their affairs until they were truly "civilized."

In the summer of 1889, a commission led by General George Crook arrived at the Great Sioux Reservation. When he tried to get the Lakota to sign, he met strong opposition. Sitting Bull, like most chiefs, denounced the act as just another white-man swindle. The Americans, he warned, had always made grand promises, only to break them when they got what they wanted. Furthermore, he suspected a trick. If they signed, he feared that Congress would cut their food rations.

General Crook knew the Lakota did not have a chance. Whether they liked it or not, he told the chiefs, they would have to give in to the government's demands. Instead of complaining about the past, they should try to save whatever they could for their children. If they signed, he, Crook, promised to ask Congress not to reduce rations; it was the best he could do. That seemed better than nothing, especially when they remembered what refusing to sell the Black Hills had cost their people. So, against Sitting Bull's advice, the majority made their mark beside their names on the list; the chief, of course, refused to touch the pen. Whites celebrated with bonfires and fireworks. That fall, North Dakota, South Dakota, and Montana became the thirty-ninth, fortieth, and forty-first states to join the Union.[20]

Congress ignored Crook's appeal. Two weeks after the vote, it cut the Lakotas' daily beef ration by 40 percent and other supplies by 10 percent, claiming a shortage of funds. Yet that was just the beginning, as disaster followed disaster. Drought and grasshopper plagues swept the Great Plains in 1889; even experienced white farmers lost their crops. That winter, entire herds of cattle froze in record-breaking blizzards; ranchers called it "the die-up of '89." To make matters worse, the government banned the killing of wild game on reservations as a "conservation" measure. Disease followed hunger. Epidemics of measles, whooping cough, and influenza struck the reservations. Despair gripped the people. Many said they had nothing to live for, so they might as well crawl under their blankets and die.

And then hope suddenly returned. It came as a new religion called the Ghost Dance. Within a year, that religion would cost Sitting Bull his life.

For many years afterward, the Paiute tribe of Nevada called January 1, 1889, the Day the Sun Died. Early that afternoon, an eclipse blotted out the sun. Moments later, in Mason Valley, a medicine man named Wovoka "died," too. Wovoka went to bed with a high fever and lay unconscious for two days. During that time, he claimed, a strange and wonderful thing happened. His spirit left his body and rose into the sky. Higher and higher he went, until he reached a land beyond the stars. There Wovoka met the Great Spirit, who showed him all his ancestors living as in the long-ago time. They rode fine horses over endless green prairies teeming with buffalo. After a while, the Great Spirit sent him back to earth with a message.

Wovoka's spirit fell back into his body. When he awoke, he repeated the message. The Great Spirit had promised to visit the earth sometime soon. He would come out of the West, bringing herds of buffalo to restock the Great Plains. Every Indian who had ever died would rejoin their loved ones and live forever, never growing old or getting sick. Wovoka then spoke with the Great Spirit's very own voice: "When your friends die you must not cry. You must not hurt anybody or do harm to anyone. You must not fight. Do right always. . . . Do not refuse to work for the whites and do not make any trouble with them. . . . Do not tell lies."[21] Finally, they must do a dance the Great Spirit had taught the medicine man. Wovoka called it the Dance of the Returning Spirits—or the Ghost Dance.

The Ghost Dance "religion" spread throughout the West, particularly among the former buffalo-hunting tribes of the Great Plains. It spread because it promised a better life, precisely what the tribes needed. It also spread because of the white man's post offices and railroads. Native Americans had learned to use these to their own advantage. Having schoolchildren write letters in English enabled them to "speak" over vast distances in a common language. Similarly, railroads served all the major western areas. Indians simply "rode the rails"—that is, hopped freight cars with little if any trouble from white trainmen.

Delegates from thirty tribes visited Wovoka, who told his story over and over. All became believers. So did the Lakota delegates, only with a difference. Somehow they got the idea that the Great Spirit would come behind a tidal wave of fresh earth. As it rolled onward, the wave would cover the spoiled land and push the whites into the sea. No one should fear the whites, because the Great Spirit had also sent the secret of the ghost shirt. Made of white cotton cloth and decorated with magical designs, the shirt made its owners impervious to bullets.

A *Ghost Dance* shirt decorated with magical symbols.

By 1890, the Ghost Dance was sweeping the Lakota reservations. Its leading supporter was Kicking Bear, a Miniconjou who had spent many weeks in Mason Valley. Following Wovoka's instructions, he taught believers to join hands and form a large dance circle. Following his lead, they began by singing a sad song. Each tribe developed its own songs, although they always had the same theme:

> *Father, have pity on me,*
> *Father, have pity on me;*
> *I am crying for thirst,*
> *I am crying for thirst;*
> *All is gone—I have nothing to eat,*
> *All is gone—I have nothing to eat.*[22]

Kicking Bear brought the Ghost
Dance religion to the Lakota.

Dancers moved in slow, shuffling steps, singing in unison. Hours passed. Gradually, the pace quickened. The circle moved faster, faster, whirling like the wheels of a locomotive barreling down the tracks. Dancers wailed and moaned until overcome by emotion and dizziness. Dozens fell unconscious and had visions as they lay thrashing on the ground. Fellow dancers stepped over them, changing the songs from time to time. Finally, they burst into a song of joy:

> *The whole world of the dead is returning,*
> *   returning*
> *Our nation is coming, is coming.*
> *The spotted eagle brought us the message,*
> *Bearing the Father's word—*
> *The word and wish of the Father.*
> *Over the glad new earth they are coming,*
> *Our dead come driving the elk and the*
> *   deer.*
> *See them hurrying the herds of buffalo!*
> *This the Father has promised,*
> *This the Father has given.*[23]

People fear what they do not understand. Whites living near the Lakota reservations had never heard of Wovoka or his warnings against violence. All they knew was that Indians—thousands of them—were dancing furiously. Why? The only reason the whites could imagine was that dancers were building up their courage for an all-out war. Articles about the dances began to appear in local newspapers. Before long, several large eastern newspapers learned of these articles, reprinted them, and sent reporters to investigate. Without realizing it, they were setting the stage for an immense human tragedy.

The reporters were dudes, city people who knew little, if anything,

Arapaho Indians doing the Ghost Dance.

about Native Americans. What they did know was that their editors wanted exciting stories to get the public to buy more newspapers. As one reporter recalled, his impatient editor burned up the telegraph wires with demands for "More Blood!"[24]

Since there was no blood (so far), reporters used their imaginations to create an atmosphere of danger, excitement, and confusion. Describing themselves as "war correspondents," they presented every rumor and tidbit of gossip as a fact. Reporters enlivened otherwise dull articles by recalling, in gory detail, events like the Minnesota uprising of 1862 and Custer's defeat at the Little Bighorn. Editors pitched in with screaming headlines: "Dark Is the Outlook," "Bound to Be Trouble," "Redskins Prepare for War," "Getting Ready to Fight," "The Dance of Death to Come."[25]

Fear fed on itself. Settlers' fears had attracted the reporters to begin with. Reporters' stories now turned settlers' fears into panic. Expecting to be killed at any moment, ranchers fled to Rapid City in the Black Hills. Farmers living south of Mandan, North Dakota, bundled their families into wagons and ran to town. "They urgently demand protection," thundered a Chicago newspaper. "Many a farm house in North Dakota will soon be deserted unless settlers receive some assurance that they will not be left to the mercy of the murderous redskins, who are now whetting their knives in anticipation of the moment when they may begin their bloody work."[26]

Fear, however, is a contagious emotion. As fear of a massacre spread among whites, the Lakota caught the same fever. Although they had no newspapers, rumors spread from camp to camp with lightning speed. According to these, whites planned to break up the Ghost Dance and murder the dancers. So, in self-defense, Lakota men sold their possessions to buy guns and ammunition. Although the government banned weapons sales on reservations, there were always traders eager to make a deal. Some traders sold Winchester repeating rifles. The army, however, still used the old single-shot Springfield carbines.

Like any group, the Lakota had their share of hotheads. A few of these hotheads got carried away and said stupid things. Wearing their "bullet-proof" ghost shirts, they visited ranches with Winchesters cradled in their arms. When cowboys got their own rifles, the visitors backed down. Shouting threats as they rode away, they promised to return in force. And when they did, watch out! They would smash open the heads of white children and drink the blood of white women.[27]

Reporters described these hotheads as "Sitting Bull's men." Some may have been members of his band; we simply do not know. Although their threats were bad enough, reporters went further. In story after story, they said the chief hated whites. That was true. They also accused him of plotting to drown the West in blood. That was nonsense. Nobody has ever found evidence of a Lakota plot, let alone a plot led by Sitting Bull. There *were* plenty of rumors spread by reporters out for the "big story."

Historians disagree on whether Sitting Bull did the Ghost Dance himself. Yet all agree that he favored the new religion. He welcomed Kicking Bear to his camp. Ignoring Sitting Bull's protests, Major McLaughlin forced Kicking Bear to leave Standing Rock. The chief then built a dance circle near his cabins and wore a ghost shirt painted with black stars and a blue-black moon. When dancers dropped to the ground, he interpreted their visions.[28]

The Ghost Dance, however, gave Sitting Bull little satisfaction. He knew he did not have long to live. That knowledge came to him from a source he trusted: the spirit world. One day, probably in 1889, while going to saddle Buffalo Bill's gift horse, he crossed a field of flowers growing up to his waist. Halfway across, he heard a meadowlark singing. This bird, we recall, had been his special friend since youth. In its song he had always heard the truth. This time Brother Meadowlark said: "Lakotas will kill you." That prediction upset him deeply. Although he tried to forget it, he could not. It preyed on his mind.[29]

Meanwhile, the government decided that the Ghost Dance had gone too far. Unless the government acted forcefully, and soon, the "dance craze" seemed sure to explode into wholesale violence. Again telegraph keys clattered, sending troop reinforcements to the Dakotas. Bear Coat Miles, recently promoted to general, got orders to stop the dancing, arrest the dance leaders, and disarm the Lakota. In Oklahoma, for example, Quanah Parker, the Comanche leader, kept dancers under control and steered them clear of confrontations with the soldiers. Given the Lakotas' history, however, the authorities felt they could not afford to take any chances. So on November 20, Miles's soldiers occupied the Pine Ridge and Rosebud reservations. A few days later, Custer's old outfit, the 7th Cavalry, arrived at Pine Ridge. Fearing for their lives, six hundred Ghost Dancers and their families fled to a plateau at the northwest corner of the reservation. Known as the Stronghold, this place was a natural fortress. There the fugitives danced in their "bulletproof" shirts while daring the soldiers to come and get them.

Bear Coat refused to be drawn into an unnecessary battle. With the dancers bottled up in the Stronghold, he knew they could not cause trouble elsewhere. So, while his officers tried to talk them down, the general turned his attention to Standing Rock and Sitting Bull. Nobody had died so far, and he meant to keep it that way, if possible.

Miles knew that any attempt to take Sitting Bull by force would cost lives. Hoping to avoid bloodshed, he asked Buffalo Bill Cody, an old friend, for a favor. The general knew that Sitting Bull liked the showman. Would Cody, then, try to bring him to the agency jail without a fight? Cody promised to try his best. As they parted, Miles gave him a signed order for the chief's arrest.

Cody intended to make the most of his mission. Before setting out, he called a press conference to announce that he was starting "the most dangerous undertaking of my career."[30] That was the publicity-hungry showman talking. His actions told quite a different story.

After leaving the train at Bismarck, Cody "armed" himself thoroughly—with candy! "Why, I've got a hundred dollars' worth of stuff in that wagon for every pound old Bull weighs," he told reporters, a twinkle in his eye.[31] He knew that Sitting Bull, like most people, had a sweet tooth. There was nothing like a hefty dose of sugar to put him in a good mood. Cody would invite the chief to meet Miles, who would jail him until things calmed down. Then he would send him back to Standing Rock. It would simply be a holding action.

Major McLaughlin was shocked when Cody walked into his office at the agency. If anyone got the credit for arresting Sitting Bull, McLaughlin wanted it. So, while some friends tried to get the showman drunk, McLaughlin sent a telegram to the Department of Indian Affairs in Washington.

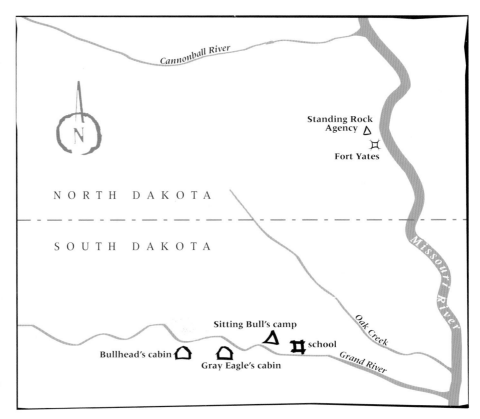

Sitting Bull's camp and the surrounding area on the day of his death, December 15, 1890.

Cody could hold his liquor. After drinking most of the night, he left at the crack of dawn, November 28, fit as a fiddle. His drinking partners had pounding headaches.

McLaughlin, however, had thought of everything. As Cody drove his candy wagon, he met an agency interpreter. The interpreter, another friend of McLaughlin's, said that Sitting Bull had left his cabin for parts unknown. That was an outright lie, but nevertheless Cody believed it. When he returned to the agency, he found a telegram canceling Miles's order and giving McLaughlin the authority to arrest Sitting Bull. The telegram came from President Benjamin Harrison. It was all most unfortunate. "If they had left Cody alone," a soldier remarked, "he'd have captured Sitting Bull with an all-day sucker."[32]

McLaughlin chose a loyal Metal Breast, Lieutenant Bull Head, to make the arrest. Bull Head gathered a squad of men at his cabin in the early evening of December 14, 1890. That cabin stood on almost the exact spot where Sitting Bull had come into the world fifty-nine years earlier.[33]

The Metal Breasts passed the night retelling war stories and downing "liquid courage," jugs of whiskey sent by McLaughlin. After outlining his plan, Bull Head read the agent's arrest order. To set their minds at ease, McLaughlin told them that arresting Sitting Bull was for the good of their people. He ended with the imperative: "You must not let him escape under any circumstances."[34]

On Tuesday, December 15, 1890, at 4:30 A.M., Lieutenant Bull Head led forty-two men across the Grand River east of Sitting Bull's cabins. Meanwhile, a squadron of cavalry left Fort Yates to back up the police, should they get into trouble. Capturing the chief, however, was to be an all-Lakota affair. That way, if anything went wrong, the Metal Breasts would have to take the blame.

Sitting Bull's camp on the day of his death, December 15, 1890.

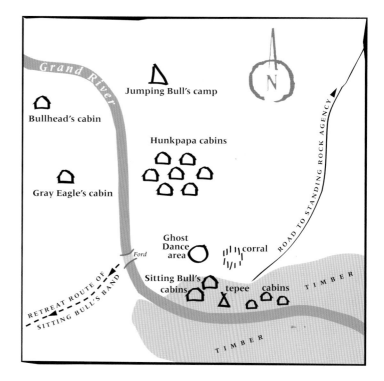

The police officers shivered, not from the biting cold, but from fear. They had reason to be frightened. Nobody had ever gone into a Hunkpapa camp to seize a chief and lived to tell about it. As they rode, the night creatures "spoke" to them. An owl's hooting sounded like the sobbing of a woman in mourning. Howling coyotes seemed to say "beware, beware."[35]

After an hour's ride, they saw the outlines of cabins in the distance. In the gray half-light of dawn, they rode into the settlement at a full gallop. Dogs barked, waking their masters. Men instinctively threw off their blankets and reached for their guns.

The Metal Breasts dismounted and surrounded Sitting Bull's cabin. Bull Head sprang from the saddle, ran through the ring of guards, and banged on the door with the butt of his pistol. A match flared inside and the yellow light of a kerosene lamp outlined the space between the door and its frame. "All right!" a man's voice called. "Come in!"

Bull Head entered the cabin, followed by Sergeants Shave Head and Red Tomahawk. They found Sitting Bull sitting on the edge of a bed, naked; he always slept without clothes, even in wintertime. Nearby stood one of his wives and his son, Crow Foot, now seventeen years old.

Nervous and fearful, the intruders wanted to do their job as fast as possible. Bull Head grabbed Sitting Bull by the shoulder, saying, "I've come after you to take you to the agency. You are under arrest." The chief did not resist. "Let me put my clothes on and go with you," he replied.

Meanwhile, a large crowd had gathered outside the cabin. Angry shouts filled the air. Women cried. Men fingered the triggers of their rifles. The police officers, both outside and inside the cabin, grew more jittery by the moment.

The arrest of Sitting Bull, as portrayed by an anonymous eyewitness.

When he thought Sitting Bull had spent enough time dressing, Bull Head flung open the cabin door. The crowd gasped. There stood their chief, a prisoner, only partly clothed and flanked by Metal Breasts. How they hated these men—these traitors!

Sitting Bull saw the upturned faces and hesitated in the doorway. With Bull Head leading the way, Shave Head and Red Tomahawk pushed him forward. Once outside, Shave Head kept punching him in the back with his pistol to get him to move faster. Off to the side, the chief may have noticed a gray horse, Buffalo Bill's gift, saddled and waiting.

As they moved toward the horse, the chief's wife, Seen by Her Nation, chanted in a high-pitched voice:

> *Sitting Bull, you have always been a*
> *   brave man,*
> *What is going to happen now?*

Sitting Bull hesitated for a moment. What *would* happen now? He probably did not know himself. Then, from the cabin door, Crow Foot cried: "You have always called yourself a brave chief. Now you are allowing yourself to be taken by the Metal Breasts."

Crow Foot's words seemed to trigger something deep within his father. Although we can never know Sitting Bull's thoughts, we can try to reconstruct them based upon his actions. Suddenly, it seems, everything became clear as the years melted away. During those last seconds of his life, Sitting Bull was no longer an old man facing arrest. Again he was a mighty chief with many coups and scalps to his credit. At the very least, he was determined to remain true to himself and his tradition—and not to walk this white man's road. "I am not going," he shouted. "Do with me as you like. I am not going. Come on! Come on! Take action! Let's go!"

Those words electrified his listeners. "You shall not take away our chief!" a villager shouted. A shot rang out and Bull Head pitched forward, mortally wounded. As he fell, he, too, fired a shot. The bullet plowed into Sitting Bull's chest, shattered his spine, and came out his back through a hole two inches across. Just then, Red Tomahawk shot the chief in the back of the head. Sitting Bull died instantly, dropping to the ground as dead-weight.

Enraged Lakotas swarmed over the Metal Breasts with guns, knives,

Sitting Bull's son, Crow Foot, was killed moments after his father.

The killing of Sitting Bull, as portrayed by an anonymous eyewitness.

clubs, and axes. In the midst of that wild scene, the gray horse remembered its part in Buffalo Bill's Wild West Show. With bullets whining overhead, the horse sat down and raised a hoof as if it wanted to shake hands. Sitting Bull's followers, thinking their chief's spirit had entered the animal, panicked for a moment. This allowed the Metal Breasts to retreat into the cabin, where they found Crow Foot hiding under a mattress.

"Uncles, I want to live! You have killed my father! Let me go!" the boy pleaded. The police officers turned to Bull Head. "Kill him," the dying man growled, "they have killed me." So they shot Crow Foot and tossed his body through the door.

Sitting Bull's followers pressed their attack, trying to wipe out the Metal Breasts. The police backup, however, arrived just in time. Cavalrymen dispersed the attackers. When the smoke cleared, they found the bodies of twelve Hunkpapas, including Jumping Bull, the chief's adopted brother. They also found four dead police officers sprawled outside the cabin. Bull Head and Shave Head died of their wounds the following day.

Relatives of the police officers rushed from their homes nearby. When they saw their loved ones' bodies, they pounded Sitting Bull's head into a shapeless mass of bone and gore. Soldiers later buried the body in a corner of the Fort Yates cemetery. They buried it in an unmarked grave, without any prayers or signs of respect. None of his followers saw the burial. When the cavalry had appeared, they had fled the village, scattering to the west and south.[36]

News of the shootout spread quickly. Lakota people still tell how their ancestors, even those living hundreds of miles from the scene, learned of Sitting Bull's death moments after it happened. A ghostly warrior is supposed to have appeared on a high butte and cried: "Sitting Bull is dead!"[37]

James Morrow Walsh had left the Royal Northwest Mounted Police to become a businessman in Winnipeg, Canada. Walsh learned of the chief's death from an article in a local newspaper. Stunned by the news, he wrote a long, thoughtful obituary. The former Mountie was proud to have known "Bull," as he called him. Here is part of what he wrote:

> I am glad to hear that Bull is relieved of his miseries even if it took the bullet to do it. A man who wields such power as Bull once did . . . cannot endure abject poverty, slavery and beggary without suffering great mental pain, and death is a relief. . . . History does not tell us that a greater Indian than Bull ever lived. . . . This man, that so many look upon as a bloodthirsty villain . . . was not a cruel man. He was kind of heart. He was not dishonest. He was truthful. He loved his people and was glad to give his hand in friendship to any man who believed he was not an enemy and was honest with him. . . . The war between the U.S. and Bull was a strange one. A nation against one man. On the U.S. side there were numbers; on Bull's side there was principle. The one man was murdered by the nation to destroy the principle he advocated—that no man against his will should be forced to be a beggar.[38]

Nobody has ever given a better, more truthful appraisal of Sitting Bull as a man and leader. Walsh, however, may have gone too far in accusing the authorities of deliberate murder.

Did McLaughlin want Sitting Bull dead? Nobody can answer that question. What we can say, however, is that he wanted the chief arrested at all costs. He must have known, as the Metal Breasts knew, that trying to arrest Sitting Bull would probably lead to trouble. If so, and the chief died in a shootout, McLaughlin would not have wanted it to look like an assassination. Captain E. G. Fechet, who led the backup force, believed that the major had set up the situation to blame Sitting Bull's people for whatever happened. "The attempt to arrest Sitting Bull," wrote Fechet, "was so managed as to place the responsibility for the fight that ensued upon Sitting Bull's band which began the firing."[39]

Yet there is no evidence that the Metal Breasts *intended* to kill the

Lakota chief. Had they, they could easily have done it in the cabin and escaped before the crowd gathered in force. Instead, they risked their own lives by taking him outside and into the crowd. They understood Major McLaughlin's order: Bring in Sitting Bull dead or alive. Rather than see him escape, they would see him dead. And that is what happened.

Postscript

DEATH OF A DREAM

"When I look back now from this high hill of my old age, I can still see the butchered women and children . . . as plain as when I saw them with eyes still young. And I can see that something else died there in that bloody mud, and was buried in the blizzard. A people's dream died there."

—BLACK ELK

OUR STORY DOES NOT END with Sitting Bull's death. The final act in the Lakota tragedy came fifteen days later, at a place called Wounded Knee. Only thirty-eight of Sitting Bull's people managed to evade the cavalry patrols. Seventy miles south of Grand River, they found their cousins, 332 Miniconjous, bound for the Stronghold. General Miles had also marked their leader, Big Foot, for arrest. The chief did not know that his fellow Ghost Dancers had already surrendered and were leaving the plateau. "We cannot live on words," they had told the waiting soldiers.[1]

On December 28, 1890, a detachment of the 7th Cavalry caught up to Big Foot's band near the Badlands. The chief was glad to see the troopers. It was winter—one of those bitter, bone-chilling South Dakota winters. His people were hungry, cold, and exhausted. Most wanted nothing more than to return to the reservation. Big Foot himself had fallen ill with pneumonia and was coughing blood. A fight was the last thing anyone needed.

Big Foot surrendered to Major Samuel Whiteside, the detachment's

Colonel George A. Forsyth led the 7th Cavalry during the fight at Wounded Knee.

leader. Since many of his warriors had Winchester repeaters, Whiteside did not try to disarm them immediately. Instead, he decided to escort them to his base camp at Wounded Knee Creek ten miles northeast of the Pine Ridge Agency. As a goodwill gesture, and to make the journey easier for his ailing prisoner, the major put him in an ambulance wagon. After arriving at the camp, the women set up their lodges along the edge of a dry ravine, or gulch, which led into the creek. After that, the major issued army rations. Later that afternoon, Colonel George A. Forsyth arrived with the rest of the 7th Cavalry and camped on a rise to the north.

Big Foot's warriors must have thought back fourteen years to that hot day on the Little Bighorn as the regiment trotted past their lodges. Some, no doubt, shuddered when they recognized the fork-tailed pennants with the number seven on them. Yet the 7th Cavalry was no longer a topnotch outfit. Colonel Forsyth, a Civil War veteran, had never led troops against Indians. Only six of his officers had served in the regiment since Custer's time, and five of these had fought beside Reno and Benteen. Apart from a handful of old-timers, none of the enlisted men had ever seen combat. One in five was a greenhorn, a recent recruit from big-city slums. Some barely knew how to ride a horse.

Nevertheless, Forsyth had about 500 men to handle 370 Lakotas (Miniconjous and Hunkpapas), of whom only 106 were warriors; the rest were old people, women, and children. In addition, the regiment had four Hotchkiss guns, light cannons able to shoot fifty explosive shells a minute. Still, nobody expected to use such devastating firepower. Neither the colonel nor his officers thought Big Foot's people had any fight left in them. Yet, just in case, Forsyth ringed their camp with guards on foot and trained the Hotchkiss guns on it from a hill nearby. While the guards shivered at their posts, everyone else turned in for the night.

Next morning, at 8:00 A.M., Forsyth asked Big Foot's warriors to come to a council near the cavalry encampment. The warriors sat in a semicircle, each with a woolen blanket draped over his shoulders against the cold. The

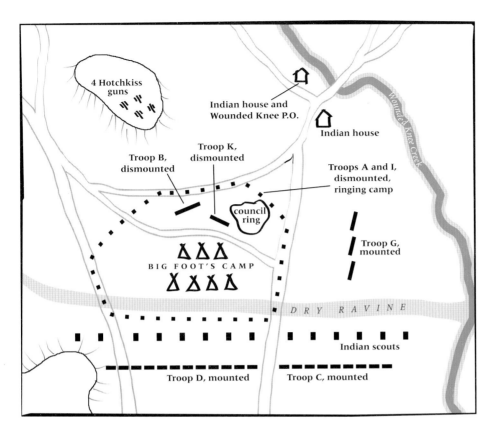

Within the map:

4 Hotchkiss guns

Indian house and Wounded Knee P.O.

Indian house

Troop K, dismounted

Troop B, dismounted

Troops A and I, dismounted, ringing camp

council ring

Wounded Knee Creek

Troop G, mounted

ΔΔΔ
BIG FOOT'S CAMP
ΧΧΧΧ

DRY RAVINE

Indian scouts

Troop D, mounted

Troop C, mounted

Wounded Knee and the surrounding area, December 29, 1890.

guards remained at their posts. Other units drew up on horseback around the warriors and their camp. When all his troops were in place, Forsyth ordered the warriors to hand in their weapons.

Big Foot did not like that idea. From a pile of blankets placed on the ground, the sick man whispered to his warriors, "Give them some of the bad guns, but keep the good ones."[2] He saw no reason to trust Forsyth more than any other white man he had met, particularly after hearing about Sitting Bull. Besides, those soldiers yonder belonged to the 7th Cavalry. He feared a massacre if his warriors disarmed completely. Although his fear was unjustified, it was very real. Yet the worse danger lay not in handing over the guns but in keeping them.

Forsyth sent some warriors to the lodges to get their rifles. They returned with two broken carbines of the sort children used as toys.

That would not do! Major Whiteside had seen Winchesters the day before, and these could not have vanished into thin air. So Forsyth intensified the search. After placing a line of dismounted troopers between the warriors and their camp, he sent a search party to the lodges. Although most searchers acted properly, some did not. They cut open bundles and scattered the contents on the ground. A few rifles turned up.

Several women sat on bundles. When they refused to stand up, soldiers lifted them bodily. That caused an outcry. An officer recalled that the first rifle he found lay under a woman. She was "moaning and . . . so indisposed to the search that I had her displaced, and under her was a beautiful Winchester rifle."[3] The searchers found thirty-eight rifles, most of them old and useless.

Meanwhile, the warriors were growing restless as they heard the commotion behind them, in the lodges. A medicine man called Yellow Bird made matters worse. Yellow Bird was a Ghost Dance leader. He had danced often, and expected the new world to come any day. Clad in an elaborately decorated ghost shirt, he walked around the seated warriors, blowing on an eagle-bone whistle. Occasionally he paused, threw a handful of dust into the air, and reminded the warriors of the power of their ghost shirts. "Do not be afraid," he chanted. "Let your hearts be strong to meet what is before you. . . . As you saw me throw up the dust and it floated away, so will the bullets float harmlessly over the prairie."[4] When he finished chanting, he sat down.

Where were those Winchesters? If they were not in the lodges or the baggage, they must be on the warriors themselves, hidden under their blankets. Forsyth announced that each warrior must be searched personally.

The warriors began to fidget and exchange glances with their eyes. One by one, they stood up and opened their blankets. The first three had two rifles and a pouch full of cartridges. Then it was Black Coyote's turn.

Black Coyote was deaf and, his fellow tribesmen said, "a crazy man."[5] He had a Winchester. Pulling it from under his blanket, he waved it over his head and began shouting that it was his gun. When they saw that, two soldiers sprang forward and grabbed him from behind, trying to twist the weapon out of his hands.

Black Coyote struggled and—*bang!* His rifle went off, firing harmlessly into the air. We do not know if his comrades had a plan of action. What we do know is that Yellow Bird immediately threw a handful of dust in the soldiers' direction. Then it happened. Warriors sprang to their feet, pulled rifles from under their blankets, and aimed at the soldiers.

"Look out! They are going to fire!" an officer shouted.[6]

Another officer remembered saying to himself, "The pity of it! What can they be thinking of!"[7]

Both sides fired at once; an Indian later compared the sound to the tearing of a gigantic sheet of canvas. The warriors could not have been thinking clearly or aiming carefully. Every one of their bullets that missed a soldier slammed into the lodges behind them, striking women and children. Soldiers also fired without thinking of the consequences. In shooting at the warriors, some of their bullets hit comrades posted on the other side of the council area. Perhaps this tells us of the atmosphere of desperation, fear, and surprise. Exploding cannon shells shredded the lodges and filled the air with hot iron splinters. Some

The fight at Wounded Knee as seen by Black Elk. Notice the soldiers firing a Hotchkiss gun on the right and the fleeing women being shot down in the ravine at the lower left.

villagers fled westward over the prairie. Nearly all these were women and children. Many had been wounded and would eventually bleed to death or die of exposure. Apparently, too, a few mounted troopers broke ranks and chased them, yelling, "Remember Custer!"[8]

Other villagers ran toward the ravine, later called the "ravine of death." Officers tried to prevent them from being shot as they ran. "Don't fire, let them go, they are squaws," a captain shouted to his men.

Yet that was impossible. Warriors escaping from the council area followed close on the fugitives' heels. Now mixed up with women and children, they handled their Winchesters with deadly effect. In reply, the Hotchkiss guns poured a murderous fire into the ravine. The shells exploded on all without regard to age or sex. Troopers also rode along the rim, firing downward with carbines and six-guns. Since both warriors and women wore ghost shirts, they could not be told apart amid the smoke and confusion. Warriors also shot at the troopers from between the women and children. They were not deliberately using them as shields, but the soldiers fired at innocent people in order to get at the warriors.[9]

Meanwhile, over at Pine Ridge, Black Elk heard shooting in the distance. He joined some 150 warriors who rode out to investigate. They were too few and too late to help the people at Wounded Knee. The scene there burned itself into Black Elk's mind. Many years later, as an old man, he described it:

We stopped on the ridge not far from the head of the dry gulch. Wagon guns [cannons] were still going off over there on the little hill, and they were going off again where they hit along the gulch. Cavalrymen were riding along the gulch and shooting into it, where the women and children were running away and trying to hide in the gullies and the stunted pines. . . . We followed them down along the dry gulch, and what we saw was terrible. Dead and wounded women and children and little babies were scattered all along there, where they had been trying to run away. The soldiers were following along the gulch, as they ran, and murdered them in there. Sometimes they were in heaps because they had huddled together, and some were scattered all along. Sometimes bunches of them had been killed and torn to pieces where the wagon guns hit them. I saw a little baby trying to suck its mother, but she was bloody and dead. . . . When I saw this I wished that I had died, too, but I was not sorry for the women and children. It was better for them to be happy in the other world, and I wanted to be there, too.[10]

Finally, those in the ravine surrendered. By late afternoon, Forsyth left for Pine Ridge. His wagons carried twenty-five dead and thirty-nine wounded troopers, and an unspecified number of prisoners. Within hours of Forsyth's return, a blizzard swept in from the north, lasting three days.

On January 1, 1891, soldiers, civilian gravediggers, and Lakota volunteers returned to Wounded Knee to search for survivors and bury the dead. Dr. Charles A. Eastman, a full-blooded Santee with a degree from Boston University, led the volunteers. Dr. Eastman had seen many dead people during his medical career. But he had never seen anything like Wounded Knee. "It took all my nerve to keep my composure in the face of this spectacle," he wrote years later.[11]

Bodies lay everywhere, each under a mantle of snow. Many were stuck to the ground by clots of frozen blood. Dr. Eastman's men found the charred remains of Yellow Bird and, frozen in a half-sitting position, the body of Big Foot. They also found four babies alive under the snow. All were sick and only one, a girl of about four months, lived. She lay beside her dead mother, wrapped in a blanket and wearing a buckskin cap deco-

The body of Big Foot lies frozen at Wounded Knee.

rated with an American flag embroidered in beads. The Lakota called her Zinkta Lanuni—"Lost Bird."

The gravediggers set to work with picks and shovels. Before placing the bodies in a long trench, they joined the soldiers in stripping off the ghost shirts for souvenirs. Then they stacked the stiffened remains of 128 men and women and 18 children in the trench. Historians believe that residents of Pine Ridge found and hid another 70 or 80 bodies on the night of December 29. This brought the total number of Lakota dead to at least 226.

After the gravediggers finished, they posed for a photograph with the soldiers in a half-circle around the trench. Then they shoveled in the dirt and left. In spring, the Lakota put a wire fence around the site and painted the posts red as a sign of respect for the victims. Eventually, they built a permanent monument on the site. A mason carved these words into the stone slab: "Many innocent women and children who knew no wrong died here."

Frozen bodies of men, women, and children about to be buried in a mass grave at Wounded Knee.

Whites refer to the events at Wounded Knee as a battle. Native Americans have another name: the Wounded Knee Massacre. In some sense, both are right—and wrong. It was a battle because the Lakota killed and wounded one in eight white soldiers, a heavy loss even by the standards of twentieth-century warfare. Yet it was also a massacre, because the soldiers fired into a village and then into a ravine crowded with women and children. Given their greater numbers, the soldiers could easily have waited until those in the ravine grew cold enough and hungry enough to surrender. This tactic had always worked in the past. Any frontiersman knew that warriors would do anything to spare the lives of their families. Lacking frontier experience, Colonel Forsyth and his men overreacted. Outraged at the slaughter of innocents, General Miles relieved the colonel of his command.

Whether we call it a battle or a massacre, Wounded Knee represented two things. First, it represented the end of the thirty-year struggle between Indians and government for the northern Great Plains. Second, it signaled the end of the Ghost Dance. The shirts had offered no protection. Spring came and went, but the buffalo did not return. Nor did a wave of new earth push the whites into the sea. Religion had been the Lakotas' last hope of bringing back the life they loved. After Wounded Knee, they realized it would never return. They had no choice but to submit to the new life—a life made for them mostly by strangers.

Wovoka understood this, too. When news of Wounded Knee reached him in Nevada, he pulled his blanket over his head and remained silent for a long time. Then he spoke not as Wovoka, but as the Great Spirit speaking though his lips. His words, like those of Drinks Water in the long-ago time, foretold the future. "Hoo-oo! My children! My children!" Wovoka cried. "In days behind, many times I called you to travel the hunting trail or to follow the war trail. Now those trails are choked with sand; they are covered with grass, the young men cannot find them. My children, today I call you to travel a new trail, the only trail now open—the White's Man's Road."[12]

It was, and has continued to be, a difficult road. Forced onto reservations, their cultural traditions under constant assault, the Great Plains tribes became almost totally dependent on government handouts. By 1900, their population had shrunk by more than half, from nearly 250,000 at the time of Sitting Bull's birth to just over 100,000. Nevertheless, during the twentieth century their population began a slow increase, reaching 1.4 million today. Despite ongoing economic hardship, the pride, spirit, and culture of the Plains Indians have survived all efforts to eradicate them. Surely this perseverance and commitment to their own heritage is part of the enduring legacy of Sitting Bull.

Notes

Prologue: THEY SAY THEY ARE INDIANS

1. Don Diessner, *There Are No Indians Left But Me! Sitting Bull's Story* (El Segundo, Calif.: Upton & Sons, 1993), 150, 155.
2. Fairfax Downey, *Indian-Fighting Army* (New York: Scribner's, 1941), 35; Major General John K. Herr and Edward S. Wallace, *The Story of the United States Cavalry, 1775–1942* (Boston: Little, Brown, 1953), 150; Don Russell, "How Many Indians Were Killed? White Man Versus Red Man: The Facts and the Legend," *The American West* (July 1973): 62.
3. Hiram M. Chittenden, *History of Early Steamboat Navigation on the Missouri River: Life and Adventures of Joseph LaBarge*. 2 vols. (New York: Macmillan, 1903), II: 253–54.
4. *Report of the Secretary of War, House Executive Documents,* 45th Cong. 3d sess., I (1878), 36.
5. Frances Densmore, *Teton Sioux Music.* Washington, D.C.: Smithsonian Institution, Bureau of American Ethnology, Bulletin 61 (1918), 458.
6. "Sitting Bull Talks," *New York Herald,* 17 November 1877.
7. Thomas B. Marquis, *Wooden Leg: A Warrior Who Fought Custer* (Lincoln, Nebr.: University of Nebraska Press, 1931), 383.
8. Philippe Régis de Trobriand, *Military Life in Dakota* (St. Paul, Minn.: Alvord Memorial Commission, 1951), 289.
9. Christopher Columbus probably used the word first, because he believed he had found an all-water route to India, not a New World.
10. Tom McHugh, *The Time of the Buffalo* (New York: Alfred A. Knopf, 1972), 9.
11. Julius Lester, ed., *To Be a Slave* (New York: Scholastic Books, 1968), 85.
12. Katherine Gibson Fougera, *With Custer's Cavalry: From the Memoirs of the Late Katherine Gibson, Widow of Captain Francis M. Gibson of the Seventh Cavalry . . .* (Lincoln: University of Nebraska Press, 1986), 282.

Chapter One: GROWING UP LAKOTA

1. Erik H. Erikson, "Observations of Sioux Education," *The Journal of Psychology* VII (1939): 136–37.
2. Stanley Vestal, *Sitting Bull: Champion of the Sioux* (Norman, Okla.: University of Oklahoma Press, 1957), 3.
3. Marie Sandoz, *These Were the Sioux* (Lincoln, Nebr.: University of Nebraska Press, 1985), 33.
4. Royal B. Hassrick, *The Sioux: Life and Customs of a Warrior Society* (Norman, Okla.: University of Oklahoma Press, 1964), 276.
5. Luther Standing Bear, *Land of the Spotted Eagle* (Lincoln, Nebr.: University of Nebraska Press, 1960), 9.
6. Ibid., 159–60.
7. Wakantanka also means Spirit of the World, Great Mystery, Grandfather Spirit, and Everywhere Spirit.
8. Doane Robinson, *A History of the Dakota or Sioux Indians* (Minneapolis: Rosee & Haines, Inc., 1967), 31, 33.
9. Stanley Vestal, *New Sources of Indian History, 1850–1891* (Norman, Okla.: University of Oklahoma Press, 1934), 202.
10. Stanley Vestal, *The Missouri* (New York: Farrar & Rinehart, 1945), 70.
11. The states are Colorado, Kansas, Montana, Nebraska, New Mexico, North Dakota, South Dakota, Oklahoma, Texas, and Wyoming.

12. Washington Irving, *Astoria* (New York: Century Company, 1911), 198–99.
13. Ibid., 138–39.
14. Tom McHugh, *Time of the Buffalo* (New York: Alfred A. Knopf, 1972), 171.
15. Ibid., 15.
16. Gerald F. Kreyche, *Visions of the American West* (Lexington: University Press of Kentucky, 1989), 71; Vestal, *New Sources of Indian History,* 32; Francis Harris, *The Buffalo* (Norman, Okla.: University of Oklahoma Press, 1995), 42–43.
17. E. Adamson Hoebel, *The Cheyennes: Indians of the Great Plains* (New York: Holt, Rinehart & Winston, 1960), 38.
18. Black Elk, *Black Elk Speaks* (New York: William Morrow, 1932), 60.
19. Hassrick, *The Sioux,* 143–45.
20. Hassrick, *The Sioux,* 36.
21. Luther Standing Bear, *Land of the Spotted Eagle,* 22.
22. J. Frank Dobie, "Indian Horses and Horsemanship," *Southwest Review* XXXV (1950), 268; Richard Irving Dodge, *Our Wild Indians: Thirty-Three Years' Personal Experience Among the Red Men of the Great West* (New York: Archer House, 1959), 426–27.
23. Black Elk, *Black Elk Speaks,* 15.
24. Vestal, *Sitting Bull,* 33.
25. George Catlin, *Letters and Notes on the Manners, Customs, and Conditions of the North American Indians,* 2 vols. (New York: Dover, 1973), I, 200–201.
26. Maria R. Audubon, ed., *Audubon and His Journals,* 2 vols. (New York: Dover Publications, 1968), II, 141.
27. Robert M. Utley, *The Lance and the Shield: The Life and Times of Sitting Bull* (New York: Henry Holt & Co., 1993), 29.

28. Utley, *The Lance and the Shield,* 29–30; Vestal, *Sitting Bull,* 30.

29. Utley, *The Lance and the Shield,* 30.

Chapter Two: WAR AND MORE

1. For a detailed account of the Lakota idea of war and its place in their society, see Royal B. Hassrick, *The Sioux: Life and Customs of a Warrior Society* (Norman, Okla.: University of Oklahoma Press, 1964), 76–100.

2. Pedro de Castañeda, *An Account of the Expedition to Cibola Which Took Place in the Year 1540* (New York: Greenwood Press, 1969), 84.

3. Hassrick, *The Sioux,* 33.

4. Ibid., 21.

5. Luther Standing Bear, *Land of the Spotted Eagle* (Lincoln, Nebr.: University of Nebraska Press, 1960), 40.

6. Black Elk, *Black Elk Speaks* (New York: William Morrow, 1932), 89.

7. K. D. Iain Murray, "Who Started Scalping?" *The West* (July 1964), 30–31, 54; "Scalping," in *Encyclopedia of the American West;* Axtell, 209–13; James Axtell, "Scalping: The Ethnohistory of a Moral Question," in *The European and the Indian: Essays in the Ethnohistory of Colonial North America* (New York: Oxford University Press, 1981), 207–41.

8. Anthony McGinnis, "A Contest of Wits and Daring: Plains Indians at War with the U.S. Army," *North Dakota History* 48 (Spring 1981): 24–32.

9. Ibid.

10. Thomas B. Marquis, *Wooden Leg: A Warrior Who Fought Custer* (Lincoln, Nebr.: University of Nebraska Press, 1931), 12; Stanley Vestal, *Sitting Bull: Champion of the Sioux* (Norman, Okla.: University of Oklahoma Press, 1957), 9.

11. Vestal, *Sitting Bull,* 8.

12. Ibid.

13. A butte is a hill, with sloping sides and a flat top, which rises abruptly from the surrounding area.

14. Philippe Régis de Trobriand, *Military Life in Dakota* (St. Paul, Minn.: Alvord Memorial Commission), 62.

15. Marquis, *Wooden Leg,* 66.

16. Vestal, *Sitting Bull,* 12.

17. From that day on, Father took the second name the mysterious buffalo had given him: Jumping Bull. Later, he gave the other names—Lone Bull and Bull Standing with Cow—to the sons of Good Feather Woman, his eldest daughter.

18. Vestal, *Sitting Bull,* 77.

19. Robert M. Utley, *The Lance and the Shield: The Life and Times of Sitting Bull* (New York: Henry Holt & Co., 1993), 19.

20. Ibid.

21. Hassrick, *The Sioux,* 24.

22. Vestal, *Sitting Bull,* 39–42.

23. Colin Taylor, *The Warriors of the Plains* (New York: Arco Publishing Co., 1975), 30.

24. Vestal, *Sitting Bull,* 22.

25. Ibid.

26. Ibid., 23.

27. Ibid., 29.

28. Utley, *The Lance and the Shield,* 32.

29. James R. Walker, *Lakota Society* (Lincoln, Nebr.: University of Nebraska Press, 1982), 98.

30. Utley, *The Lance and the Shield,* 33.

31. Vestal, *Sitting Bull,* 33–34.

32. Ibid., 46.

Chapter Three: HAIRY MEN FROM THE EAST

1. Reuben Gold Thwaites, ed., *Original Journals of the Lewis and Clark Expedition. 1804–1806,* vol. 6 (1904–1905; reprint, New York: Antiquarian Press, 1959), 98.

2. Michael M. Mooney, ed., *George Catlin: Letters and Notes on the North American Indians* (New York: Gramercy Books, 1995), 23.

3. Ibid., 256. Italics in original.

4. Lloyd McFarling. *Exploring the Northern Plains, 1804–1876* (Caldwell, Idaho: Caxton Printers, 1955), 68, 167.

5. Ibid., 141; LeRoy R. Hafen and Francis M. Young. *Fort Laramie and the Pageant of the West, 1834–1900* (Glendale, Calif.: Arthur M. Clark Co., 1938), 164.

6. Remi Nadeau, *Fort Laramie and the Sioux Indians* (Englewood Cliffs, N.J.: Prentice-Hall, 1967), 50.

7. Ibid., 62; Glenda Riley, *Women and Indians on the Frontier, 1825–1915* (Albuquerque: University of New Mexico Press, 1984), 152; Sandra L. Myres, *Westering Women and the Frontier Experience, 1800–1915* (Albuquerque: University of New Mexico Press, 1982), 57.

8. Gen. I:28.

9. Riley, *Women and Indians on the Frontier,* 129.

10. Ibid., 128, 130.

11. Ibid., 130.

12. Ibid., 22.

13. Ibid., 22; Evan S. Connell, *Son of the Morning Star* (New York: Promontory Press, 1993), 133.

14. Riley, *Women and Indians on the Frontier,* 86.

15. Elliott West, *Growing Up with the Country: Childhood on the Far Western Frontier* (Albuquerque: University of New Mexico Press, 1990), 35, 41; Riley, *Women and Indians on the Frontier,* 102; Colin Taylor, *The Warriors of the Plains* (New York: Arco Publishing Co., 1975), 85.

16. Hafen, *Fort Laramie and the Pageant of the West,* 164.

17. Josiah Gregg, *The Commerce of the Prairies* (New York: Citadel Press, 1968), 317–18.

18. Russell Thornton, *American Indian Holocaust and Survival: A Population History Since 1492* (Norman, Okla.: University of Oklahoma Press, 1987), 46.

19. John D. Unruh, Jr., *The Plains Across: The Overland Emigrants and the Trans-Mississippi West, 1840–60* (Urbana, Ill.: University of Illinois Press, 1978), 185.

20. Robert M. Utley, *The Lance and the Shield: The Life and Times of Sitting Bull,* (New York: Henry Holt & Co., 1993), 45.

21. Black Elk, *Black Elk Speaks* (New York: William Morrow, 1932), 13; John W. G. MacEwan, *Sitting Bull: The Years in Canada* (Edmonton, Alberta: Hurtig Publishers, 1973), 16.

22. Stan Hoig, ed., *The Sand Creek Massacre* (Norman, Okla.: University of Oklahoma Press, 1961), 185–86.

23. Colin G. Calloway, ed., *Our Hearts Fell to the Ground: Plains Indian Views of How the West Was Lost* (New York: St. Martin's Press, 1996), 92.

24. *New York Tribune,* 23 August 1862; Calloway, *Our Hearts Fell to the Ground,* 92.

25. Robert W. Rochmond and Robert W. Mardock, eds., *A Nation Moving West: Readings in the History of the American Frontier* (Lincoln, Nebr.: University of Nebraska Press, 1966), 247.

26. Edward Lazarus, *Black Hills/White Justice: The Sioux Nation Versus the United States, 1775 to the Present* (New York: HarperCollins, 1991), 32.

27. Utley, *The Lance and the Shield,* 51.

28. Black Elk, *Black Elk Speaks,* 79.

29. Stanley Vestal, *Sitting Bull: Champion of the Sioux* (Norman, Okla.: University of Oklahoma Press, 1957), 51–52.

30. Utley, *The Lance and the Shield,* 57.

31. Fanny Kelly, *My Captivity Among the Sioux Indians* (Secaucus, N.J.: Citadel Press, 1973), 106; Utley, *The Lance and the Shield,* 63.

32. Vestal, *Sitting Bull,* 61.

Chapter Four: A Tipi Word

1. Joe De Barthe, *The Life and Adventure of Frank Grouard* (St. Joseph, Mo.: Combe Printing Co., 1894), 387.

2. Louise Barnett, *Touched with Fire: The Life, Death, and Mythic Afterlife of George Armstrong Custer* (New York: Henry Holt, 1996), 114.

3. Ibid., 76.

4. Neil B. Thompson, *Crazy Horse Called Them Walk-a-Heaps: The Story of the Foot Soldiers in the Prairie Indian Wars* (St. Cloud, Minn.: North Star Press, 1979), 113.

5. John C. Ewers, "Intertribal Warfare as a Precursor of Indian-White Warfare on the Northern Great Plains," *The Western Historical Quarterly* VI (October 1975): 409.

6. Thompson, *Crazy Horse Called Them Walk-a-Heaps,* 47.

7. Philippe Régis de Trobriand, *Military Life in Dakota* (St. Paul, Minn.; Alvord Memorial Commission, 1951), 313–14.

8. Ibid., 295.

9. Sherry L. Smith, *The View from Officers' Row: Army Perceptions of Western Indians* (Tucson: University of Arizona Press, 1990), 24.

10. On the use of torture by Indians, see Francis Jennings, *The Invasion of North America* (New York: W. W. Norton & Co., 1976), 160–64; Bill Neeley, *Quanah Parker and His People* (Slaton, Tex.: Brazos Press, 1986), 28–29; T. R. Fehrenbach, *Comanches: The Destruction of a People* (New York: Alfred A. Knopf, 1974), 77; Richard

Irving Dodge, *Our Wild Indians: Thirty-Three Years' Personal Experience Among the Red Men of the Great West* (1882; reprint, New York: Archer House, 1959), 523–29.

11. Stanley Vestal, *New Sources of Indian History 1850–1891* (Norman, Okla.: University of Oklahoma Press, 1934), 156; Thomas B. Marquis, *Wooden Leg: A Warrior Who Fought Custer* (Lincoln, Nebr.: University of Nebraska Press, 1931), 66; Edwin T. Denig, *Five Indian Tribes of the Upper Missouri* (Norman, Okla.: University of Oklahoma Press, 1969), 21.

12. Elizabeth B. Custer, *"Boots and Saddles," or Life in Dakota with General Custer* (New York: Harper & Brothers, 1885), 56.

13. Robert M. Utley, *The Lance and the Shield: The Life and Times of Sitting Bull* (New York: Henry Holt & Co., 1993), 72.

14. *Helena Herald,* 11 April 1867, in Trobriand, *Military Life in Dakota,* 46, n. 30.

15. Dee Brown, *Bury My Heart at Wounded Knee: An Indian History of the American West* (New York: Holt, Rinehart & Winston, 1970), 97.

16. Evan S. Connell, *Son of the Morning Star* (New York: Promontory Press, 1993), 130. Historian Dee Brown believes these mutilations were in imitation of, and revenge for, the horrors of Sand Creek. Perhaps they were, but we have no evidence for this either way. Brown, *Bury My Heart at Wounded Knee,* 137.

17. Trobriand, *Military Life in Dakota,* 17, italics in original; Robert G. Athearn, *William Tecumseh Sherman and the Settlement of the West* (Norman, Okla.: University of Oklahoma Press, 1995), 99.

18. Utley, *The Lance and the Shield,* 80.

19. Utley, *The Lance and the Shield,* 79–80.

20. Stanley Vestal, *Sitting Bull, Champion of the Sioux* (Norman, Okla.: University of Oklahoma Press, 1957), 107–08.

21. Robert M. Utley, *Cavalier in Buckskin: George Armstrong Custer and the Western Military Frontier* (Norman, Okla.: University of Oklahoma Press, 1988), 59, italics in original.

22. Doane Robinson, *A History of the Dakota or Sioux Indians* (1904; reprint, Minneapolis: Rosee & Haines, Inc., 1967), 197.

23. Brown, *Bury My Heart at Wounded Knee,* 188.

24. Milo M. Quaife, ed., *Forty Years a Fur Trader on the Upper Missouri, 1833–1872,* by Charles Larpenteur (Chicago: Lakeside Press, 1933), 359–60. Hardtack was a type of bread baked hard as a dog biscuit. It was a standard part of army rations.

25. Edward Lazarus, *Black Hills/White Justice: The Sioux Nation Versus the United States, 1775 to the Present* (New York: HarperCollins, 1991), 51.

26. Vestal, *Sitting Bull,* 120.

27. William Tecumseh Sherman, *Memoirs of General W. T. Sherman* (New York: Library of America, 1990), 601.

28. Philip Weeks, ed., *The American Indian Experience: A Profile, 1524 to the Present* (Arlington Heights, Ill.: Forum Press, 1975), 144–45.

29. Vestal, *Sitting Bull,* 94.

30. Ibid., 95.

31. Anthony McGinnis, *Intertribal Warfare on the Northern Plains, 1738–1889* (Evergreen, Colo.: Cordillera Press, 1990), 82–83.

32. Vestal, *New Sources of Indian History,* 177.

33. Utley, *Cavalier in Buckskin,* 112.

34. Ibid., 36.

35. James Welch, *Killing Custer: The Battle of the Little Big Horn and the Fate of the Plains Indians* (New York: W. W. Norton, 1994), 57.

36. Custer, *"Boots and Saddles,"* 5.

37. Ibid., 234.

38. Welch, *Killing Custer,* 59.

39. Utley, *Cavalier in Buckskin,* 120.

40. Vestal, *Sitting Bull,* 127.

41. Ibid.

42. Ibid.

43. Ibid., 128.

44. Ibid., 129.

45. Ibid.

46. Ibid.

47. Watson Parker, *Gold in the Black Hills* (Norman, Okla.: University of Oklahoma Press, 1966), 39.

Chapter Five: War for the Black Hills

1. Black Elk, *Black Elk Speaks* (New York: William Morrow, 1932), 79.

2. Lazarus, *Black Hills/White Justice: The Sioux Nation Versus the United States, 1775 to the Present* (New York: HarperCollins, 1991), 73.

3. Marie Sandoz, *Crazy Horse: The Strange Man of the Oglalas* (Lincoln, Nebr.: University of Nebraska Press, 1961), 287.

4. Lazarus, *Black Hills/White Justice*, 73; Harold E. Briggs, "The Black Hills Gold Rush," *North Dakota Historical Quarterly* V (1931): 77.

5. Stephen E. Ambrose, *Crazy Horse and Custer: The Parallel Lives of Two American Warriors* (Garden City, N.Y.: Doubleday & Co., 1975), 377.

6. Donald Jackson, *Custer's Gold: The United States Cavalry Expedition of 1874* (New Haven: Yale University Press, 1966), 76.

7. Doane Robinson, *A History of the Dakota or Sioux Indians* (1904; reprint, Minneapolis: Rosee & Haines, Inc., 1967), 408.

8. John F. Reiger, ed., *The Passing of the Great West: Selected Papers of George Bird Grinnell* (New York: Winchester Press, 1972), 106.

9. Robinson, *A History of the Dakota or Sioux Indians*, 413.

10. Donald Jackson, *Custer's Gold: The United States Cavalry Expedition of 1874* (New Haven, Conn.: Yale University Press, 1966), 89–90.

11. Watson Parker, *Gold in the Black Hills* (Norman, Okla.: University of Oklahoma Press, 1966), 141.

12. Lazarus, *Black Hills/White Justice*, 79.

13. Evan S. Connell, *Son of the Morning Star* (New York: Promontory Press, 1993), 241.

14. Alvin M. Josephy, Jr. *The Patriot Chiefs* (New York: Penguin Books, 1980), 293–94; James Welch, *Killing Custer: The Battle of Little Big Horn and the Fate of the Plains Indians* (New York: W. W. Norton, 1994), 89.

15. Stanley Vestal, *Sitting Bull: Champion of the Sioux* (Norman, Okla.: University of Oklahoma Press, 1957), 133.

16. Lazarus, *Black Hills/White Justice*, 81; see also George E. Hyde, *Spotted Tail's Folk: A History of the Brulé Sioux* (Norman, Okla.: University of Oklahoma Press, 1976), 236–37.

17. Ambrose, *Crazy Horse and Custer*, 396.

18. P. E. Byrne, "The Custer Myth," *North Dakota Historical Quarterly* VI (1932): 190.

19. Vestal, *Sitting Bull*, 139–40.

20. George Crook, *Address to the Graduates of the United States Military Academy, West Point, New York, Class 1884*. West Point: West Point: U.S. Military Academy, 1884. n.p.

21. John G. Bourke, *On the Border with Crook* (New York: Charles Scribner's Sons, 1891), 262.

22. John S. Gray, *Centennial Campaign: The Sioux War of 1876* (Fort Collins, Colo.: Old Army Press, 1976), 48.

23. Thomas B. Marquis, *Wooden Leg: A Warrior Who Fought Custer* (Lincoln, Nebr.: University of Nebraska Press, 1931), 171–72.

24. Vestal, *Sitting Bull*, 141.

25. Ibid.

26. Col. W. A. Graham, ed., *The Custer Myth: A Source Book of Custeriana* (New York: Bonanza Books, 1953), 79–81.

27. Vestal, *Sitting Bull*, 144.

28. Ibid.

29. Robert M. Utley, *The Lance and the Shield: The Life and Times of Sitting Bull* (New York: Henry Holt & Co., 1993), 136.

30. Utley, *The Lance and the Shield*, 137–38.

31. Vestal, *Sitting Bull*, 150–51.

32. Graham, *The Custer Myth*, 81.

33. John F. Finerty, *War-Path and Bivouac: or, The Conquest of the Sioux* (Norman: University of Oklahoma Press, 1961), 67–68.

34. Vestal, *Sitting Bull*, 153.

35. Finerty, *War-Path and Bivouac*, 121.

Chapter Six: SOLDIERS FALLING INTO CAMP

1. Elizabeth B. Custer, *"Boots and Saddles," or Life in Dakota with General Custer* (New York: Harper & Brothers, 1885), 218, 220.

2. Stephen E. Ambrose, *Crazy Horse and Custer: The Parallel Lives of Two American Warriors* (Garden City, N.Y.: Doubleday & Co., 1975), 427.

3. O. G. Libby, ed., "The Arikara Narrative of the Campaign Against the Hostile Dakotas, June 1876," *North Dakota State Historical Society Collections* 6 (1920): 75–80.

4. Robert M. Utley, *Cavalier in Buckskin: George Armstrong Custer and the Western Military Frontier* (Norman, Okla.: University of Oklahoma Press, 1988), 65.

5. Stanley Vestal, *Sitting Bull: Champion of the Sioux* (Norman, Okla.: University of Oklahoma Press, 1957), 158: Robert M. Utley, *The Lance and the Shield: The Life and Times of Sitting Bull* (New York: Henry Holt & Co., 1993), 144.

6. John S. Gray, *Centennial Campaign: The Sioux War of 1876* (Fort Collins, Colo.: Old Army Press, 1976), 165.

7. David Humphreys Miller, *Custer's Fall. The Indian Side of the Story* (Lincoln, Nebr.: University of Nebraska Press, 1985), 8.

8. Charles K. Mills, *Harvest of Barren Regrets: The Army Career of Frederick William Benteen, 1834–1898* (Glendale, Calif.: Arthur H. Clark Co., 1985), 247–48.

9. Miller, *Custer's Fall*, 16.

10. Ibid., 44–45.

11. Evan S. Connell, *Son of the Morning Star* (New York: Promontory Press, 1993), 270.

12. Ibid., 21.

13. Ibid., 81.

14. Black Elk, *Black Elk Speaks* (New York: William Morrow, 1932), 109.

15. James McLaughlin, *My Friend the Indian* (Lincoln, Nebr.: University of Nebraska Press, 1989), 169; Thomas B. Marquis, *She Watched Custer's Last Battle* (Scottsdale, Ariz.: Cactus Pony Press, 1933).

16. Utley, *The Lance and the Shield*, 148; Col. W. A. Graham, ed., *The Custer Myth: Source Book of Custeriana* (New York: Bonanza Books, 1953), 90.

17. Utley, *The Lance and the Shield*, 150.

18. Utley, *The Lance and the Shield*, 150.

19. Miller, *Custer's Fall*, 92.

20. P. E. Byrne, "The Custer Myth," *North Dakota Historical Quarterly* VI (1932): 193.

21. Thomas B. Marquis, *Save the Last Bullet for Yourself: The True Story of Custer's Last Stand* (New York: Two Continents Publishing Group, 1976), 110.

22. Miller, *Custer's Fall*, 102.

23. Black Elk, *Black Elk Speaks*, 111.

24. James Welch, *Killing Custer: The Battle of Little Big Horn and the Fate of the Plains Indians* (New York: W. W. Norton, 1994), 161.

25. Thomas B. Marquis, *Wooden Leg: A*

Warrior Who Fought Custer (Lincoln, Nebr.: University of Nebraska Press, 1931), 221.

26. Black Elk, *Black Elk Speaks*, 112–13.

27. Vestal, *Sitting Bull*, 165.

28. Miller, *Custer's Fall*, 119.

29. Utley, *The Lance and the Shield*, 154.

30. Graham, *Custer Myth*, 18.

31. Their names were Roan Bear, White Cow Bull, Bobtail Horse, Calf, and White Shield.

32. Utley, *The Lance and the Shield*, 156–57.

33. Marquis, *She Watched Custer's Last Battle.*

34. Frazier Hunt and Robert Hunt. *I Fought with Custer: The Story of Sergeant Windolph, Last Survivor of the Battle of the Little Bighorn* (New York: Scribner's, 1947), 102–103.

35. Vestal, *Sitting Bull*, 174.

36. Black Elk, *Black Elk Speaks*, 118.

37. Utley, *The Lance and the Shield*, 160.

38. Hunt and Hunt, *I Fought with Custer*, 106.

39. P. E. Byrne, *Soldiers of the Plains* (New York: Minto, Balch & Co., 1926), 119.

40. Barnett, *Touched with Fire: The Life, Death, and Mythic Afterlife of George Armstrong Custer* (New York: Henry Holt, 1996), 299.

41. Graham, *Custer Myth*, 376–77.

42. Connell, *Son of the Morning Star*, 325.

43. Robert M. Utley, *Custer and the Great Controversy: The Origin and Development of a Legend* (Los Angeles: Westernlore Press, 1962), 37.

44. Ibid., 120.

45. Utley, *Cavalier in Buckskin: George Armstrong Custer and the Western Military Frontier* (Norman, Okla.: University of Oklahoma Press, 1988), 5–6.

46. Connell, *Son of the Morning Star*, 281.

47. E. A. Brininstool, *The Custer Fight: Capt. Benteen's Story of the Battle of the Little Big Horn* (Hollywood, Calif.: E. A. Brininstool, 1933), 85.

48. Joseph Manzione, *I Am Looking North for My Life: Sitting Bull, 1876–1881* (Salt Lake City: University of Utah Press, 1991), 17; Watson Parker, *Gold in the Black Hills* (Norman, Okla.: University of Oklahoma Press, 1966), 123; Lazarus, *Black Hills/White Justice: The Sioux Nation Versus the United States, 1775 to the Present* (New York: HarperCollins, 1991), 89.

Chapter Seven: A Hard Time

1. Roy Morris, Jr., *Sheridan: The Life and Wars of General Phil Sheridan* (New York: Crown Publishers, 1992), 328.

2. Robert M. Utley, *The Lance and the Shield: The Life and Times of Sitting Bull* (New York: Henry Holt & Co., 1993), 166. Historians are unsure of the boy's name.

3. Stanley Vestal, *Sitting Bull: Champion of the Sioux* (Norman, Okla.: University of Oklahoma Press, 1957), 187–88.

4. Ibid., 188–89.

5. John F. Finerty, *War-Path and Bivouac: or, The Conquest of the Sioux* (Norman, Okla.: University of Oklahoma Press, 1961), 212.

6. U.S. Commissioner of Indian Affairs, *Annual Report, 1876*, 336–37.

7. Vestal, *Sitting Bull*, 191.

8. Nelson A. Miles, *The Personal Recollections and Observations of General Nelson A. Miles* (Chicago: The Werner Company, 1897), 226.

9. Miles, *Personal Recollections*, 226.

10. Ibid., 207.

11. Black Elk, *Black Elk Speaks* (New York: William Morrow, 1932), 134.

12. Marie Sandoz, *Crazy Horse: The Strange Man of the Oglalas* (Lincoln, Nebr.: University of Nebraska Press, 1961), 346. The "Strange Man" was Crazy Horse himself.

13. Utley, *The Lance and the Shield*, 186.

14. MacEwan, *Sitting Bull: The Years in Canada* (Edmonton, Alberta: Hurtig Publishers, 1973), 80; C. F. Turner, *Across the Medicine Line* (Toronto: McClelland & Stewart, 1973), 64–65.

15. Turner, *Across the Medicine Line*, 211.

16. MacEwan, *Sitting Bull*, 87.

17. Turner, *Across the Medicine Line*, 79–81.

18. Ibid., 106–107.

19. Vestal, *Sitting Bull*, 208.

20. Gary Pennanen, "Sitting Bull: Indian Without a Country," *Canadian Historical Review* 51 (June 1970): 123; MacEwan, *Sitting Bull*, 21.

21. Black Elk, *Black Elk Speaks*, 147.

22. Utley, *The Lance and the Shield*, 193.

23. Vestal, *New Sources of Indian History: 1850–1891* (Norman, Okla.: University of Oklahoma Press, 1934), 242; Colin Taylor, *Warriors of the Plains* (New York, Arco Publishing, 1975), 120.

24. Turner, *Across the Medicine Line*, 124.

25. U.S. Commissioner of Indian Affairs, *Annual Report, 1877*, 722–30.

26. Vestal, *Sitting Bull*, 216–17.

27. Turner, *Across the Medicine Line*, 133.

28. Don Russell, *The Lives and Legends of Buffalo Bill* (Norman, Okla.: University of Oklahoma Press, 1960), 90.

29. DeBenneville Randolph Keim, *The Lives and Legends of Buffalo Bill* (Norman, Okla.: University of Oklahoma Press, 1960), 38–40; originally published in 1870.

30. Wayne Gard, *The Great Buffalo Hunt* (New York: Alfred A. Knopf, 1960), 97.

31. Ibid., 127–30.

32. Richard Irving Dodge, *The Plains of the Great West and Their Inhabitants* (New York: Archer House, 1959), 133.

33. E. Douglas Branch, *The Hunting of the Buffalo* (Lincoln, Nebr.: University of Nebraska Press, 1962), 181.

34. John R. Cook, *The Border and the Buffalo* (New York: Citadel Press, 1969), 163–64.

35. Archibald Oswald MacRae, *History of the Province of Alberta*, 2 vols. (Calgary, Alberta: Western Canada History Co., 1912), I, 377. By 1889, only 1,091 buffalo remained alive in the United States. At that point, conservationists mounted an all-out campaign to save it from extinction. Finally the American Bison Society, founded in 1905 with President Theodore Roosevelt as its honorary president, got Congress to establish the National Bison Range in western Montana. Today there are nearly 200,000 of these magnificent animals in the United States and Canada. They are increasing so rapidly that hunting is necessary to keep the herds in balance with their food supply. Ranchers raise them instead of cattle, and restaurants serve "buffalo burgers."

36. W. A. Graham, *The Custer Myth: A Source Book of Custeriana* (New York: Bonanza Books, 1953), 67.

37. Utley, *The Lance and the Shield*, 207.

38. Turner, *Across the Medicine Line*, 199–202; MacEwan, *Sitting Bull*, 148–50.

39. MacEwan, *Sitting Bull*, 160–61.

40. Turner, *Across the Medicine Line*, 215; MacEwan, *Sitting Bull*, 118.

Chapter Eight: AFTER THE BUFFALO WENT AWAY

1. Robert M. Utley, *The Lance and the Shield: The Life and Times of Sitting Bull* (New York: Henry Holt & Co., 1993), 232.
2. John C. Ewers, "Intertribal Warfare as a Precursor of Indian-White Warfare on the Northern Plains," *The Western Historical Quarterly* VI (October 1975), 176.
3. Stanley Vestal, *New Sources of Indian History: 1850–1891* (Norman, Okla.: University of Oklahoma Press, 1934), 284.
4. Black Elk, *Black Elk Speaks* (New York: William Morrow), 10.
5. Vestal, *New Sources of Indian History*, 288.
6. Barnett, *Touched with Fire: The Life, Death, and Mythic Afterlife of George Custer Armstrong* (New York: Henry Holt, 1996), 117. The idea that Native Americans had no rights became the law of the land. In 1903, the U.S. Supreme Court ruled they had no rights that Congress was bound to respect and that Congress had unlimited power over the tribes. In other words, the government could violate its own treaties and Congress could do whatever it pleased with Native American lands. See Blue Clark, *Lone Wolf v. Hitchcock: Treaty Rights and Indian Law to the End of the Nineteenth Century* (Lincoln, Nebr.: University of Nebraska Press, 1994).
7. Utley, *The Lance and the Shield*, 249; Vestal, *New Sources of Indian History*, 308.
8. Stanley Vestal, *Sitting Bull: Champion of the Sioux* (Norman, Okla.: University of Oklahoma Press, 1957), 232.
9. Robert M. Utley, *The Last Days of the Sioux Nation* (New Haven: Yale University Press, 1963), 133.
10. Ibid., 35.
11. William T. Hagan, *United States–Comanche Relations: The Reservation Years* (New Haven: Yale University Press, 1976), 162.
12. Philip Weeks, ed., *Farewell, My Nation: The American Indian and the United States, 1820–1890* (Arlington Heights, Ill: Harlan Davidson, 1990), 223.
13. Ibid., 223–26; David Wallace Adams, "From Bullets to Boarding Schools: The Educational Assault on the American Indian Identity," in *The American Indian Experience: A Profile, 1524 to the Present*, ed. Philip Weeks (Arlington Heights, Ill.: Forum Press, 1975), 218–39, 282.
14. Utley, *The Lance and the Shield*, 269.
15. Vestal, *Sitting Bull*, 256; Usher L. Burdick, *The Last Days of Sitting Bull* (Baltimore: Wirth Brothers, 1941), 21; Vestal, *New Sources of Indian History*, 282–83; Gary C. Anderson, *Sitting Bull and the Paradox of Lakota Nationhead* (New York: HarperCollins, 1996), 147.
16. Vestal, *New Sources of Indian History*, 273–74.
17. "A Group of Howling Savages Pursue a Defenseless Stage Coach," *Washington Post*, 24 June 1885.
18. Anderson, *Sitting Bull*, 143.
19. Vestal, *Sitting Bull*, 250–51.
20. The General Allotment Act cost Native Americans dearly. The Lakota immediately lost 11 million acres of prime grazing land. By 1934, when Congress repealed the act, all the western tribes had lost 102 million acres of land, or about half their original holdings. Arrell Morgan Gibson, *The American Indian: Prehistory to the Present* (Lexington, Mass.: D.C. Heath, 1980), 506.
21. James Mooney, "The Ghost Dance Religion and the Sioux Outbreak of 1890," *14th Annual Report of the Bureau of American Ethnology, 1892–1893, Part 2* (Washington, D.C.: U.S. Government Printing Office, 1896), 781.
22. Ibid., 977.
23. David Humphreys Miller, *Ghost Dance* (New York: Duell, Sloan, and Pearce, 1959), 102.
24. Elmo Scott Watson, "The Last Indian War, 1890–91—A Study of Newspaper Jingoism," *Journalism Quarterly* 20 (1943): 210.
25. Watson, "The Last Indian War," 208, 210; Rex Alan Smith, *Moon of the Popping Trees: The Tragedy at Wounded Knee and the End of the Indian Wars* (Lincoln, Nebr.: University of Nebraska Press, 1981), 137; Miller, *Ghost Dance*, 140.
26. *Chicago Daily Tribune*, 16 November 1890.
27. Utley, *Last Days of the Sioux Nation*, 107.
28. Utley, *The Lance and the Shield*, 285; Vestal, *Sitting Bull*, 272; McLaughlin, *My Friend the Indian* (1910; reprint, Lincoln, Nebr.: University of Nebraska Press, 1989), 191.
29. Utley, *The Lance and the Shield*, 290.
30. Vestal, *Sitting Bull*, 281.
31. Ibid.
32. Ibid., 280.
33. Utley, *The Lance and the Shield*, 298.
34. Utley, *Last Days of the Sioux Nation*, 155.
35. John M. Carroll, ed. *The Arrest and Killing of Sitting Bull* (Glendale, Calif.: The Arthur H. Clark Co., 1986), 81.
36. I have based my description of Sitting Bull's death on these sources: Vestal, *Sitting Bull*, 293–307; Utley, *The Lance and the Shield*, 291–307; Carroll, *The Arrest and Killing of Sitting Bull* (Glendale, Calif.: Arthur H. Clark Co., 1986).
37. C. F. Turner, *Across the Medicine Line* (Toronto: McClelland & Stewart, 1973), 263.
38. Ibid., 260–63.
39. Vestal, *Sitting Bull*, 293.

Postscript: DEATH OF A DREAM

1. David Humphreys Miller, *Ghost Dance* (New York: Duell, Sloan, and Pearce, 1959), 214.
2. Rex Alan Smith, *Moon of the Popping Trees: The Tragedy of Wounded Knee and the End of the Indian Wars* (Lincoln, Nebr., University of Nebraska Press, 1981), 184.
3. Ibid., 186.
4. Ibid., 187.
5. Robert M. Utley, *Last Days of the Sioux Nation* (New Haven, Conn.: Yale University Press, 1963), 212.
6. Smith, *Moon of the Popping Trees*, 190.
7. Ibid.
8. Miller, *Ghost Dance*, 234.
9. Utley, *Last Days of the Sioux Nation*, 217; Smith, *Moon of the Popping Trees*, 192–95.
10. Black Elk, *Black Elk Speaks* (New York: William Morrow, 1932), 260, 265–66.
11. Charles A. Eastman, *From the Deep Woods to Civilization* (Boston: Little, Brown, 1929), 112.
12. Smith, *Moon of the Popping Trees*, 200. Wovoka died in 1932 at the age of seventy-eight.

Some More Books to Read

Adams, Alexander B. *Sitting Bull: An Epic of the Plains.* New York: G. P. Putnam's Sons, 1973.

Adams, David Wallace. "From Bullets to Boarding Schools: The Educational Assault on the American Indian Identity." In *The American Indian Experience,* edited by Philip Weeks. New York: Facts on File, 1997, pp. 218–39.

Allison, Edwin H. "Surrender of Sitting Bull," *South Dakota Historical Collections* 6 (1912): 231–70.

Ambrose, Stephen E. *Crazy Horse and Custer: The Parallel Lives of Two American Warriors.* Garden City, N.Y.: Doubleday & Co., 1975.

Anderson, Gary C. *Sitting Bull and the Paradox of Lakota Nationhood.* New York: HarperCollins, 1996.

Athearn, Robert G. *William Tecumseh Sherman and the Settlement of the West.* Norman, Okla.: University of Oklahoma Press, 1995.

Audubon, Maria R., ed. *Audubon and His Journals.* 2 vols. New York: Dover Publications, 1968. Reprint of a book first published in 1897.

Axelrod, Alan. *Chronicle of the Indian Wars: From Colonial Times to Wounded Knee.* New York: Prentice Hall, 1993.

Axtell, James. "Scalping: The Ethnohistory of a Moral Question." In *The European and the Indian: Essays in the Ethnohistory of Colonial North America,* edited by James Axtell. New York: Oxford University Press, 1981, pp. 207–41.

Barnett, Louise. *Touched with Fire: The Life, Death, and Mythic Afterlife of George Armstrong Custer.* New York: Henry Holt, 1996.

Barry, David E. *Indian Notes on the Custer Battle.* Baltimore: Proof Press, 1937.

Bell, Gordon and Beth L. "General Custer in North Dakota." *North Dakota History* 32 (1964): 101–13.

Black Elk. *Black Elk Speaks.* New York: William Morrow, 1932.

Blish, Helen H. *A Pictographic History of the Oglala Sioux.* Lincoln, Nebr.: University of Nebraska Press, 1967.

Bourke, John G. *On the Border with Crook.* New York: Charles Scribner's Sons, 1891.

Boyes, William. *Custer's Black White Man.* Washington, D.C.: South Capitol Press, 1972.

Branch, E. Douglas. *The Hunting of the Buffalo.* Lincoln, Nebr.: University of Nebraska Press, 1962.

Briggs, Harold E. "The Black Hills Gold Rush." *North Dakota Historical Quarterly* V (1931): 71–99.

Brininstool, E.A. *The Custer Fight: Capt. Benteen's Story of the Battle of the Little Big Horn.* Hollywood, Calif.: E. A. Brininstool, 1933.

Brown, Dee. *Bury My Heart at Wounded Knee: An Indian History of the American West.* New York: Holt, Rinehart & Winston, 1970.

Burdick, Usher L. *The Last Days of Sitting Bull.* Baltimore: Wirth Brothers, 1941.

Byrne, P. E. "The Custer Myth." *North Dakota Historical Quarterly* VI (1932): 187–200.

———. *Soldiers of the Plains.* New York: Minto, Balch & Co., 1926.

Calloway, Colin G., ed. *Our Hearts Fell to the Ground: Plains Indian Views of How the West Was Lost.* New York: St. Martin's Press, 1996.

Carroll, John M., ed. *The Arrest and Killing of Sitting Bull.* Glendale, Calif.: Arthur H. Clark Co., 1986.

———, ed. *The Benteen-Goldin Letters on Custer and His Last Battle.* New York: Liveright, 1974.

————, ed. *Camp Talk: The Very Private Letters of Frederick W. Benteen of the Seventh U.S. Cavalry to His Wife, 1871 to 1888.* Bryan, Tex.: J. M. Carroll Co., 1983.

Catlin, George. *Letters and Notes on the Manners, Customs, and Conditions of the North American Indians.* 2 vols. New York: Dover, 1973.

Connell, Evan S. *Son of the Morning Star.* New York: Promontory Press, 1993.

Coffman, Edward M. *The Old Army: A Portrait of the American Army in Peacetime, 1784–1898.* New York: Oxford University Press, 1986.

Cook, John R. *The Border and the Buffalo.* New York: Citadel Press, 1969. Reprint of a book first published in 1907.

Crook, George. *Address to the Graduates of the United States Military Academy, West Point, New York, Class 1884.* West Point, N.Y.: U.S. Military Academy, 1884.

Custer, Elizabeth B. *"Boots and Saddles," or Life in Dakota with General Custer.* New York: Harper & Brothers, 1885.

————. *Following the Guidon.* Norman, Okla.: University of Oklahoma Press, 1966.

Custer, George A. *My Life on the Plains.* Edited by Milo M. Quaife. Lincoln, Nebr.: University of Nebraska Press, 1966.

De Barthe, Joe. *The Life and Adventures of Frank Grouard, Chief of Scouts, U.S.A.* St. Joseph, Mo.: Combe Printing Co., 1894.

Denig, Edwin T. *Indian Tribes of the Upper Missouri.* Washington, D.C.: Smithsonian Institution, Bureau of American Ethnology, Annual Report 46, 1930, 377–628. From a manuscript prepared in 1854.

————. *Five Indian Tribes of the Upper Missouri.* Norman, Okla.: University of Oklahoma Press, 1969.

Densmore, Frances. *Teton Sioux Music.* Washington, D.C.: Smithsonian Institution, Bureau of American Ethnology, Bulletin 61, 1918.

Diessner, Don. *There Are No Indians Left But Me! Sitting Bull's Story.* El Segundo, Calif.: Upton & Sons, 1993.

Dobie, J. Frank. "Indian Horses and Horsemanship." *Southwest Review* XXXV (1950): 265–75.

Dodge, Richard Irving. *Our Wild Indians: Thirty-Three Years' Personal Experience Among the Red Men of the Great West.* New York: Archer House, 1959. Reprint of a book first published in 1882.

————. *The Plains of the Great West and Their Inhabitants.* New York: Archer House, 1959. Reprint of a classic work that first appeared in 1877.

Downey, Fairfax. *Indian-Fighting Army.* New York: Scribner's, 1941.

Dunlay, Thomas W. *Wolves of the Blue Soldiers: Indian Scouts and Auxiliaries with the United States Army, 1860–90.* Lincoln, Nebr.: University of Nebraska Press, 1982.

Eastman, Charles A. *From the Deep Woods to Civilization.* Boston: Little, Brown, 1929.

Erikson, Erik H. "Observations of Sioux Education," *The Journal of Psychology* VII (1939): 101–56.

Ewers, John C. *Indian Life on the Upper Missouri.* Norman, Okla.: University of Oklahoma Press, 1968.

————. "Intertribal Warfare as a Precursor of Indian-White Warfare on the Northern Great Plains," *The Western Historical Quarterly* VI (October 1975), 397–410.

Finerty, John F. *War-Path and Bivouac: or, The Conquest of the Sioux.* Norman, Okla.: University of Oklahoma Press, 1961.

Fiske, Frank B. *Life and Death of Sitting Bull.* Fort Yates, N. Dak.: Pioneer-Arrow Print, 1933.

Forsyth, George A. *The Story of the Soldier.* New York: D. Appleton & Co., 1900.

Fougera, Katherine Gibson. *With Custer's Cavalry: From the Memoirs of the Late Katherine Gibson, Widow of Captain Francis M. Gibson of the Seventh Cavalry.* Lincoln, Nebr.: University of Nebraska Press, 1986. Reprint of a book first published in 1940.

Fox, Richard Allan, Jr., "A New View of Custer's Last Battle." *American History Illustrated* (September/October 1993): 30–37, 64–66.

Gard, Wayne. *The Great Buffalo Hunt.* New York: Alfred A. Knopf, 1960.

Garretson, Martin S. *The American Bison.* New York: New York Zoological Society, 1938.

Gibson, Arrell Morgan. *The American Indian: Prehistory to the Present.* Lexington, Mass.: D. C. Heath, 1980.

Goodrich, Thomas. *Scalp Dance: Indian Warfare on the High Plains, 1865–1879.* Mechanicsburg, Pa.: Stackpole, 1997.

Graham, Col. W. A., ed. *The Custer Myth: A Source Book of Custeriana.* New York: Bonanza Books, 1953.

———. *The Story of the Little Big Horn: Custer's Last Fight.* Lincoln, Nebr.: University of Nebraska Press, 1988 [first published in 1926].

Gray, John S. *Centennial Campaign: The Sioux War of 1876.* Fort Collins, Colo.: Old Army Press, 1976.

Greene, Jerome A., ed. *Battles and Skirmishes of the Great Sioux War. 1876–1877: The Military View.* Norman, Okla.: University of Oklahoma Press, 1993.

———. *Lakota and Cheyenne: Indian Views of the Great Sioux War, 1876–1877.* Norman, Okla.: University of Oklahoma Press, 1993.

Grinnell, George Bird. "Coup and Scalping Among the Plains Indians," *American Anthropologist* XII (1910): 296–310.

———. *The Fighting Cheyennes,* Williamstown, Mass.: Corner House Publishers, 1976. Reprint of a book first published in 1915.

Hafen, LeRoy R., and Francis M. Young. *Fort Laramie and the Pageant of the West, 1834–1900.* Glendale, Calif.: Arthur M. Clark Co., 1938.

Hagan, William T. "Reformers' Images of the Native Americans: The Late Nineteenth Century." In *The American Indian Experience,* edited by Philip Weeks. New York: Facts on File, 1997, pp. 207–17.

Hardorff, Richard G. *Hookahey! A Good Day to Die! The Indian Casualties of the Custer Fight.* Spokane, Wash.: Arthur H. Clark Co., 1993.

———, ed. *Lakota Recollections of the Custer Fight.* Spokane, Wash.: Arthur H. Clark Co., 1991.

Harris, Francis. *The Buffalo.* Norman, Okla.: University of Oklahoma Press, 1995.

Hassrick, Royal B. *The Sioux: Life and Customs of a Warrior Society.* Norman, Okla.: University of Oklahoma Press, 1964.

Herr, Major General John K., and Edward S. Wallace. *The Story of the United States Cavalry, 1775–1942.* Boston: Little, Brown, 1953.

Hoebel, E. Adamson. *The Cheyennes: Indians of the Great Plains.* New York: Holt, Rinehart & Winston, 1960.

Hunt, Frazier, and Robert Hunt. *I Fought with Custer: The Story of Sergeant Windolph, Last Survivor of the Battle of the Little Bighorn.* New York: Scribner's, 1947.

Hutton, Paul H., ed. *The Custer Reader.* Lincoln, Nebr.: University of Nebraska Press, 1992.

———. *Phil Sheridan and His Army.* Lincoln, Nebr.: University of Nebraska Press, 1985.

Hyde, George E. *Red Cloud's Folk: A History of the Oglala Sioux Indians.* Norman, Okla.: University of Oklahoma Press, 1974.

———. *Spotted Tail's Folk: A History of the Brulé Sioux.* Norman, Okla.: University of Oklahoma Press, 1976.

Innis, Ben. *Bloody Knife!* Fort Collins, Colo.: Old Army Press, 1973.

Jackson, Donald. *Custer's Gold: The United States Cavalry Expedition of 1874.* New Haven, Conn.: Yale University Press, 1966.

Jeffrey, Julie Roy. *Frontier Women: The Trans-Mississippi West, 1849–1880.* New York: Hill and Wang, 1979.

Keim, DeBenneville Randolph. *Sheridan's Troopers on the Borders: A Winter Campaign on the Plains.* Lincoln, Nebr.: University of Nebraska Press, 1985 [first published in 1870].

Kelly, Fanny. *My Captivity Among the Sioux Indians.* Secaucus, N.J.: Citadel Press, 1973.

Larsen, Arthur J., ed. "The Black Hills Gold Rush: Letters from the Men Who Participated." *North Dakota Historical Quarterly* VI (1932): 302–18.

Laubin, Reginald, and Gladys Laubin. *The Indian Tipi: Its History, Construction, and Use.* Norman, Okla.: University of Oklahoma Press, 1977.

———. *Indian Dances of North America.* Norman, Okla.: University of Oklahoma Press, 1977.

Lavender, David. *Let Me Be Free: The Nez Percé Tragedy.* New York: Doubleday, 1992.

Lazarus, Edward. *Black Hills/White Justice: The Sioux Nation Versus the United States, 1775 to the Present.* New York: HarperCollins, 1991.

Libby, O.G., ed. "The Arikara Narrative of the Campaign Against the Hostile Dakotas, June 1876," *North Dakota State Historical Society Collections* 6 (1920): 75–80.

Linderman, Frank B. *Plenty Coups: Chief of the Crows.* Lincoln, Nebr.: University of Nebraska Press, 1962.

Lowie, Robert H. *Indians of the Plains.* Lincoln, Nebr.: University of Nebraska Press, 1982.

Luther Standing Bear. *Land of the Spotted Eagle.* Lincoln, Nebr.: University of Nebraska Press, 1960.

———. *My People the Sioux.* Lincoln, Nebr.: University of Nebraska Press, 1975. Reprint of a book first published in 1928.

MacEwan, John W. G. *Sitting Bull: The Years in Canada.* Edmonton, Alberta: Hurtig Publishers, 1973.

McFarling, Lloyd. *Exploring the Northern Plains, 1804–1876.* Caldwell, Idaho: Caxton Printers, 1955.

McGinnis, Anthony. "A Contest of Wits and Daring: Plains Indians at War with the U.S. Army." *North Dakota History: Journal of the Northern Plains,* 48 (Spring 1981): 24–32.

———. *Intertribal Warfare on the Northern Plains. 1738–1889.* Evergreen, Colo.: Cordillera Press, 1990.

McGregor, James H. *The Wounded Knee Massacre from the Viewpoint of the Sioux.* Baltimore: Wirth Brothers, 1940.

McHugh, Tom. *The Time of the Buffalo.* New York: Alfred A. Knopf, 1972.

McLaughlin, James. *My Friend the Indian.* Lincoln, Nebr.: University of Nebraska Press, 1989. Reprint of a book first published in 1910.

MacRae, Archibald Oswald. *History of the Province of Alberta.* 2 vols. Calgary, Alberta: Western Canada History Co., 1912.

Mails, Thomas E. *The Mystic Warriors of the Plains.* Garden City, N.Y.: Doubleday, 1972.

Manzione, Joseph. *I Am Looking North for My Life: Sitting Bull, 1876–1881.* Salt Lake City: University of Utah Press, 1991.

Marquis, Thomas B. *Save the Last Bullet for Yourself: The True Story of Custer's Last Stand.* New York: Two Continents Publishing Group, 1976.

———. *She Watched Custer's Last Battle.* Scottsdale, Ariz.: Cactus Pony Press, 1933.

———. *Wooden Leg: A Warrior Who Fought Custer.* Lincoln, Nebr.: University of Nebraska Press, 1931.

Mattison, Ray H. *The Army Post on the Northern Plains, 1865–1885.* Gering, Nebr.: 1982.

Mayer, Frank H., and Roth, Charles B. *The Buffalo Harvest.* Denver: Sage Books, 1958.

Mekeel, Scudder. "A Short History of the Teton-Dakota." *North Dakota Historical Quarterly* X (1943): 137–205.

Merington, Marguerite, ed. *The Custer Story: The Life and Intimate Letters of General Custer and His Wife Elizabeth.* New York: Devin-Adair, 1950.

Meyers, Augustus. "Dakota in the Fifties." *South Dakota Historical Collections* 10 (1920): 130–94.

Miles, Nelson A. *Personal Recollections and Observations of General Nelson A. Miles.* Chicago: Werner Co., 1896.

Miller, David Humphreys. *Custer's Fall: The Indian Side of the Story.* Lincoln, Nebr.: University of Nebraska Press, 1985.

———. *Ghost Dance.* New York: Duell, Sloan, and Pearce, 1959.

Mills, Charles K. *Harvest of Barren Regrets: The Army Career of Frederick William Benteen, 1834–1898.* Glendale, Calif.: Arthur H. Clark Co., 1985.

Milner, Clyde A., et al., eds. *The Oxford History of the American West.* New York: Oxford University Press, 1994.

Mooney, James. "The Ghost Dance Religion and the Sioux Outbreak of 1890." *14th Annual Report of the Bureau of American Ethnology, 1892–1893, Part 2.* Washington, D.C.: U.S. Government Printing Office, 1896.

Mooney, Michael M., ed. *George Catlin: Letters and Notes on the North American Indians.* New York: Gramercy Books, 1995.

Morris, Roy, Jr. *Sheridan: The Life and Wars of General Phil Sheridan.* New York: Crown Publishers, 1992.

Murray, K. D. Iain. "Who Started Scalping?" *The West* (July 1964): 30–31, 54.

Myres, Sandra L. *Westering Women and the Frontier Experience, 1800–1915.* Albuquerque: University of New Mexico Press, 1982.

Nadeau, Remi. *Fort Laramie and the Sioux Indians.* Englewood Cliffs, N.J.: Prentice-Hall, 1967.

Nelson, Bruce. *The Land of the Dacotahs.* Minneapolis: University of Minnesota Press, 1946.

Parker, Watson. *Gold in the Black Hills.* Norman, Okla.: University of Oklahoma Press, 1966.

Parkman, Francis. *The Oregon Trail.* Garden City, N.Y.: Doubleday & Co., 1946.

Pennanen, Gary. "Sitting Bull: Indian Without a Country." *Canadian Historical Review* 51 (June 1970): 123–40.

Praus, Alexic A. *A New Pictographic Autobiography of Sitting Bull.* Washington, D.C.: Smithsonian Institution, 1955.

Quaife, Milo M., ed. *War Path and Bivouac: The Big Horn and Yellowstone Expedition,* by John F. Finerty. Chicago: R. R. Donnelley, 1955.

———. *Forty Years a Fur Trader on the Upper Missouri, 1833–1872,* by Charles Larpenteur. Chicago: Lakeside Press, 1933.

Rankin, Charles E., ed. *Legacy: New Perspectives on the Battle of the Little Bighorn.* Helena: Montana Historical Society Press, 1996.

Reiger, John F., ed. *The Passing of the Great West: Selected Papers of George Bird Grinnell.* New York: Winchester Press, 1972.

Rickey, Don, Jr. *Forty Miles a Day on Beans and Hay: The Enlisted Soldier Fighting the Indian Wars.* Norman, Okla.: University of Oklahoma Press, 1989.

Riley, Glenda. *Women and Indians on the Frontier, 1825–1915.* Albuquerque: University of New Mexico Press, 1984.

Rister, Carl C. *Border Command: General Phil Sheridan in the West.* Norman, Okla.: University of Oklahoma Press, 1944.

Robertson, Francis B. " 'We Are Going to Have a Big Sioux War': Colonel David S. Stanley's Yellowstone Expedition, 1872." *Montana, the Magazine of Western History* 34 (Autumn 1984): 2–15.

Robinson, Charles M. *A Good Year to Die: The Story of the Great Sioux War.* New York: Random House, 1995.

———. *Bad Hand: A Biography of General Ranald S. Mackenzie.* Austin, Tex.: State House Press, 1993.

Robinson, Doane. *A History of the Dakota or Sioux Indians.* Minneapolis: Rosee & Haines, Inc., 1967. Reprint of a book first published in 1904.

———. "Some Sidelights on the Character of Sitting Bull." *Collections of the Nebraska State Historical Society* (1911): 187–92.

Rochmond, Robert W., and Mardock, Robert W., eds. *A Nation Moving West: Readings in the History of the American Frontier.* Lincoln, Nebr.: University of Nebraska Press, 1966.

Roe, Frank G. *The Indian and the Horse.* Norman, Okla.: University of Oklahoma Press, 1951.

Russell, Don. *Custer's Last: or, The Battle of the Little Big Horn in Picturesque Perspective, Being a Pictorial Representation of the Late and Unfortunate Incident in Montana.* Fort Worth, Tex.: Amon Carter Museum of Western Art, 1968.

———. "How Many Indians Were Killed? White Man Versus Red Man: The Facts and the Legend." *The American West* (July 1973), pp. 42–47, 61–63.

———. *The Lives and Legends of Buffalo Bill.* Norman, Okla.: University of Oklahoma Press, 1960.

Sandoz, Marie. *The Battle of the Little Big Horn.* Philadelphia: J. B. Lippincott, 1966.

———. *The Buffalo Hunters: The Story of the Hide Men.* New York: Hastings House, 1954.

———. *Crazy Horse: The Strange Man of the Oglalas.* Lincoln, Nebr.: University of Nebraska Press, 1961.

———. *These Were the Sioux.* Lincoln, Nebr.: University of Nebraska Press, 1985.

Schmitt, Martin F., ed. *General George Crook: His Autobiography.* Norman, Okla.: University of Oklahoma Press, 1986.

Smith, Rex Alan. *Moon of the Popping Trees: The Tragedy at Wounded Knee and the End of the Indian Wars.* Lincoln, Nebr.: University of Nebraska Press, 1981.

Smith, Sherry L. *Sagebrush Soldier: Private William Earl Smith's View of the Great Sioux War of 1876.* Norman, Okla.: University of Oklahoma Press, 1989.

———. *The View from Officers' Row: Army Perceptions of Western Indians.* Tucson: University of Arizona Press, 1990.

Smits, Davis D. "The Frontier Army and the Destruction of the Buffalo: 1865–1883." *Western Historical Quarterly* 25 (1994): 313–38.

Sterling, Matthew William, *Three Pictographic Autobiographies of Sitting Bull.* Smithsonian Miscellaneous Collections, vol. 97, no. 5. Washington, D.C.: Smithsonian Institution, 1938.

Taylor, Colin. *The Warriors of the Plains.* New York: Arco Publishing Co., 1975.

Terrill, John Upton, and George Walton. *Faint the Trumpet Sounds: The Life and Trial of Major Reno.* New York: David McKay Co., 1966.

Thompson, Neil B. *Crazy Horse Called Them Walk-a-Heaps: The Story of the Foot Soldiers in the Prairie Indian Wars.* St. Cloud, Minn.: North Star Press, 1979.

Thornton, Russell. *American Indian Holocaust and Survival: A Population History Since 1492.* Norman, Okla.: University of Oklahoma Press, 1987.

Thwaites, Reuben Gold, ed. *Original Journals of the Lewis and Clark Expedition, 1804–1806.* 7 vols. New York: Antiquarian Press, 1959. Reprint of a work first published in 1904–1905.

Tillett, Leslie. *Wind on the Buffalo Grass: The Indians' Own Account of the Battle at the Little Big Horn River, and the Death of Their Life on the Plains.* New York: Thomas Y. Crowell, 1976.

Trobriand, Philippe Régis de. *Military Life in Dakota.* St. Paul, Minn.: Alvord Memorial Commission, 1951.

Turner, C. F. *Across the Medicine Line.* Toronto: McClelland & Stewart, 1973.

Unruh, John D., Jr. *The Plains Across: The Overland Emigrants and the Trans-Mississippi West, 1840–60.* Urbana, Ill.: University of Illinois Press, 1978.

Utley, Robert M. *Cavalier in Buckskin: George Armstrong Custer and the Western Military Frontier.* Norman, Okla.: University of Oklahoma Press, 1988.

———. *The Contribution of the Frontier to the American Military Tradition.* Colorado Springs: U.S. Air Force Academy, 1977.

———. *Custer and the Great Controversy: The Origin and Development of a Legend.* Los Angeles: Westernlore Press, 1962.

———. *Frontier Regulars: The United States Army and the Indian, 1866–1891.* New York: Macmillan, 1973.

———. *The Indian Frontier of the American West, 1846–1890.* Albuquerque: University of New Mexico Press, 1984.

———. *The Lance and the Shield: The Life and Times of Sitting Bull.* New York: Henry Holt & Co., 1993.

———. *The Last Days of the Sioux Nation.* New Haven, Conn.: Yale University Press, 1963.

———. ed. *Life in Custer's Cavalry: Diaries and Letters of Albert and Jennie Barnitz, 1867–1868.* Lincoln, Nebr.: University of Nebraska Press, 1987.

Vestal, Stanley. *The Missouri.* New York: Farrar & Rinehart, 1945.

———. *New Sources of Indian History, 1850–1891.* Norman, Okla.: University of Oklahoma Press, 1934.

———. *Sitting Bull: Champion of the Sioux.* Norman, Okla.: University of Oklahoma Press, 1957.

———. *Warpath: The True Story of the Fighting Sioux Told in a Biography of Chief White Bull.* Lincoln, Nebr.: University of Nebraska Press, 1984.

Walker, James R. *Lakota Society.* Lincoln, Nebr.: University of Nebraska Press, 1982.

Watson, Elmo Scott. "The Last Indian War, 1890–91—A Study of Newspaper Jingoism." *Journalism Quarterly* 20 (1943): 205–19.

Webb, Walter Prescott. *The Great Plains.* Boston: Ginn & Co., 1931.

Weeks, Philip, ed. *The American Indian Experience: A Profile, 1524 to the Present.* Arlington Heights, Ill.: Forum Press, 1975.

———. *Farewell, My Nation: The American Indian and the United States, 1820–1890.* Arlington Heights, Ill.: Harlan Davidson, 1990.

Welch, James. *Killing Custer: The Battle of the Little Big Horn and the Fate of the Plains Indians.* New York: W. W. Norton, 1994.

Wert, Jeffrey D. *Custer: The Controversial Life of George Armstrong Custer.* New York: Simon & Schuster, 1996.

West, Elliott. *Growing Up with the Country: Childhood on the Far Western Frontier.* Albuquerque: University of New Mexico Press, 1990.

White, Richard. "The Winning of the West: The Expansion of the Western Sioux in the Eighteenth and Nineteenth Centuries." *Journal of American History* 65 (September 1978): 319–43.

Whitman, S. E. *The Troopers: An Informal History of the Plains Cavalry, 1865–1890.* New York: Hastings House, 1962.

Wiltsey, Norman B. "The Great Buffalo Slaughter." In *The American West,* edited by Raymond Friday Locke. New York: Hawthorn Books, 1971, 109–40.

Wishart, Bruce. "Grandmother's Land: Sitting Bull in Canada." *True West* 37 (May 1990): 14–20; (June 1990): 26–32; (July 1990):2 0–17; (August 1990): 28–32.

Wooster, Robert. *Nelson A. Miles and the Twilight of the Frontier Army,* Lincoln, Nebr.: University of Nebraska Press, 1993.

Index